Contents

0037784

KV-288-474

Contents

ONS, Family Spending 2000-01, © Crown copyright 2002

United Kingdom

ISSN 0965–1403

0037784
R 314.2

LEARNING CENTRE
CARSHALTON COLLEGE

03/02.

Family Spending

A report on the 2000-2001 Family Expenditure Survey

Editor: Denis Down

London: The Stationery Office

© Crown copyright 2002.
Published with the permission of the Controller of Her
Majesty's Stationery Office (HMSO).

ISBN 0 11 621478 3
ISSN 0965–1403

A National Statistics publication

Official statistics bearing the National Statistics logo are
produced to high professional standards set out in the
National Statistics Code of Practice. They undergo regular
quality assurance reviews to ensure that they meet customer
needs. They are produced free from any political interference.

Applications for reproduction should be submitted to HMSO
under HMSO's Class Licence:
www.clickanduse.hmso.gov.uk

Alternatively applications can be made in writing to:
HMSO Licensing Division
St Clement's House
2-16 Colegate
Norwich NR3 1BQ

Contact points

For enquiries about this publication, contact the Editor,
Denis Down
Tel: 020 7533 5760
E-mail: denis.down@ons.gov.uk

To order this publication, call The Stationery Office
on **0870 600 5522**. See also back cover.

For general enquiries, contact the National Statistics
Public Enquiry Service on **0845 601 3034**
(minicom: 01633 812399)
E-mail: info@statistics.gov.uk
Fax: 01633 652747
Letters: Room 1.001, Government Buildings,
Cardiff Road, Newport NP10 8XG

You can also find National Statistics on the internet -
go to **www.statistics.gov.uk**

About the Office for National Statistics

The Office for National Statistics (ONS) is the government
agency responsible for compiling, analysing and disseminating
many of the United Kingdom's economic, social and
demographic statistics, including the retail prices index, trade
figures and labour market data, as well as the periodic census
of the population and health statistics. The Director of ONS is
also the National Statistician and the Registrar General for
England and Wales, and the agency administers the statutory
registration of births, marriages and deaths there.

Introduction

The Family Expenditure Survey

This report presents information from the Family Expenditure Survey (FES) for the financial year April 2000 to March 2001. The FES is a survey of a random sample of private households in the United Kingdom carried out by the Office for National Statistics (ONS). It provides a wealth of information about household expenditure and household income.

The Expenditure and Food Survey

Plans to launch a new survey, the Expenditure and Food Survey (EFS), to replace the FES and the National Food Survey (NFS) have been mentioned in the last two reports. The decision to go ahead with the new survey was made shortly after last year's report was published and fieldwork started on 1 April 2001. The background to the decision was the substantial overlap between the FES and NFS, both asking respondents to keep a diary of expenditure. The NFS, sponsored by the Department for Environment, Food and Rural Affairs (DEFRA) asked about expenditure only on food but recorded this in more detail than the FES and asked for the weight as well as the cost. The decision to go ahead with the new survey followed successful piloting. It will be more cost effective than the two surveys separately, and an associated development of the processing system will improve the timeliness and quality of the data. The design is based on the FES design and the information currently provided by the FES will continue to be provided by the new survey.

During the developmental period, ONS and MAFF (now DEFRA) consulted widely with users. A full account of the development is in the January 2001 Survey Methodology Bulletin published by ONS. For further details about the new survey please contact

> Denis Down
> D1/23
> 1 Drummond Gate
> London SW1V 2QQ
>
> telephone: 020 7533 5760
> e-mail: denis.down@ons.gov.uk.

Purpose of the Family Expenditure Survey

The FES has been in operation since 1957. The original reason for the survey was to provide information on spending patterns for the Retail Prices Index. Over the years the range of uses has grown and the survey is now multi-purpose. It is an invaluable source of economic and social data for central government, other public and commercial organisations and for researchers in universities and independent research institutes.

The 2000-01 survey

In 2000-01 6,637 households took part in the FES. The response rate was 59 per cent in Great Britain and 56 per cent in Northern Ireland. The response was lower than the 63 per cent achieved in Great Britain in 1999-2000 but is still comparable with response in the year before. The fieldwork was undertaken by the Social Survey Division of ONS and by the Northern Ireland Statistics and Research Agency.

A large scale survey is a collaborative effort and the authors wish to thank the interviewers and other ONS staff who contributed to the study. The survey would not be possible without the co-operation of the respondents who gave up their time to be interviewed and keep a diary of their spending. Their help is gratefully acknowledged.

Data quality and definitions

The results shown in this report are of the data collected by the FES, without adjustment for outliers or non-sampling errors. These issues are discussed in the section on reliability in Appendix A. As for the last two years, results are based on data that have been re-weighted to reduce the effect of non-response bias and include spending recorded in the diaries kept by children aged 7 to 15. Appendix F describes the differential grossing method which re-weights the data and shows its effect on expenditure and income estimates.

Figures in the report are subject to sampling variability. Percent standard errors are indicated in most tables and are described in Appendix C. Figures shown for particular groups of households (e.g. income groups or household composition groups), regions or other sub-sets of the sample are subject to larger sampling variability, and are more sensitive to possible extreme values than are figures for the sample as a whole.

The definitions used in the report are set out in Appendix D, and changes made since 1991 are described in Appendix E. Note particularly that housing benefit and council tax rebate (rates rebate in Northern Ireland), unlike other social security benefits, are not included in income but are shown as a reduction in housing costs.

Change in definition of the household

The FES changed to the harmonised definition of the household for the 2000-01 survey to bring it into line with other government surveys. The definition groups together some households who would have been treated as separate households under the previous FES definition. The new and old definitions are set out in full in Appendix E and there is an analysis of the effect of the change in Chapter 9. The new definition probably increased the average number of persons per household by 0.6 per cent, and therefore average household expenditure by the same amount.

Changes in definition in 2001-02

COICOP

The Expenditure and Food Survey is being coded to a new set of expenditure codes, called EFS codes, based on the European standard Classification of Individual Consumption by Purpose, or COICOP. The EFS codes sub-divide the lowest level of COICOP codes where that is necessary to provide a good mapping to the current FES codes. The report on the 2001-02 survey will be based on COICOP but will include an analysis of the effect of the change.

Household reference person

In 2001 all government surveys stopped classifying households by the characteristics of the head of household and started using the household reference person (HRP) instead. The definition of head of household had a strong male bias, always counting as head the male partner in a couple. The new definition counts as household reference person the householder, that is the person in whose name the accommodation is owned or rented. If there are joint householders, the one with the highest income is the HRP. The HRP was recorded alongside the head of household in the 2000-01 survey. A number of tables in the report are based on the HRP, for comparison with those based on the head of household. Tables affected are those showing the age, employment status and social class of the head of household/HRP.

Social class

A new classification by social class is being introduced in government surveys from 2001. Only one table in Family Spending will be affected.

Related data sources

More detailed income information is available from the Family Resources Survey (FRS) conducted by the Department for Work and Pensions. Further information about food consumption, and in particular details of food quantities, is available from the National Food Survey (NFS) conducted by the Department for Environment, Food and Rural Affairs.

In Northern Ireland, a companion survey to the GB FES is conducted by the Northern Ireland Statistics and Research Agency using an enhanced sample. Results from this sample will be published in a separate report, *The Northern Ireland Family Expenditure Survey Report for 2000-2001.* Further information and copies of this report can be obtained from:

> Northern Ireland Statistics and Research Agency,
> Central Survey Unit
> McAuley House
> 2-14 Castle Street
> Belfast BT1 1SY
> Tel: 02890 348 215

Additional tabulations

The report gives a broad overview of the results of the survey, and provides more detailed information about some aspects of expenditure. However, many users of FES data have very specific data requirements which may not appear in the desired form in this report. The ONS can provide more detailed analysis of the tables in this report, and can also provide additional tabulations to meet specific requests. A charge will be made to cover the cost of providing additional information.

The tables in Family Spending 2000-01 are available as Excel spreadsheets (with unrounded data).

Contact points

Please address all enquiries to:

Family Expenditure Survey,
Office for National Statistics,
Room D1/23,
1 Drummond Gate,
London SW1V 2QQ.

Tel: 020 7533 5756 (answering machine outside office hours)
Fax: 020 7533 5300

Symbols and conventions used in this report

..   Data not available due to unreliability, as a result of:

1.   too few reporting households, generally less than 10, or
2.   sampling error too large, generally 50 per cent or more

[ ]   Figures to be used with extra caution because based on fewer than 20 reporting households.

Rounding: Individual figures have been rounded independently. The sum of component items does not therefore necessarily add to the totals shown.

Averages: These are averages (means) for all households included in the column or row, and are not restricted to those households reporting expenditure on a particular item or income of a particular type.

Period covered: Financial year 2000-01 (1 April 2000 to 31 March 2001).

ONS, Family Spending 2000-01, © Crown copyright 2002

Chapter *1*

Expenditure by income

- Average weekly expenditure in 2000-01 was £390. It ranged from £130 a week in the lowest of the ten income groups to £850 a week in the highest.

- The increase in spending with income was especially large between the one-from-highest and the highest of the ten groups, of £250 a week.

- **Leisure goods and services** was the largest item of spending by an increased margin, with an average of £70 a week. Spending on **housing**, £64 a week, was the next largest, overtaking **food and non-alcoholic drink**, £62 a week, for the first time.

- For households in the lower half of the income range, however, **food and non-alcoholic drink** was the largest item of spending, with **housing** second. They were both overtaken by **leisure** spending for households in the upper half of the range. Spending on **housing** was greater than on **food** at higher incomes.

- Spending on **motoring**, at £55 a week, was lower than on **leisure, housing** and **food** overall and was lower than on leisure and housing in all income groups. It was higher than spending on **food**, however, in the highest three out of the ten income groups.

- As a proportion of all expenditure, spending on **fares and other travel costs** did not vary much with income. But the proportion going on **bus and coach travel** fell from 35 per cent in the lowest two income groups to only 5 per cent in the highest group. A particularly high proportion of travel spending went on **rail** travel for the two highest income groups, over a quarter.

- The proportion of motoring spending going on the **purchase of vehicles** increased with income, from 20 per cent in the lowest income groups to about 45 per cent in the higher groups.

- The proportion of spending on reading matter that went on **newspapers** fell with income from over 60 per cent in the three lowest income groups to 30 per cent in the highest group, though amounts went up in money terms. **Books** showed the reverse pattern, the proportion spent on them increasing from under 20 per cent at low incomes to nearly 50 per cent for the highest group.

Expenditure by income

1.1 Average weekly expenditure on the main commodities and services

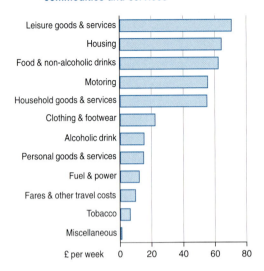

£ per week

Tables 1.1 to 1.3 show household expenditure on commodities and services by gross income group. As in the other reports from 1998-99 onwards, the figures include the information from the expenditure diaries kept by children aged 7 to 15 and use re-weighted data, which compensates for the under-representation of some types of household in the sample.

Ten income groups are shown, based on gross income, with an equal number of households in each group (decile). The characteristics of households varied across income groups. Differences in spending may therefore be the result of other factors as well as income. Household size is particularly important and is shown in the top part of the table. It can be seen that as the average number of people in each household increases, the income decile group is also higher. The highest income group had more than twice the average household size of the lowest income group (3.2 people compared with 1.3 people).

Tables 1.4 and **1.5** show how expenditure varies with disposable income instead of gross income.

Total household expenditure

The estimate of total household expenditure per household in the 2000-01 survey was £390 a week. This was £26 a week higher than in 1999-2000, equivalent to a 7 per cent increase. Some of this was the result of a slightly higher average number of persons per household, and the increase per person was only 5.5 per cent.

1.2 Average weekly expenditure by gross income decile group

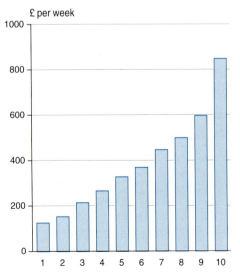

£ per week

Figure 1.1 shows how expenditure is spread between the main commodities and services. Leisure goods and services, when combined, were again the largest item of spending in 2000-01. They first became the largest item in 1998-99. For the first time housing and food had the next largest weekly expenditures.

Table 1.1 and **Figure 1.2** illustrate that the average weekly expenditure ranged from £130 per week in the lowest income decile group to £850 per week in the highest income decile. Expenditure increased steadily with income with the exception of the highest group which showed a steeper rise. This increase of £250 between the ninth and the highest group was more than three times the average increase of £80 between consecutive groups. The highest income group spent more than double the average expenditure

ONS, Family Spending 2000-01, © Crown copyright 2002

for all households. Increases in spending compared with 1999-2000 were below average for the two lowest groups, about £7 a week or 5 per cent.

In general, expenditure for all 14 main commodity / service headings increased with income except for tobacco where expenditure did not vary very much with income from the third income group onwards.

Expenditure patterns

Although spending on leisure was highest overall, **Table 1.1** and **Figure 1.3a** shows that for the half of households with the lowest incomes, food was the largest item of spending with housing second. **Figure 1.3b** shows that leisure was the largest item for the half of households with the highest incomes, and spending on housing was generally higher than on food for this group. Expenditure on leisure goods and services ranged from £20 per week for the lowest income group to £188 per week for the highest. The amount spent on housing ranged from £21 to £141, and on food from £26 to £111. Spending on motoring was the lowest of the four items when comparing all households.

Table 1.2 shows expenditure on each commodity as a percentage of total expenditure. Spending on most commodities increased broadly in line with total expenditure, so that the proportion spent on them did not vary much with income. However, it shows that the proportion spent on leisure goods and services increased with income, particularly at the highest incomes. It ranged from a proportion of 16 per cent at the low incomes to 22 per cent at the highest. The proportion of spending going on housing, however, remained fairly constant around the 17 per cent mark regardless of income group. It can be seen that the proportion spent on food and non-alcoholic drink decreased with income. The lowest group spent 20 per cent on food whereas the highest spent only 13 per cent. The pattern for motoring is distinctive, as can be seen in **Figure 1.4**. The proportion of expenditure on motoring increased for the first eight decile income groups, then decreased for the last group. The smallest proportion spent on motoring was by the lowest income group at 7 per cent a week. The highest proportion spent was by the seventh, eighth and ninth groups at 16 per cent a week.

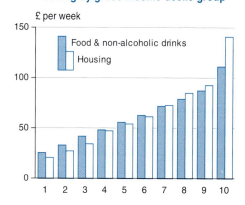

1.3a **Food and non-alcoholic drinks and housing by gross income decile group**

£ per week

1.3b **Motoring and leisure by gross income decile group**

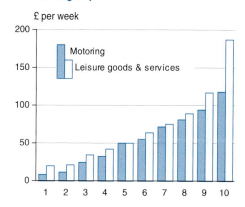

£ per week

1.4 **Food & non-alcoholic drinks and motoring as a percentage of total expenditure by gross income decile group**

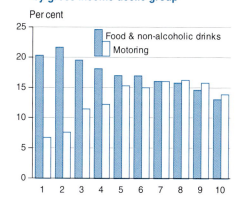

Per cent

1.5 Holidays in the UK and abroad as a percentage of holiday expenditure by gross income decile group

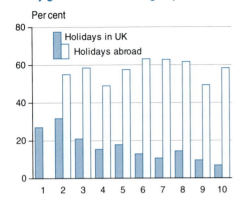

Per cent

1.6 Rail & bus fares as a percentage of travel expenditure by gross income decile group

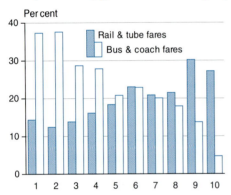

Per cent

1.7 Vehicle purchase and motor fuel as a percentage of expenditure on motoring by gross income quintile group

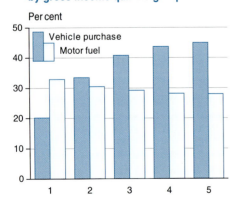

Per cent

Detailed expenditure patterns

Table 1.3 shows a more detailed breakdown of expenditure categories for the income groups.

Holidays

Figure 1.5 shows how holiday expenditure was divided between holidays abroad and in the UK. (The share of holiday spending on holidays abroad is not shown for the lowest income group because of high sampling variability.) It is noticeable that the largest proportion of holiday money was spent on holidays abroad for all income groups shown. In general, the higher the income group, the smaller the proportion of money spent on UK holidays. The three lowest income groups spent the highest proportion on holidays within the UK at around 20 to 30 per cent. The highest income group spent only 10 per cent, but nevertheless spent the most in absolute terms, along with the eighth and ninth deciles, at £4.70 per week.

Fares and other travel costs

As a proportion of all expenditure, total spending on fares and other travel costs did not vary much with income. But **Figure 1.6** shows that the shares taken by different types of fares did vary. The proportions are of all spending on fares and travel, including taxis, air and combined tickets. Rail and tube fares, as a percentage of this total, increased with income group. This is particularly evident for groups nine and ten who both spent over a quarter of fares money on rail and tube fares. Lower income groups spent a larger proportion on bus and coach tickets compared with the higher groups. Over 35 per cent of spending on fares and travel was spent on bus and coach journeys by the lowest two income groups, at about £1.20 a week. The highest income group spent the smallest proportion on buses and coaches, at only 5 per cent.

Motoring

Quintile income groups have been displayed in **Figure 1.7** for a better comparison. It shows the proportion of motoring which is spent on petrol, diesel and other motor oils. For the lowest quintile, a larger proportion was used on fuel, at 33 per cent, compared to vehicle purchase. However, as this group spent one of the smallest amounts on motoring overall at £10.20 per week, this proportion amounted to only £3.30. The largest expenditure on petrol, diesel

ONS, Family Spending 2000-01, © Crown copyright 2002

and other motor fuels was by the highest quintile at £29.90 although, as more was spent on motoring overall, this meant that the proportion was smaller. There is a general trend of an increase in proportion spent on vehicle purchase, the higher the income group is. The highest three income quintiles spent the largest proportion on vehicle purchase, each spending over 40 per cent of their motoring expenditure.

Reading materials

Figure 1.8 shows the expenditure on three headings from leisure goods as a percentage of total expenditure on reading materials – magazines and periodicals, books, maps and diaries, and newspapers. The higher the income decile, the lower the proportion that was spent on newspapers. From the eighth income decile onwards, the proportion spent on books, maps and diaries exceeded the proportion spent on newspapers. The third decile through to the ninth spent similar amounts to one another on newspapers at around £2.10 per week. All income groups spent a higher proportion on books, maps and diaries than they did on magazines and periodicals, although this difference was small for the three lowest income groups. The higher the income group, the larger the proportion spent on books. The proportion spent on magazines rose at a smaller rate up to the sixth decile group, then dropped down to the highest income group. As can be seen in the figure, this had the effect of widening the gap between proportions spent on books compared with magazines. The highest income group spent £4.50 on books, diaries and maps. This is more than twice the amount they spent on magazines and periodicals at £1.90 a week.

Expenditure by disposable income

Tables 1.4 and **1.5** show how expenditure varied with disposable income, that is, gross income less income tax and National Insurance contributions. Some households will be in a different income decile when defined by disposable income than by gross income decile. If this is the case, they will normally move only one group up or down. **Figure 1.9** shows that the variation of total expenditure with income depended very little on the measure of income used. Comparisons of **Table 1.1** with **1.4** and of **1.2** with **1.5** show that the pattern of expenditure was also similar.

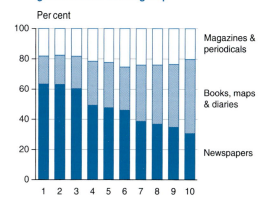

1.8 Selected leisure goods as a percentage of expenditure on reading materials by gross income decile group

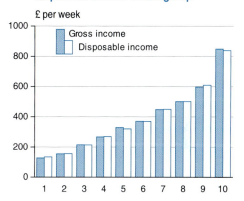

1.9 Average weekly expenditure by gross and disposable income decile group

1.1 Household expenditure by gross income decile group

based on weighted data and including children's expenditure

2000-01

Commodity or service	Lowest ten per cent	Second decile group	Third decile group	Fourth decile group	Fifth decile group	Sixth decile group
Lower boundary of group (£ per week)		107	163	231	310	397
Grossed number of households (thousands)	2,500	2,500	2,500	2,500	2,500	2,500
Total number of households in sample	664	709	710	695	668	664
Total number of persons in sample	893	1,263	1,399	1,518	1,582	1,724
Total number of adults in sample	722	935	1,118	1,175	1,182	1,224
Weighted average number of persons per household	1.3	1.7	1.9	2.1	2.3	2.5

Commodity or service	Average weekly household expenditure (£)					
1 Housing (Net)	**21.00**	**27.60**	**34.60**	**47.50**	**54.40**	**61.60**
Percentage standard error	*7*	*5*	*4*	*3*	*2*	*2*
2 Fuel and power	**8.60**	**9.40**	**11.80**	**10.60**	**11.20**	**11.50**
"	*3*	*3*	*6*	*2*	*3*	*3*
3 Food and non-alcoholic drinks	**25.80**	**33.40**	**42.10**	**48.50**	**56.10**	**62.90**
"	*3*	*2*	*2*	*2*	*2*	*2*
4 Alcoholic drink	**4.20**	**4.80**	**7.80**	**9.90**	**13.00**	**16.40**
"	*11*	*8*	*7*	*6*	*5*	*5*
5 Tobacco	**3.90**	**4.30**	**6.00**	**5.90**	**7.00**	**6.90**
"	*8*	*7*	*7*	*8*	*7*	*7*
6 Clothing and footwear	**6.70**	**8.20**	**11.50**	**14.90**	**19.90**	**20.30**
"	*10*	*7*	*7*	*6*	*7*	*6*
7 Household goods	**11.20**	**14.20**	**18.30**	**22.60**	**27.50**	**31.10**
"	*12*	*9*	*6*	*7*	*7*	*6*
8 Household services	**8.50**	**9.70**	**12.00**	**16.00**	**16.90**	**17.50**
"	*7*	*6*	*5*	*7*	*4*	*5*
9 Personal goods and services	**5.00**	**5.50**	**7.40**	**9.60**	**12.40**	**14.10**
"	*11*	*6*	*6*	*6*	*6*	*5*
10 Motoring	**8.60**	**11.80**	**24.80**	**32.80**	**50.50**	**55.70**
"	*15*	*7*	*7*	*6*	*5*	*5*
11 Fares and other travel costs	**2.70**	**3.40**	**3.90**	**5.60**	**8.70**	**7.20**
"	*10*	*12*	*9*	*8*	*20*	*9*
12 Leisure goods	**6.10**	**7.00**	**11.00**	**11.30**	**18.00**	**20.30**
"	*11*	*7*	*7*	*6*	*8*	*10*
13 Leisure services	**14.10**	**14.40**	**23.70**	**31.10**	**32.50**	**44.00**
"	*14*	*8*	*6*	*8*	*6*	*6*
14 Miscellaneous	**0.20**	**0.30**	**0.30**	**0.40**	**0.90**	**0.70**
"	*23*	*20*	*19*	*18*	*21*	*16*
1-14 All expenditure groups	**126.70**	**153.80**	**215.10**	**266.70**	**329.00**	**370.20**
Percentage standard error	*5*	*3*	*2*	*2*	*2*	*2*
Average weekly expenditure per person (£)						
All expenditure groups	**97.00**	**90.20**	**111.80**	**126.60**	**143.40**	**148.40**

ONS, Family Spending 2000-01, © Crown copyright 2002

1.1 Household expenditure by gross income decile group (cont.)

2000-01

based on weighted data and including children's expenditure

	Seventh decile group	Eighth decile group	Ninth decile group	Highest ten per cent	All house-holds
Lower boundary of group (£ per week)	489	597	739	993	
Grossed number of households (thousands)	2,500	2,500	2,500	2,510	25,030
Total number of households in sample	667	631	619	610	6,637
Total number of persons in sample	1,847	1,853	1,854	1,992	15,925
Total number of adults in sample	1,340	1,336	1,366	1,454	11,852
Weighted average number of persons per household	2.7	2.9	2.9	3.2	2.4

Commodity or service	Average weekly household expenditure (£)				
1 **Housing (Net)**	73.10	85.20	92.90	141.10	63.90
Percentage standard error	*2*	*3*	*2*	*4*	*1*
2 **Fuel and power**	12.50	13.30	13.40	16.60	11.90
"	*2*	*3*	*2*	*2*	*1*
3 **Food and non-alcoholic drinks**	72.20	79.30	87.60	111.40	61.90
"	*2*	*2*	*2*	*2*	*1*
4 **Alcoholic drink**	17.70	19.70	22.70	33.80	15.00
"	*4*	*4*	*4*	*5*	*2*
5 **Tobacco**	6.60	7.00	6.40	6.50	6.10
"	*7*	*8*	*9*	*10*	*3*
6 **Clothing and footwear**	26.80	28.30	37.30	45.80	22.00
"	*5*	*5*	*5*	*5*	*2*
7 **Household goods**	38.70	37.40	54.60	70.60	32.60
"	*7*	*6*	*7*	*7*	*3*
8 **Household services**	25.70	27.70	30.80	54.80	22.00
"	*7*	*5*	*5*	*7*	*2*
9 **Personal goods and services**	16.90	20.10	23.30	32.70	14.70
"	*4*	*6*	*5*	*5*	*2*
10 **Motoring**	72.10	81.60	94.60	118.30	55.10
"	*4*	*4*	*4*	*4*	*2*
11 **Fares and other travel costs**	9.30	10.30	15.30	28.20	9.50
"	*14*	*11*	*16*	*10*	*5*
12 **Leisure goods**	22.00	28.20	31.90	41.70	19.70
"	*6*	*8*	*8*	*8*	*3*
13 **Leisure services**	53.60	61.30	85.40	145.80	50.60
"	*5*	*6*	*6*	*6*	*2*
14 **Miscellaneous**	0.80	1.00	1.20	1.60	0.70
"	*17*	*13*	*15*	*16*	*6*
1-14 **All expenditure groups**	448.00	500.50	597.30	849.00	385.70
Percentage standard error	*2*	*2*	*2*	*2*	*1*

Average weekly expenditure per person (£)					
All expenditure groups	165.60	173.80	203.90	266.20	163.90

1.2 Household expenditure as a percentage of total expenditure by gross income decile group

2000-01

based on weighted data and including children's expenditure

	Lowest ten per cent	Second decile group	Third decile group	Fourth decile group	Fifth decile group	Sixth decile group
Lower boundary of group (£ per week)		107	163	231	310	397
Grossed number of households (thousands)	2,500	2,500	2,500	2,500	2,500	2,500
Total number of households in sample	664	709	710	695	668	664
Total number of persons in sample	893	1,263	1,399	1,518	1,582	1,724
Total number of adults in sample	722	935	1,118	1,175	1,182	1,224
Weighted average number of persons per household	1.3	1.7	1.9	2.1	2.3	2.5
Commodity or service	**Percentage of total expenditure**					
1 Housing (Net)	17	18	16	18	17	17
2 Fuel and power	7	6	5	4	3	3
3 Food and non-alcoholic drinks	20	22	20	18	17	17
4 Alcoholic drink	3	3	4	4	4	4
5 Tobacco	3	3	3	2	2	2
6 Clothing and footwear	5	5	5	6	6	5
7 Household goods	9	9	8	8	8	8
8 Household services	7	6	6	6	5	5
9 Personal goods and services	4	4	3	4	4	4
10 Motoring	7	8	12	12	15	15
11 Fares and other travel costs	2	2	2	2	3	2
12 Leisure goods	5	5	5	4	5	5
13 Leisure services	11	9	11	12	10	12
14 Miscellaneous	0	0	0	0	0	0
1-14 All expenditure groups	100	100	100	100	100	100

ONS, Family Spending 2000-01, © Crown copyright 2002

1.2 Household expenditure as a percentage of total expenditure by gross income decile group (cont.)

2000-01

based on weighted data and including children's expenditure

	Seventh decile group	Eighth decile group	Ninth decile group	Highest ten per cent	All house-holds
Lower boundary of group (£ per week)	489	597	739	993	
Grossed number of households (thousands)	2,500	2,500	2,500	2,510	25,030
Total number of households in sample	667	631	619	610	6,637
Total number of persons in sample	1,847	1,853	1,854	1,992	15,925
Total number of adults in sample	1,340	1,336	1,366	1,454	11,852
Weighted average number of persons per household	2.7	2.9	2.9	3.2	2.4
Commodity or service	**Percentage of total expenditure**				
1 Housing (Net)	16	17	16	17	17
2 Fuel and power	3	3	2	2	3
3 Food and non-alcoholic drinks	16	16	15	13	16
4 Alcoholic drink	4	4	4	4	4
5 Tobacco	1	1	1	1	2
6 Clothing and footwear	6	6	6	5	6
7 Household goods	9	7	9	8	8
8 Household services	6	6	5	6	6
9 Personal goods and services	4	4	4	4	4
10 Motoring	16	16	16	14	14
11 Fares and other travel costs	2	2	3	3	2
12 Leisure goods	5	6	5	5	5
13 Leisure services	12	12	14	17	13
14 Miscellaneous	0	0	0	0	0
1-14 All expenditure groups	100	100	100	100	100

1.3 Detailed household expenditure by gross income decile group
based on weighted data and including children's expenditure

2000-01

	Lowest ten per cent	Second decile group	Third decile group	Fourth decile group	Fifth decile group	Sixth decile group
Lower boundary of group (£ per week)		107	163	231	310	397
Grossed number of households (thousands)	2,500	2,500	2,500	2,500	2,500	2,500
Total number of households in sample	664	709	710	695	668	664
Total number of persons in sample	893	1,263	1,399	1,518	1,582	1,724
Total number of adults in sample	722	935	1,118	1,175	1,182	1,224
Weighted average number of persons per household	1.3	1.7	1.9	2.1	2.3	2.5

Commodity or service	Average weekly household expenditure (£)					
1 Housing (Net)	**21.00**	**27.60**	**34.60**	**47.50**	**54.40**	**61.60**
Percentage standard error	*7*	*5*	*4*	*3*	*2*	*2*
1.1 Gross rent, mortgage interest payments, water charges, council tax, etc	54.20	48.90	46.30	49.50	52.40	56.90
1.2 *less* housing benefit, rebates and allowances received	36.00	25.40	17.50	8.30	4.30	2.90
1.3 Net rent, mortgage interest payments, water charges, council tax, etc	18.20	23.50	28.80	41.30	48.10	54.00
1.4 Repairs, maintenance and decorations	2.80	4.10	5.80	6.30	6.30	7.60
2 Fuel and power	**8.60**	**9.40**	**11.80**	**10.60**	**11.20**	**11.50**
Percentage standard error	*3*	*3*	*6*	*2*	*3*	*3*
2.1 Gas	3.40	3.80	4.10	4.20	4.50	4.60
2.2 Electricity	4.50	4.80	6.30	5.40	5.80	6.00
2.3 Other fuels	0.80	0.90	1.50	0.90	0.80	0.90
3 Food and non-alcoholic drinks	**25.80**	**33.40**	**42.10**	**48.60**	**56.10**	**62.90**
Percentage standard error	*3*	*2*	*2*	*2*	*2*	*2*
3.1 Bread, rolls etc	1.00	1.30	1.50	1.60	1.70	1.90
3.2 Pasta, rice, flour and other cereals	0.30	0.20	0.40	0.40	0.40	0.40
3.3 Biscuits, cakes etc	1.50	2.20	2.60	2.60	2.80	3.10
3.4 Breakfast cereals	0.40	0.60	0.60	0.70	0.80	0.80
3.5 Beef and veal (uncooked)	0.70	0.90	1.30	1.40	1.30	1.60
3.6 Mutton and lamb (uncooked)	0.40	0.50	0.50	0.60	0.60	0.40
3.7 Pork (uncooked)	0.30	0.50	0.50	0.60	0.70	0.60
3.8 Bacon and ham (uncooked)	0.50	0.70	0.80	0.70	0.80	0.80
3.9 Poultry (uncooked)	0.90	1.10	1.40	1.70	1.90	1.90
3.10 Cold meats, ready to eat meats	0.70	1.00	1.10	1.10	1.40	1.50
3.11 Meat pies, sausages and other meats	0.80	1.10	1.30	1.20	1.30	1.30
3.12 Fish, shellfish and fish products	0.70	1.00	1.50	1.40	1.40	1.40
3.13 Butter	0.20	0.30	0.30	0.30	0.20	0.20
3.14 Margarine	0.20	0.30	0.40	0.40	0.40	0.40
3.15 Cooking oils and fats	0.10	0.10	0.20	0.20	0.20	0.20
3.16 Fresh milk	1.30	1.70	2.00	1.90	2.10	2.10
3.17 Milk products including cream	0.60	0.90	1.00	1.20	1.30	1.50
3.18 Cheese	0.50	0.80	0.90	1.00	1.20	1.30
3.19 Eggs	0.30	0.30	0.40	0.40	0.40	0.40
3.20 Potatoes, potato products (excluding crisps)	0.70	0.90	1.10	1.10	1.20	1.30
3.21 Other vegetables	1.50	2.00	2.40	2.60	2.80	3.10
3.22 Fruit, nuts	1.30	1.70	2.20	2.40	2.50	2.60

1.3 Detailed household expenditure by gross income decile group (cont.)
based on weighted data and including children's expenditure

2000-01

	Seventh decile group	Eighth decile group	Ninth decile group	Highest ten per cent	All house-holds
Lower boundary of group (£ per week)	489	597	739	993	
Grossed number of households (thousands)	2,500	2,500	2,500	2,510	25,030
Total number of households in sample	667	631	619	610	6,637
Total number of persons in sample	1,847	1,853	1,854	1,992	15,925
Total number of adults in sample	1,340	1,336	1,366	1,454	11,852
Weighted average number of persons per household	2.7	2.9	2.9	3.2	2.4

Commodity or service	Average weekly household expenditure (£)				
1 Housing (Net)	**73.10**	**85.20**	**92.90**	**141.10**	**63.90**
Percentage standard error	*2*	*3*	*2*	*4*	*1*
1.1 Gross rent, mortgage interest payments, water charges, council tax, etc	63.50	73.80	80.90	120.90	64.70
1.2 *less* housing benefit, rebates and allowances received	1.20	0.70	0.60	0.30	9.70
1.3 Net rent, mortgage interest payments, water charges, council tax, etc	62.30	73.10	80.40	120.70	55.00
1.4 Repairs, maintenance and decorations	10.80	12.10	12.50	20.40	8.90
2 Fuel and power	**12.50**	**13.30**	**13.40**	**16.60**	**11.90**
Percentage standard error	*2*	*3*	*2*	*2*	*1*
2.1 Gas	5.40	5.60	5.70	7.30	4.80
2.2 Electricity	6.10	6.70	6.60	7.80	6.00
2.3 Other fuels	1.00	1.00	1.10	1.50	1.00
3 Food and non-alcoholic drinks	**72.20**	**79.30**	**87.60**	**111.40**	**61.90**
Percentage standard error	*2*	*2*	*2*	*2*	*1*
3.1 Bread, rolls etc	2.00	2.20	2.20	2.60	1.80
3.2 Pasta, rice, flour and other cereals	0.50	0.50	0.70	0.90	0.50
3.3 Biscuits, cakes etc	3.30	3.50	3.50	3.60	2.90
3.4 Breakfast cereals	1.10	1.00	1.20	1.40	0.90
3.5 Beef and veal (uncooked)	1.60	1.80	1.90	2.10	1.50
3.6 Mutton and lamb (uncooked)	0.70	0.70	0.70	0.80	0.60
3.7 Pork (uncooked)	0.80	0.70	0.70	0.90	0.60
3.8 Bacon and ham (uncooked)	1.00	1.00	1.10	1.30	0.90
3.9 Poultry (uncooked)	2.40	2.50	3.00	3.20	2.00
3.10 Cold meats, ready to eat meats	1.80	1.70	1.90	2.20	1.40
3.11 Meat pies, sausages and other meats	1.50	1.50	1.40	1.40	1.30
3.12 Fish, shellfish and fish products	1.70	1.80	1.90	2.40	1.50
3.13 Butter	0.30	0.30	0.30	0.40	0.30
3.14 Margarine	0.50	0.40	0.50	0.40	0.40
3.15 Cooking oils and fats	0.20	0.20	0.20	0.30	0.20
3.16 Fresh milk	2.30	2.50	2.40	2.60	2.10
3.17 Milk products including cream	1.70	1.90	2.00	2.10	1.40
3.18 Cheese	1.50	1.50	1.80	2.30	1.30
3.19 Eggs	0.40	0.50	0.50	0.50	0.40
3.20 Potatoes, potato products (excluding crisps)	1.40	1.50	1.50	1.60	1.20
3.21 Other vegetables	3.80	4.10	4.80	5.50	3.30
3.22 Fruit, nuts	3.00	3.30	3.90	4.90	2.80

1.3 Detailed household expenditure by gross income decile group (cont.)
based on weighted data and including children's expenditure

2000-01

	Lowest ten per cent	Second decile group	Third decile group	Fourth decile group	Fifth decile group	Sixth decile group
Commodity or service	**Average weekly household expenditure (£)**					
3 Food and non-alcoholic drinks (continued)						
3.23 Sugar	0.20	0.20	0.20	0.20	0.20	0.20
3.24 Jam, jellies, preserves and other spreads	0.20	0.20	0.20	0.20	0.20	0.30
3.25 Sweets and chocolates	0.90	1.10	1.60	1.70	2.00	2.40
3.26 Ice cream and sorbets	0.20	0.30	0.40	0.40	0.50	0.50
3.27 Tea	0.30	0.40	0.50	0.50	0.50	0.40
3.28 Coffee	0.30	0.40	0.40	0.50	0.40	0.50
3.29 Drinking chocolate, other food drinks	0.10	0.10	0.10	0.20	0.20	0.20
3.30 Fruit juice, squashes, bottled water	0.50	0.70	0.90	0.90	1.10	1.30
3.31 Fizzy drinks	0.50	0.50	0.80	0.90	1.00	1.10
3.32 Soup	0.20	0.20	0.30	0.20	0.30	0.30
3.33 Pizzas, vegetarian pies, quiches	0.30	0.40	0.50	0.60	0.70	0.80
3.34 Other convenience foods	1.00	1.40	1.50	1.70	2.00	2.20
3.35 Potato crisps and savoury snacks	0.50	0.60	0.70	0.80	0.90	1.10
3.36 Restaurant and café meals	2.40	2.70	4.20	6.50	8.20	9.90
3.37 Take-away meals eaten at home	1.30	1.50	1.70	2.40	3.30	3.80
3.38 Other take-away food and snack food	1.10	1.50	2.00	2.70	3.90	5.20
3.39 State school meals and meals at work	0.40	0.30	0.50	1.30	1.90	2.40
3.40 Other foods	0.70	0.90	1.10	1.30	1.40	1.40
4 Alcoholic drink	**4.20**	**4.80**	**7.80**	**9.90**	**13.00**	**16.40**
Percentage standard error	*11*	*8*	*7*	*6*	*5*	*5*
4.1 Beer, cider	2.40	2.60	4.30	4.90	7.40	9.20
4.2 Wines, fortified wines	0.80	0.90	1.20	2.10	2.80	3.50
4.3 Spirits, liqueurs	0.90	1.00	1.80	2.00	1.70	2.20
4.4 Other drinks	0.20	0.30	0.50	0.90	1.10	1.40
5 Tobacco	**3.90**	**4.30**	**6.00**	**5.90**	**7.00**	**6.90**
Percentage standard error	*8*	*7*	*7*	*8*	*7*	*7*
5.1 Cigarettes	3.40	3.90	5.20	5.30	6.30	5.90
5.2 Tobacco and other tobacco products	0.50	0.40	0.90	0.70	0.70	1.00
6 Clothing and footwear	**6.70**	**8.20**	**11.50**	**14.90**	**19.90**	**20.30**
Percentage standard error	*10*	*7*	*7*	*6*	*7*	*6*
6.1 Men's outerwear	0.90	1.30	2.20	2.60	3.50	4.30
6.2 Men's underwear and hosiery	[0.10]	0.20	0.30	0.40	0.40	0.50
6.3 Women's outerwear	2.50	2.80	3.50	5.50	6.80	5.40
6.4 Women's underwear and hosiery	0.40	0.60	0.80	0.90	0.70	1.00
6.5 Boys' outerwear	[0.20]	0.20	0.40	0.30	0.90	0.90
6.6 Girls' outerwear	0.30	0.40	0.60	1.10	0.90	1.20
6.7 Babies' outerwear	0.30	0.30	0.30	0.50	0.50	0.90
6.8 Boys', girls' and babies' underwear	0.20	0.20	0.20	0.30	0.30	0.40
6.9 Ties, belts, hats, gloves, etc	0.20	0.20	0.20	0.30	0.50	0.60
6.10 Haberdashery, textiles and clothes hire	0.20	0.10	0.30	0.40	0.40	0.30
6.11 Footwear	1.50	1.80	2.60	2.70	5.00	4.70

ONS, Family Spending 2000-01, © Crown copyright 2002

1.3 Detailed household expenditure by gross income decile group (cont.)

2000-01

based on weighted data and including children's expenditure

		Seventh decile group	Eighth decile group	Ninth decile group	Highest ten per cent	All house- holds
Commodity or service		Average weekly household expenditure (£)				
3	**Food and non-alcoholic drinks (continued)**					
3.23	Sugar	0.20	0.20	0.20	0.20	0.20
3.24	Jam, jellies, preserves and other spreads	0.30	0.30	0.30	0.40	0.30
3.25	Sweets and chocolates	2.40	2.40	2.60	2.70	2.00
3.26	Ice cream and sorbets	0.60	0.60	0.70	0.70	0.50
3.27	Tea	0.50	0.50	0.60	0.60	0.50
3.28	Coffee	0.70	0.60	0.70	0.90	0.50
3.29	Drinking chocolate, other food drinks	0.20	0.20	0.20	0.20	0.20
3.30	Fruit juice, squashes, bottled water	1.60	1.70	2.10	2.80	1.40
3.31	Fizzy drinks	1.30	1.40	1.30	1.70	1.00
3.32	Soup	0.30	0.30	0.40	0.50	0.30
3.33	Pizzas, vegetarian pies, quiches	1.00	1.10	1.10	1.20	0.80
3.34	Other convenience foods	2.60	2.90	3.20	3.50	2.20
3.35	Potato crisps and savoury snacks	1.30	1.40	1.30	1.50	1.00
3.36	Restaurant and café meals	10.90	13.90	17.60	27.40	10.40
3.37	Take-away meals eaten at home	4.80	5.40	5.10	6.50	3.60
3.38	Other take-away food and snack food	5.70	6.30	7.00	9.80	4.50
3.39	State school meals and meals at work	2.70	3.00	3.30	4.20	2.00
3.40	Other foods	1.80	2.00	2.20	3.10	1.60
4	**Alcoholic drink**	**17.70**	**19.70**	**22.70**	**33.80**	**15.00**
	Percentage standard error	*4*	*4*	*4*	*5*	*2*
4.1	Beer, cider	9.20	10.90	11.60	14.80	7.70
4.2	Wines, fortified wines	4.30	4.40	5.90	10.30	3.60
4.3	Spirits, liqueurs	2.40	2.50	3.20	4.50	2.20
4.4	Other drinks	1.70	1.90	2.00	4.30	1.40
5	**Tobacco**	**6.60**	**7.00**	**6.40**	**6.50**	**6.10**
	Percentage standard error	*7*	*8*	*9*	*10*	*3*
5.1	Cigarettes	5.90	6.20	5.90	5.80	5.40
5.2	Tobacco and other tobacco products	0.70	0.70	0.50	0.80	0.70
6	**Clothing and footwear**	**26.80**	**28.30**	**37.30**	**45.80**	**22.00**
	Percentage standard error	*5*	*5*	*5*	*5*	*2*
6.1	Men's outerwear	5.60	5.80	7.70	10.20	4.40
6.2	Men's underwear and hosiery	0.60	0.50	0.70	1.00	0.50
6.3	Women's outerwear	8.70	9.60	13.70	17.00	7.60
6.4	Women's underwear and hosiery	1.40	1.70	1.70	2.90	1.20
6.5	Boys' outerwear	1.30	1.20	1.30	1.60	0.80
6.6	Girls' outerwear	1.60	1.50	2.20	2.10	1.20
6.7	Babies' outerwear	0.80	1.10	0.90	1.20	0.70
6.8	Boys', girls' and babies' underwear	0.50	0.70	0.70	0.60	0.40
6.9	Ties, belts, hats, gloves, etc	0.70	0.80	0.80	1.30	0.60
6.10	Haberdashery, textiles and clothes hire	0.30	0.60	1.00	0.70	0.40
6.11	Footwear	5.20	4.80	6.40	7.20	4.20

1.3 Detailed household expenditure by gross income decile group (cont.)
based on weighted data and including children's expenditure

	Lowest ten per cent	Second decile group	Third decile group	Fourth decile group	Fifth decile group	Sixth decile group
Commodity or service	Average weekly household expenditure (£)					
7 Household goods	**11.20**	**14.20**	**18.30**	**22.60**	**27.50**	**31.10**
Percentage standard error	*12*	*9*	*6*	*7*	*7*	*6*
7.1 Furniture	2.60	4.00	4.50	5.60	6.50	7.70
7.2 Floor coverings	1.50	1.20	1.80	3.00	3.40	3.60
7.3 Soft furnishings and bedding	0.50	0.90	1.00	1.40	1.20	2.90
7.4 Gas and electric appliances, inc repairs	2.40	1.70	3.30	3.00	4.50	4.10
7.5 Kitchen\garden equipment, household hardware	1.10	1.90	2.30	3.30	4.00	4.60
7.6 Kitchen and electrical consumables	0.40	0.50	0.70	0.80	0.90	0.90
7.7 Greetings cards, stationery and paper goods	0.50	0.80	1.00	1.30	1.70	1.60
7.8 Detergents and other cleaning materials	0.90	1.30	1.60	1.70	1.80	2.10
7.9 Toilet paper	0.40	0.50	0.60	0.60	0.60	0.70
7.10 Pets and pet food	0.80	1.30	1.50	1.80	2.80	2.90
8 Household services	**8.50**	**9.70**	**12.00**	**16.00**	**16.90**	**17.50**
Percentage standard error	*7*	*6*	*5*	*7*	*4*	*5*
8.1 Insurance of contents of dwelling	1.00	1.00	1.30	1.60	1.80	2.10
8.2 Postage	0.20	0.40	0.50	0.40	0.50	0.50
8.3 Telephone	4.70	5.10	5.70	6.70	7.90	7.90
8.4 Domestic help and childcare	0.80	1.20	2.10	1.50	1.70	1.70
8.5 Repairs to footwear, watches, etc	..	..	[0.10]	[0.00]	[0.10]	..
8.6 Laundry, cleaning and dyeing	0.10	0.10	0.20	0.20	0.30	0.20
8.7 Subscriptions	0.10	0.10	0.20	0.40	0.60	0.90
8.8 Professional fees	[0.50]	[0.80]	1.00	3.00	1.70	1.10
8.9 Other services	1.00	0.50	1.00	2.10	2.20	2.70
9 Personal goods and services	**5.00**	**5.50**	**7.40**	**9.60**	**12.40**	**14.10**
Percentage standard error	*11*	*6*	*6*	*6*	*6*	*5*
9.1 Leather and travel goods, jewellery, watches etc	0.40	0.60	0.80	1.00	1.70	2.10
9.2 Baby toiletries and equipment	0.40	0.40	0.40	0.50	1.00	1.00
9.3 Medicines, prescriptions, spectacles	1.40	1.10	1.70	2.20	3.00	2.70
9.4 Medical, dental, optical and nursing fees	[0.50]	0.50	0.80	1.00	1.00	1.50
9.5 Toiletries and soap	0.70	0.80	1.10	1.40	1.50	1.80
9.6 Cosmetics and hair products	0.60	0.90	1.20	1.60	2.10	2.70
9.7 Hairdressing, beauty treatment	1.00	1.30	1.50	2.10	2.10	2.30
10 Motoring	**8.60**	**11.80**	**24.80**	**32.80**	**50.50**	**55.70**
Percentage standard error	*15*	*7*	*7*	*6*	*5*	*5*
10.1 Cars, vans and motorcycles purchase	1.80	2.30	8.10	11.20	21.00	22.30
10.2 Spares and accessories	..	0.80	1.20	1.40	1.40	1.80
10.3 Car and van repairs and servicing	..	1.30	2.50	3.60	4.60	4.60
10.4 Motor vehicle insurance and taxation	1.70	2.70	4.10	5.60	7.60	8.60
10.5 Petrol, diesel and other motor oils	2.40	4.30	7.60	9.90	14.30	16.80
10.6 Other motoring costs	0.30	0.40	1.20	1.10	1.60	1.60
11 Fares and other travel costs	**2.70**	**3.40**	**3.90**	**5.60**	**8.70**	**7.20**
Percentage standard error	*10*	*12*	*9*	*8*	*20*	*9*
11.1 Rail and tube fares	0.40	0.40	0.50	0.80	1.30	1.40
11.2 Bus and coach fares	1.00	1.20	1.00	1.50	1.50	1.40
11.3 Taxis, air and other travel	1.30	1.50	2.00	2.90	4.40	3.30
11.4 Bicycles, boats, purchase and repair	..	[0.30]	..	[0.40]	..	1.10

ONS, Family Spending 2000-01, © Crown copyright 2002

1.3 Detailed household expenditure by gross income decile group (cont.)

based on weighted data and including children's expenditure

2000-01

Commodity or service	Seventh decile group	Eighth decile group	Ninth decile group	Highest ten per cent	All house- holds
	Average weekly household expenditure (£)				
7 Household goods	**38.70**	**37.40**	**54.60**	**70.60**	**32.60**
Percentage standard error	*7*	*6*	*7*	*7*	*3*
7.1 Furniture	11.40	12.40	14.20	23.90	9.30
7.2 Floor coverings	4.10	3.10	4.80	6.80	3.30
7.3 Soft furnishings and bedding	2.30	1.80	3.20	4.00	1.90
7.4 Gas and electric appliances, inc repairs	3.80	4.40	9.40	8.80	4.60
7.5 Kitchen\garden equipment, household hardware	5.80	5.50	10.60	10.70	5.00
7.6 Kitchen and electrical consumables	1.40	1.30	1.60	1.90	1.00
7.7 Greetings cards, stationery and paper goods	2.10	2.30	2.90	3.80	1.80
7.8 Detergents and other cleaning materials	2.50	2.30	2.60	3.20	2.00
7.9 Toilet paper	0.90	0.90	1.00	1.00	0.70
7.10 Pets and pet food	4.40	3.40	4.50	6.40	3.00
8 Household services	**25.70**	**27.70**	**30.80**	**54.80**	**22.00**
Percentage standard error	*7*	*5*	*5*	*7*	*2*
8.1 Insurance of contents of dwelling	2.30	2.60	2.90	3.70	2.00
8.2 Postage	0.50	0.50	0.70	0.90	0.50
8.3 Telephone	9.40	10.00	11.00	15.20	8.40
8.4 Domestic help and childcare	4.90	4.00	4.70	11.30	3.40
8.5 Repairs to footwear, watches, etc	..	..	..	0.40	0.30
8.6 Laundry, cleaning and dyeing	0.50	0.50	0.50	1.30	0.40
8.7 Subscriptions	1.40	1.40	1.90	4.00	1.10
8.8 Professional fees	1.50	3.00	3.30	6.00	2.20
8.9 Other services	4.80	5.30	5.40	11.90	3.70
9 Personal goods and services	**16.90**	**20.10**	**23.30**	**32.70**	**14.70**
Percentage standard error	*4*	*6*	*5*	*5*	*2*
9.1 Leather and travel goods, jewellery, watches etc	2.60	3.60	3.30	5.20	2.10
9.2 Baby toiletries and equipment	1.10	0.90	1.20	0.80	0.80
9.3 Medicines, prescriptions, spectacles	3.60	3.80	4.40	7.50	3.10
9.4 Medical, dental, optical and nursing fees	1.60	2.80	3.20	3.50	1.60
9.5 Toiletries and soap	2.20	2.60	3.00	3.80	1.90
9.6 Cosmetics and hair products	2.90	3.20	4.00	5.50	2.50
9.7 Hairdressing, beauty treatment	2.90	3.20	4.30	6.40	2.70
10 Motoring	**72.10**	**81.60**	**94.60**	**118.30**	**55.10**
Percentage standard error	*4*	*4*	*4*	*4*	*2*
10.1 Cars, vans and motorcycles purchase	30.00	37.10	42.40	53.40	23.00
10.2 Spares and accessories	2.70	2.00	2.10	3.30	1.70
10.3 Car and van repairs and servicing	5.60	5.70	6.30	9.00	4.50
10.4 Motor vehicle insurance and taxation	10.80	11.50	13.40	16.20	8.20
10.5 Petrol, diesel and other motor oils	20.60	22.80	27.00	32.70	15.80
10.6 Other motoring costs	2.50	2.50	3.40	3.70	1.80
11 Fares and other travel costs	**9.30**	**10.30**	**15.30**	**28.20**	**9.50**
Percentage standard error	*14*	*11*	*16*	*10*	*5*
11.1 Rail and tube fares	1.70	2.10	4.30	7.20	2.00
11.2 Bus and coach fares	1.60	1.70	1.90	1.20	1.40
11.3 Taxis, air and other travel	4.80	5.80	7.90	17.90	5.20
11.4 Bicycles, boats, purchase and repair	1.10	0.60	1.20	1.80	0.80

1.3 Detailed household expenditure by gross income decile group (cont.)
based on weighted data and including children's expenditure

	Lowest ten per cent	Second decile group	Third decile group	Fourth decile group	Fifth decile group	Sixth decile group
Commodity or service	Average weekly household expenditure (£)					
12 Leisure goods	**6.10**	**7.00**	**11.00**	**11.30**	**18.00**	**20.30**
Percentage standard error	*11*	*7*	*7*	*6*	*8*	*10*
12.1 Books, maps, diaries	0.40	0.50	0.70	1.10	1.30	1.30
12.2 Newspapers	1.20	1.60	2.00	1.90	2.10	2.20
12.3 Magazines and periodicals	0.30	0.50	0.60	0.80	1.00	1.20
12.4 TVs, videos, computers and audio equipment	2.50	2.60	3.40	4.00	8.40	9.70
12.5 Sports and camping equipment	..	[0.10]	0.40	0.40	0.80	0.70
12.6 Toys and hobbies	0.80	0.70	1.20	1.30	2.10	2.50
12.7 Photography and camcorders	0.20	0.20	1.10	0.40	0.70	0.80
12.8 Horticultural goods, plants, flowers	0.60	0.80	1.50	1.50	1.60	1.90
13 Leisure services	**14.10**	**14.40**	**23.70**	**31.10**	**32.50**	**44.00**
Percentage standard error	*14*	*8*	*6*	*8*	*6*	*6*
13.1 Cinema and theatre	0.10	0.30	0.40	0.60	1.10	1.20
13.2 Sports admissions and subscriptions	0.50	0.70	0.60	1.20	2.30	2.40
13.3 TV, video and satellite rental, television licences and Internet	2.90	2.90	3.50	4.10	4.70	4.60
13.4 Miscellaneous entertainments	0.20	0.40	0.50	0.80	1.10	1.30
13.5 Educational and training expenses	3.30	1.80	1.00	2.80	2.90	2.80
13.6 Holiday in UK	0.80	1.20	1.90	1.90	2.10	2.30
13.7 Holiday abroad	[1.70]	2.20	5.40	5.90	6.70	11.20
13.8 Other incidental holiday expenses	..	[0.50]	[1.90]	4.30	2.90	4.20
13.9 Gambling payments	1.70	2.30	3.60	3.70	4.40	4.50
13.10 Cash gifts, donations	2.20	2.10	4.70	5.80	4.30	9.40
14 Miscellaneous	**0.20**	**0.30**	**0.30**	**0.40**	**0.90**	**0.70**
Percentage standard error	*23*	*20*	*19*	*18*	*21*	*16*
1-14 All expenditure groups	**126.70**	**153.80**	**215.10**	**266.70**	**329.00**	**370.20**
Percentage standard error	*5*	*3*	*2*	*2*	*2*	*2*
15 Other payments recorded						
15.1 Life assurance, contributions to pension funds	1.50	2.10	3.70	8.30	11.50	16.40
15.2 Medical insurance premiums	[0.20]	[0.10]	0.70	0.70	1.00	1.20
15.3 Other insurance premiums	0.10	0.20	0.40	0.60	0.70	0.90
15.4 Income tax, payments less refunds	0.60	2.60	6.60	19.20	34.70	49.20
15.5 National insurance contributions	0.40	0.40	1.30	5.40	11.20	17.40
15.6 Purchase or alteration of dwellings, mortgages	5.00	5.20	6.90	10.70	14.90	16.30
15.7 Savings and investments	..	0.40	1.60	..	2.70	3.10
15.8 Repayment of loans to clear other debts	[0.20]	[0.30]	[0.50]	1.40	2.60	3.30

1.3 Detailed household expenditure by gross income decile group (cont.)

2000-01

based on weighted data and including children's expenditure

Commodity or service	Seventh decile group	Eighth decile group	Ninth decile group	Highest ten per cent	All house-holds
	Average weekly household expenditure (£)				
12 **Leisure goods**	**22.00**	**28.20**	**31.90**	**41.70**	**19.70**
Percentage standard error	*6*	*8*	*8*	*8*	*3*
12.1 Books, maps, diaries	2.00	2.20	2.50	4.50	1.70
12.2 Newspapers	2.00	2.10	2.10	2.80	2.00
12.3 Magazines and periodicals	1.30	1.40	1.40	1.90	1.00
12.4 TVs, videos, computers and audio equipment	10.10	14.50	15.60	17.70	8.80
12.5 Sports and camping equipment	0.80	1.00	1.20	3.50	0.90
12.6 Toys and hobbies	2.90	2.90	3.10	3.10	2.10
12.7 Photography and camcorders	1.00	1.70	2.40	2.20	1.10
12.8 Horticultural goods, plants, flowers	2.00	2.60	3.70	6.00	2.20
13 **Leisure services**	**53.60**	**61.30**	**85.40**	**145.80**	**50.60**
Percentage standard error	*5*	*6*	*6*	*6*	*2*
13.1 Cinema and theatre	1.30	1.70	2.30	3.00	1.20
13.2 Sports admissions and subscriptions	3.30	5.20	7.20	9.40	3.30
13.3 TV, video and satellite rental, television licences and Internet	4.80	5.20	5.60	6.10	4.40
13.4 Miscellaneous entertainments	2.20	1.80	1.90	3.40	1.40
13.5 Educational and training expenses	5.30	8.10	9.70	27.70	6.50
13.6 Holiday in UK	2.50	3.80	3.90	4.70	2.50
13.7 Holiday abroad	15.00	16.40	20.20	40.10	12.50
13.8 Other incidental holiday expenses	6.30	6.30	16.80	23.90	6.80
13.9 Gambling payments	4.70	4.50	4.40	5.00	3.90
13.10 Cash gifts, donations	8.20	8.30	13.30	22.50	8.10
14 **Miscellaneous**	**0.80**	**1.00**	**1.20**	**1.60**	**0.70**
Percentage standard error	*17*	*13*	*15*	*16*	*6*
1-14 **All expenditure groups**	**448.00**	**500.50**	**597.30**	**849.00**	**385.70**
Percentage standard error	*2*	*2*	*2*	*2*	*1*
15 **Other payments recorded**					
15.1 Life assurance, contributions to pension funds	24.90	28.60	39.30	75.30	21.20
15.2 Medical insurance premiums	1.10	1.70	2.10	3.90	1.30
15.3 Other insurance premiums	1.50	1.20	2.00	2.80	1.00
16.4 Income tax, payments less refunds	68.20	90.40	132.40	299.40	70.40
15.5 National insurance contributions	23.70	31.50	41.40	50.90	18.40
15.6 Purchase or alteration of dwellings, mortgages	24.40	30.40	41.10	90.20	24.50
15.7 Savings and investments	10.50	13.50	19.60	46.10	10.40
15.8 Repayment of loans to clear other debts	4.80	6.10	5.70	6.10	3.10

1.4 Household expenditure by disposable income decile group
based on weighted data and including children's expenditure

	Lowest ten per cent	Second decile group	Third decile group	Fourth decile group	Fifth decile group	Sixth decile group
Lower boundary of group (£ per week)		104	158	210	271	338
Grossed number of households (thousands)	2,510	2,500	2,500	2,500	2,500	2,500
Total number of households in sample	669	703	703	687	668	676
Total number of persons in sample	918	1,220	1,324	1,448	1,586	1,793
Total number of adults in sample	738	909	1,057	1,147	1,178	1,276
Weighted average number of persons per household	1.3	1.7	1.8	2.0	2.3	2.5

Commodity or service	Average weekly household expenditure (£)					
1 Housing (Net)	**21.60**	**28.50**	**35.70**	**47.40**	**54.60**	**62.10**
Percentage standard error	*7*	*4*	*4*	*3*	*3*	*2*
2 Fuel and power	**8.80**	**9.30**	**11.30**	**10.80**	**10.90**	**11.70**
"	*3*	*3*	*6*	*3*	*3*	*2*
3 Food and non-alcoholic drinks	**26.50**	**32.70**	**40.90**	**47.20**	**56.50**	**62.80**
"	*3*	*2*	*2*	*2*	*2*	*2*
4 Alcoholic drink	**4.40**	**4.80**	**7.90**	**9.70**	**14.30**	**15.30**
"	*11*	*8*	*7*	*6*	*5*	*5*
5 Tobacco	**4.00**	**4.30**	**5.90**	**5.70**	**7.00**	**7.10**
"	*8*	*8*	*7*	*8*	*8*	*7*
6 Clothing and footwear	**6.80**	**8.20**	**11.60**	**13.80**	**18.00**	**22.60**
"	*9*	*7*	*7*	*7*	*6*	*6*
7 Household goods	**11.60**	**14.50**	**18.90**	**22.60**	**25.20**	**29.90**
"	*12*	*10*	*6*	*6*	*6*	*7*
8 Household services	**8.60**	**9.70**	**13.00**	**15.20**	**16.00**	**18.60**
"	*7*	*6*	*5*	*6*	*4*	*5*
9 Personal goods and services	**5.30**	**5.50**	**7.10**	**10.30**	**12.00**	**13.80**
"	*11*	*6*	*6*	*6*	*6*	*5*
10 Motoring	**10.30**	**11.50**	**23.50**	**37.50**	**47.50**	**52.70**
"	*14*	*8*	*7*	*6*	*5*	*6*
11 Fares and other travel costs	**2.80**	**3.50**	**4.10**	**4.40**	**9.10**	**7.50**
"	*10*	*12*	*9*	*9*	*19*	*10*
12 Leisure goods	**6.60**	**6.90**	**10.40**	**12.90**	**16.80**	**19.50**
"	*11*	*7*	*6*	*9*	*7*	*10*
13 Leisure services	**15.90**	**15.50**	**23.40**	**30.90**	**31.40**	**44.60**
"	*14*	*9*	*7*	*8*	*5*	*6*
14 Miscellaneous	**0.20**	**0.30**	**0.30**	**0.60**	**0.70**	**0.70**
"	*22*	*19*	*19*	*26*	*16*	*16*
1-14 All expenditure groups	**133.50**	**155.10**	**214.00**	**268.80**	**320.00**	**368.90**
Percentage standard error	*5*	*3*	*2*	*2*	*2*	*2*
Average weekly expenditure per person (£)						
All expenditure groups	**100.60**	**93.20**	**116.60**	**134.10**	**138.60**	**145.30**

ONS, Family Spending 2000-01, © Crown copyright 2002

1.4 Household expenditure by disposable income decile group (cont.)
based on weighted data and including children's expenditure

2000-01

	Seventh decile group	Eighth decile group	Ninth decile group	Highest ten per cent	All house-holds
Lower boundary of group (£ per week)	404	490	595	776	
Grossed number of households (thousands)	2,500	2,500	2,500	2,500	25,030
Total number of households in sample	663	643	620	605	6,637
Total number of persons in sample	1,846	1,887	1,929	1,974	15,925
Total number of adults in sample	1,328	1,349	1,405	1,465	11,852
Weighted average number of persons per household	2.7	2.9	3.0	3.2	2.4

Commodity or service	Average weekly household expenditure (£)				
1 Housing (Net)	**73.50**	**85.10**	**93.70**	**137.00**	**63.90**
Percentage standard error	*2*	*3*	*2*	*4*	*1*
2 Fuel and power	**12.70**	**12.80**	**14.00**	**16.60**	**11.90**
"	*2*	*2*	*2*	*2*	*1*
3 Food and non-alcoholic drinks	**72.10**	**79.20**	**89.00**	**112.40**	**61.90**
"	*2*	*2*	*2*	*2*	*1*
4 Alcoholic drink	**17.00**	**19.40**	**23.10**	**34.40**	**15.00**
"	*4*	*4*	*4*	*5*	*2*
5 Tobacco	**6.20**	**6.70**	**6.70**	**7.10**	**6.10**
"	*8*	*8*	*9*	*10*	*3*
6 Clothing and footwear	**26.20**	**28.60**	**38.80**	**45.30**	**22.00**
"	*5*	*5*	*5*	*5*	*2*
7 Household goods	**41.70**	**39.90**	**53.00**	**69.10**	**32.60**
"	*7*	*7*	*7*	*7*	*3*
8 Household services	**24.00**	**29.30**	**32.20**	**52.90**	**22.00**
"	*5*	*7*	*7*	*7*	*2*
9 Personal goods and services	**17.90**	**17.80**	**25.70**	**31.90**	**14.70**
"	*5*	*5*	*6*	*5*	*2*
10 Motoring	**73.90**	**84.00**	**91.10**	**119.00**	**55.10**
"	*4*	*4*	*4*	*4*	*2*
14 Fares and other travel costs	**8.30**	**10.80**	**16.10**	**28.10**	**9.50**
"	*9*	*13*	*16*	*10*	*5*
12 Leisure goods	**23.20**	**24.80**	**34.90**	**41.40**	**19.70**
"	*7*	*6*	*8*	*8*	*3*
13 Leisure services	**52.10**	**61.10**	**89.60**	**142.00**	**50.60**
"	*5*	*5*	*7*	*6*	*2*
14 Miscellaneous	**0.90**	**1.00**	**1.10**	**1.60**	**0.70**
"	*17*	*14*	*14*	*16*	*6*
1-14 All expenditure groups	**449.60**	**500.60**	**608.80**	**838.80**	**385.70**
Percentage standard error	*2*	*2*	*2*	*2*	*1*
Average weekly expenditure per person (£)					
All expenditure groups	**163.70**	**173.70**	**200.40**	**262.70**	**163.90**

1.5 Household expenditure as a percentage of total expenditure by disposable income decile group

2000-01

based on weighted data and including children's expenditure

	Lowest ten per cent	Second decile group	Third decile group	Fourth decile group	Fifth decile group	Sixth decile group
Lower boundary of group (£ per week)		104	158	210	271	338
Grossed number of households (thousands)	2,510	2,500	2,500	2,500	2,500	2,500
Total number of households in sample	669	703	703	687	668	676
Total number of persons in sample	918	1,220	1,324	1,448	1,586	1,793
Total number of adults in sample	738	909	1,057	1,147	1,178	1,276
Weighted average number of persons per household	1.3	1.7	1.8	2.0	2.3	2.5

Commodity or service	Percentage of total expenditure					
1 Housing (Net)	16	18	17	18	17	17
2 Fuel and power	7	6	5	4	3	3
3 Food and non-alcoholic drinks	20	21	19	18	18	17
4 Alcoholic drink	3	3	4	4	4	4
5 Tobacco	3	3	3	2	2	2
6 Clothing and footwear	5	5	5	5	6	6
7 Household goods	9	9	9	8	8	8
8 Household services	6	6	6	6	6	5
9 Personal goods and services	4	4	3	4	4	4
10 Motoring	8	7	11	14	15	14
11 Fares and other travel costs	2	2	2	2	3	2
12 Leisure goods	5	4	5	5	5	5
13 Leisure services	12	10	11	11	10	12
14 Miscellaneous	0	0	0	0	0	0
1-14 All expenditure groups	100	100	100	100	100	100

ONS, Family Spending 2000-01, © Crown copyright 2002

1.5 Household expenditure as a percentage of total expenditure by disposable income decile group (cont.)

based on weighted data and including children's expenditure

2000-01

	Seventh decile group	Eighth decile group	Ninth decile group	Highest ten per cent	All house-holds
Lower boundary of group (£ per week)	404	490	595	776	
Grossed number of households (thousands)	2,500	2,500	2,500	2,500	25,030
Total number of households in sample	663	643	620	605	6,637
Total number of persons in sample	1,846	1,887	1,929	1,974	15,925
Total number of adults in sample	1,328	1,349	1,405	1,465	11,852
Weighted average number of persons per household	2.7	2.9	3.0	3.2	2.4

Commodity or service	Percentage of total expenditure				
1 **Housing (Net)**	16	17	15	16	17
2 **Fuel and power**	3	3	2	2	3
3 **Food and non-alcoholic drinks**	16	16	15	13	16
4 **Alcoholic drink**	4	4	4	4	4
5 **Tobacco**	1	1	1	1	2
6 **Clothing and footwear**	6	6	6	5	6
7 **Household goods**	9	8	9	8	8
8 **Household services**	5	6	5	6	6
9 **Personal goods and services**	4	4	4	4	4
10 **Motoring**	16	17	15	14	14
14 **Fares and other travel costs**	2	2	3	3	2
12 **Leisure goods**	5	5	6	5	5
13 **Leisure services**	12	12	15	17	13
14 **Miscellaneous**	0	0	0	0	0
1-14 **All expenditure groups**	100	100	100	100	100

Chapter 2

Expenditure by age & income

- Expenditure in 2000-01 varied with age of head of household from an average of £170 a week for households with a head aged 75 or over to £470 a week for those with a head aged 30 to 49.

- **Leisure goods and services** were the largest item of spending on average for households with a head in the age ranges from 30 to 74. **Housing** was the largest item on average for households with a young head, aged under 30, and **food and non-alcoholic drink** was the largest item when the head was aged 75 or over.

- The proportion of expenditure going on **food and non-alcoholic drink** increased progressively with the age of the head from an average of 14 per cent at age under 30 to 21 per cent at age 75 or over.

- Households with a head under 30 spent the most on **take-away meals eaten at home**, an average of £6 a week. For **eating out** both the 30 to 49 and 50 to 64 age groups were high spenders, averaging about £12 a week.

- Expenditure on **reading matter** as a percentage of all leisure goods rose with age from under 20 per cent at ages below 30 to over 50 per cent in households with a head aged 75 or over.

- Expenditure on **toys and hobbies** was highest in households with a head aged 30 to 49 but spending on **horticultural goods, plants and flowers** was much the higher of the two items from ages 50 onwards. Households with a head aged 50 to 64 spent the most on horticultural goods etc., an average of £3.10 a week.

- The lower total spending of older households was mainly the result of lower incomes, but even within the same income group older households spent less. For example, for the fifth of households with the lowest incomes, total spending averaged £110 a week when the head was aged 65 or over, compared with £160 a week when the head was aged 30 to 65.

- The pattern of spending also varied with age after allowing for the effect of income. In the middle income group, for example, spending on **housing** fell progressively with the age of the head of household, from £70 a week at age under 30 to £35 a week at age 75 and over.

2

Expenditure by age and income

2.1 Expenditure by age of head of household

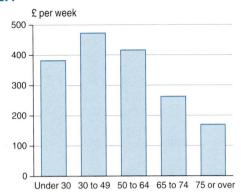

£ per week

2.2 Food and motoring as a percentage of total expenditure by age of head of household

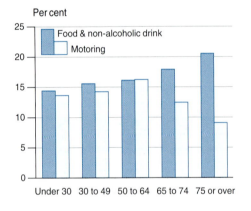

Per cent

- Food & non-alcoholic drink
- Motoring

2.3 Leisure goods and services by age of head of household

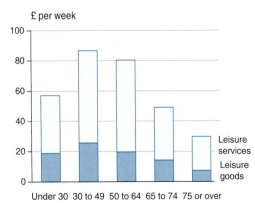

£ per week

Leisure services
Leisure goods

This chapter analyses household expenditure by the age of head of household. In addition, **Tables 2.4 to 2.8** contain an analysis of average weekly expenditure for each group by income. The way incomes are shown changed last year. The same income groups are now used in every table so that comparisons can be made between households with heads of different age but the same income. For the first time this year **Tables 2.4 to 2.8** are based on data from the last three years, 1998-99 – 2000-01. This increases sample size and reliability. Next year the tables will be based on the age of the household reference person. An explanation of the difference from head of household is in Appendix D. **Table 2.9** shows expenditure by age of household reference person for comparison with **Table 2.1**.

Characteristics of households

Table 2.1 shows how the number of households varied across the age groups. Eleven per cent of households had a head aged under 30. Households with a head aged 30 to 49 were the largest group, forming 40 per cent of the total, 25 per cent had a head aged 50 to 64, and a further 25 per cent had a head aged 65 or over. The average number of persons per household was highest for households with a head aged 30 to 49, 3.0 persons, falling to 1.4 persons for those households with a head aged 75 or over.

Aggregate expenditure patterns

Figure 2.1 shows that average weekly household expenditure was lowest at £170 a week for households where the head was aged 75 or over and highest at £470 a week where the head was 30 to 49. **Table 2.1** shows that expenditure on leisure goods and services combined was the largest item of spending on average for households with a head aged between 30 and 74. Housing was the largest item for households with young heads, under 30, and food and non-alcoholic drink was the largest item for households with a head aged 75 or over.

Table 2.2 shows expenditure as a percentage of total expenditure by age of head of household. **Figure 2.2** shows the proportions for two items, food and non-alcoholic drinks and motoring. The proportion spent on food increased steadily with the age of head, from 14 per cent at age under 30 to 21 per cent at age 75 or over. Spending on motoring was similar to spending on food up to the 50 to 64 age group, but fell after that to 9 per cent of spend at 75

ONS, Family Spending 2000-01, © Crown copyright 2002

or over. **Figure 2.3** shows that spending on leisure goods and on leisure services followed broadly the same pattern as each other, being highest for households with a head aged 30 to 49 and 50 to 64. The proportion of leisure spending going on leisure services did increase a little with age however, from about two thirds in the youngest households to three quarters of those with a head aged 75 or over.

Detailed expenditure patterns

Leisure goods and services

Table 2.3 gives a detailed breakdown of expenditure for each of the age groups. **Figure 2.4a** compares expenditure on electronic goods and electronic services across the age groups. Households headed by those in the 30 to 49 age group spent the most at £12.00 a week on TVs, videos, computers and audio equipment, and households with a head under 30 spent nearly as much. This compares to the average £4.50 a week these households spent on TV, video and satellite rental, television licences and the Internet. Spending on these items was again highest where the head of household was aged 30 to 49, £5.20 a week. Next highest were households in the 50 to 64 age group, £4.70 a week. Households with a head aged 75 or over spent an average of £2.30 a week on these electronic services, less than half the amount of those in the 50 to 64 age group but more than on electronic goods. **Figure 2.4b** compares spending on toys and hobbies with that on horticultural goods, plants and flowers. Spending on toys and hobbies was markedly higher among households headed by those in the 30 to 49 age group, over twice that of all other age groups with the exception of those under 30. Spending on horticultural goods peaked in the age group 50 to 64 however, followed by those in the 65 to 74 age group. Those aged 75 or over spent more, £1.30 a week, on these goods than did the under 30 age group who spent an average of 80p a week, almost a quarter of the amount spent by the 50 to 64 age group.

Fuel and Power

Tables 2.2, 2.3 and **Figure 2.5** show that spending on fuel and power varied relatively little with age. Spending increased with the age of the head, up to £13.00 a week at age 50 to 64, then declined. However, spending on fuel as a proportion of all spending went on increasing with age, from 3 per cent up to age 65 to 6 per cent at

2.4a Electronic goods and services by age of head of household

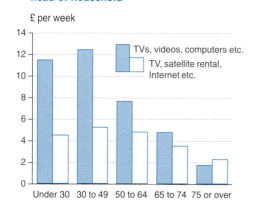

2.4b Toys & hobbies and horticultural goods by age of head of household

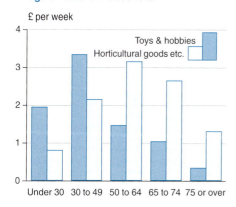

2.5 Fuel and power by age of head of household

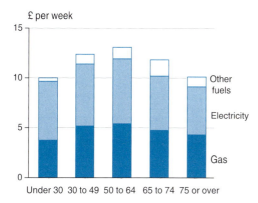

2.6 Holidays by age of head of household

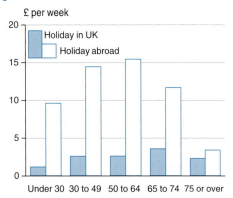

£ per week

Under 30 30 to 49 50 to 64 65 to 74 75 or over

2.7a Total expenditure by age of head of household: lowest income quintile group

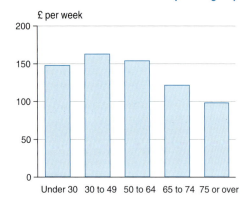

£ per week

Under 30 30 to 49 50 to 64 65 to 74 75 or over

2.7b Housing and food by age of head of household: lowest income quintile group

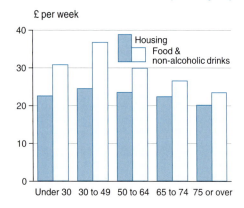

£ per week

Under 30 30 to 49 50 to 64 65 to 74 75 or over

age 75 or over. Spending per person also increased with age, from about £4.20 per person up to age 50 to £7.20 per person at 75 and over. Households spent more on electricity than gas at all ages, but the difference was largest for heads under 30, who spent an average of £6.00 a week on electricity and £3.60 on gas. Older households tended to spend slightly more on other fuels than younger age groups.

Holidays

Figure 2.6 compares spending on holidays in the UK with that on holidays abroad. Households headed by those in the 65 to 74 age group spent the most on holidays in the UK, £3.60 a week, three times as much on average as the lowest spenders, households with a head of household under 30. Spending on holidays abroad was higher than on holidays in the UK at all ages, though the difference was relatively small at age 75 or over. Spending on holidays abroad increased with age up to the 50 to 64 age group, who spent £15.40 a week on average, but then declined at higher ages. Households with heads aged 75 or over had the lowest figures for holidays abroad, £3.40 a week.

Expenditure by age and income

Much of the variation in spending with age is the result of differences in income. **Tables 2.4 to 2.8** contain an analysis of expenditure by gross income quintile group for each age group in the period 1998-99 through to 2000-01 so that the effect of age can be analysed separately.

Low income households

Figure 2.7a shows how total expenditure varies with age for the fifth of all households with the lowest incomes. It shows that households with a head aged 65 or over spent markedly less than those with similar income but a younger head, £98 among those aged 75 and over and £121 a week for those in the 65 to 74 age group. This compares with around £150 to £164 a week for those aged 64 or less. **Figure 2.7b** illustrates expenditure on food and housing for the lowest income quintile group. Expenditure on food ranged from £37 in the 30 to 49 age group to £23 a week in the 75 or over age group. Expenditure on housing was broadly similar across all age groups, ranging from £20 in the 75 or over age group to about £24 a week in the 30 to 49 age group. Looking at spending on alcoholic drink and tobacco by households with low

ONS, Family Spending 2000-01, © Crown copyright 2002

incomes, the younger age groups spent more in absolute terms on these items than those at the older end of the scale. **Tables 2.4 to 2.8** shows that spending on tobacco did not vary much with age up to 64, but declined sharply after that. Spending on alcohol was particularly high for under 30s, and generally declined with age. Households headed by those aged 65 and over spent least on these items, less than half that of the other age groups. Households headed by those in the 30 to 49 age group spent more each week on tobacco than on alcoholic drink, while the 75 or over age group spent twice as much a week on alcoholic drink as on tobacco.

Middle income households

Figure 2.8a shows total expenditure and **Figure 2.8b** shows expenditure on housing and food for the third (middle) income quintile group by age of head of household. Total expenditure did not vary much with age up to 74, but was distinctly lower at age 75 or over. Total expenditure for those households with a head aged 75 or over was about £250 a week, compared with an average of just over £340 a week for younger households with similar income. Expenditure on housing declined as age increased in the third income quintile group, from almost £70 a week among under 30s to round about half that figure for those aged 75 or over. Spending on food showed less variation, peaking at around £60 in the 30 to 49 age group, with the under 30 and the 75 or over age groups spending around about £50 a week.

Tables 2.4 to 2.8 demonstrates that in the middle income group households across every age group spent more on alcoholic drink than on tobacco, with households in the 30 to 49 age group being the only group that did not spend at least twice as much a week on alcohol as on tobacco. Spending on both declined with age from 65 onwards.

Household Reference Person

Table 2.9 shows expenditure by the age of the household reference person. A comparison with **Table 2.1** shows that there are slightly more young household reference persons and fewer old household reference persons than the equivalent heads of household, 3 per cent more under 30 and 2 per cent fewer aged 65 or older. Differences in spending are small.

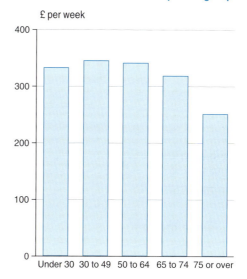

2.8a Total expenditure by age of head of household: third income quintile group

£ per week

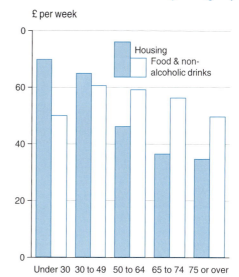

2.8b Housing and food by age of head of household: third income quintile group

£ per week

2.1 Household expenditure by age of head of household

2000-01

based on weighted data and including children's expenditure

	Under 30	30 and under 50	50 and under 65	65 and under 75	75 or over	All house-holds
Grossed number of households (thousands)	2,670	9,940	6,220	3,190	3,010	25,030
Total number of households in sample	687	2,598	1,646	956	750	6,637
Total number of persons in sample	1,620	7,989	3,617	1,622	1,077	15,925
Total number of adults in sample	1,132	4,802	3,243	1,602	1,073	11,852
Weighted average number of persons per household	2.3	3.0	2.2	1.7	1.4	2.4

Commodity or service	Average weekly household expenditure (£)					
1 Housing (Net)	**78.70**	**84.00**	**56.80**	**34.80**	**30.30**	**63.90**
Percentage standard error	*3*	*2*	*3*	*3*	*5*	*1*
2 Fuel and power	**9.90**	**12.30**	**13.00**	**11.80**	**10.00**	**11.90**
"	*7*	*1*	*2*	*2*	*2*	*1*
3 Food and non-alcoholic drinks	**55.00**	**73.60**	**67.10**	**47.00**	**34.70**	**61.90**
"	*2*	*1*	*2*	*2*	*2*	*1*
4 Alcoholic drink	**18.70**	**17.90**	**17.40**	**7.90**	**4.90**	**15.00**
"	*5*	*3*	*4*	*6*	*8*	*2*
5 Tobacco	**7.50**	**6.90**	**7.20**	**3.90**	**1.80**	**6.10**
"	*6*	*4*	*5*	*8*	*13*	*3*
6 Clothing and footwear	**25.00**	**29.80**	**21.10**	**12.20**	**5.80**	**22.00**
"	*6*	*3*	*4*	*6*	*8*	*2*
7 Household goods	**28.20**	**37.30**	**37.80**	**28.90**	**14.40**	**32.60**
"	*7*	*4*	*5*	*10*	*9*	*3*
8 Household services	**20.80**	**26.90**	**21.70**	**17.60**	**11.80**	**22.00**
"	*9*	*3*	*4*	*11*	*6*	*2*
9 Personal goods and services	**16.30**	**17.00**	**15.70**	**11.20**	**7.50**	**14.70**
"	*8*	*3*	*4*	*7*	*7*	*2*
10 Motoring	**52.00**	**67.30**	**67.60**	**32.70**	**15.40**	**55.10**
"	*6*	*3*	*4*	*5*	*9*	*2*
11 Fares and other travel costs	**12.00**	**11.80**	**10.10**	**5.40**	**2.50**	**9.50**
"	*12*	*6*	*10*	*21*	*20*	*5*
12 Leisure goods	**18.80**	**25.60**	**19.60**	**14.20**	**7.30**	**19.70**
"	*10*	*4*	*5*	*11*	*8*	*3*
13 Leisure services	**38.30**	**61.20**	**60.80**	**34.90**	**22.40**	**50.60**
"	*7*	*4*	*5*	*5*	*10*	*2*
14 Miscellaneous	**0.60**	**1.20**	**0.60**	**0.20**	**0.10**	**0.70**
"	*15*	*8*	*11*	*16*	*26*	*6*
1-14 All expenditure groups	**381.70**	**472.80**	**416.40**	**262.60**	**169.10**	**385.70**
Percentage standard error	*3*	*1*	*2*	*3*	*3*	*1*

Average weekly expenditure per person (£)						
All expenditure groups	**167.40**	**160.20**	**187.80**	**154.60**	**118.90**	**163.90**

ONS, Family Spending 2000-01, © Crown copyright 2002

2.2 Household expenditure as a percentage of total expenditure by age of head of household

2000-01

based on weighted data and including children's expenditure

	Under 30	30 and under 50	50 and under 65	65 and under 75	75 or over	All house-holds
Grossed number of households (thousands)	2,670	9,940	6,220	3,190	3,010	25,030
Total number of households in sample	687	2,598	1,646	956	750	6,637
Total number of persons in sample	1,620	7,989	3,617	1,622	1,077	15,925
Total number of adults in sample	1,132	4,802	3,243	1,602	1,073	11,852
Weighted average number of persons per household	2.3	3.0	2.2	1.7	1.4	2.4

Commodity or service	Percentage of total expenditure					
1 Housing (Net)	21	18	14	13	18	17
2 Fuel and power	3	3	3	4	6	3
3 Food and non-alcoholic drinks	14	16	16	18	21	16
4 Alcoholic drink	5	4	4	3	3	4
5 Tobacco	2	1	2	1	1	2
6 Clothing and footwear	7	6	5	5	3	6
7 Household goods	7	8	9	11	9	8
8 Household services	5	6	5	7	7	6
9 Personal goods and services	4	4	4	4	4	4
10 Motoring	14	14	16	12	9	14
11 Fares and other travel costs	3	2	2	2	1	2
12 Leisure goods	5	5	5	5	4	5
13 Leisure services	10	13	15	13	13	13
14 Miscellaneous	0	0	0	0	0	0
1-14 All expenditure groups	100	100	100	100	100	100

2.3 Detailed household expenditure by age of head of household
based on weighted data and including children's expenditure

2000-01

	Under 30	30 and under 50	50 and under 65	65 and under 75	75 or over	All house-holds
Grossed number of households (thousands)	2,670	9,940	6,220	3,190	3,010	25,030
Total number of households in sample	687	2,598	1,646	956	750	6,637
Total number of persons in sample	1,620	7,989	3,617	1,622	1,077	15,925
Total number of adults in sample	1,132	4,802	3,243	1,602	1,073	11,852
Weighted average number of persons per household	2.3	3.0	2.2	1.7	1.4	2.4

Commodity or service	Average weekly household expenditure (£)					
1 Housing (Net)	**78.70**	**84.00**	**56.80**	**34.80**	**30.30**	**63.90**
Percentage standard error	*3*	*2*	*3*	*3*	*5*	*1*
1.1 Gross rent, mortgage interest payments, water charges, council tax, etc	86.50	82.20	55.00	36.60	37.80	64.70
1.2 *less* housing benefit, rebates and allowances received	12.70	8.20	8.60	9.40	14.60	9.70
1.3 Net rent, mortgage interest payments, water charges, council tax, etc	73.80	74.00	46.40	27.20	23.10	55.00
1.4 Repairs, maintenance and decorations	4.80	10.00	10.30	7.60	7.20	8.90
2 Fuel and power	**9.90**	**12.30**	**13.00**	**11.80**	**10.00**	**11.90**
Percentage standard error	*7*	*1*	*2*	*2*	*2*	*1*
2.1 Gas	3.70	5.10	5.30	4.70	4.20	4.80
2.2 Electricity	5.90	6.20	6.50	5.40	4.80	6.00
2.3 Other fuels	0.30	1.00	1.20	1.60	1.00	1.00
3 Food and non-alcoholic drinks	**55.00**	**73.60**	**67.10**	**47.00**	**34.70**	**61.90**
Percentage standard error	*2*	*1*	*2*	*2*	*2*	*1*
3.1 Bread, rolls etc	1.40	2.00	2.00	1.70	1.20	1.80
3.2 Pasta, rice, flour and other cereals	0.50	0.60	0.50	0.30	0.20	0.50
3.3 Biscuits, cakes etc	1.70	3.10	3.10	2.90	2.50	2.90
3.4 Breakfast cereals	0.70	1.10	0.90	0.70	0.50	0.90
3.5 Beef and veal (uncooked)	0.80	1.50	1.90	1.60	1.00	1.50
3.6 Mutton and lamb (uncooked)	0.30	0.60	0.70	0.70	0.70	0.60
3.7 Pork (uncooked)	0.30	0.60	0.80	0.70	0.50	0.60
3.8 Bacon and ham (uncooked)	0.50	0.90	1.10	0.90	0.70	0.90
3.9 Poultry (uncooked)	1.70	2.40	2.20	1.60	1.00	2.00
3.10 Cold meats, ready to eat meats	1.00	1.60	1.60	1.40	1.00	1.40
3.11 Meat pies, sausages and other meats	0.80	1.40	1.40	1.30	1.00	1.30
3.12 Fish, shellfish and fish products	0.80	1.40	1.80	1.90	1.60	1.50
3.13 Butter	0.10	0.20	0.30	0.40	0.30	0.30
3.14 Margarine	0.20	0.40	0.40	0.40	0.30	0.40
3.15 Cooking oils and fats	0.10	0.20	0.20	0.20	0.10	0.20
3.16 Fresh milk	1.40	2.30	2.20	2.00	1.80	2.10
3.17 Milk products including cream	1.20	1.70	1.40	1.20	0.90	1.40
3.18 Cheese	1.00	1.50	1.50	1.10	0.70	1.30
3.19 Eggs	0.20	0.40	0.50	0.40	0.30	0.40
3.20 Potatoes, potato products (excluding crisps)	1.00	1.40	1.40	1.20	0.70	1.20
3.21 Other vegetables	2.30	3.60	3.80	3.10	2.00	3.30
3.22 Fruit, nuts	1.50	2.70	3.50	3.00	2.50	2.80

2.3 Detailed household expenditure by age of head of household (cont.)

2000-01

based on weighted data and including children's expenditure

	Under 30	30 and under 50	50 and under 65	65 and under 75	75 or over	All house-holds
Commodity or service	Average weekly household expenditure (£)					

3   Food and non-alcoholic drinks (continued)

		Under 30	30 and under 50	50 and under 65	65 and under 75	75 or over	All households
3.23	Sugar	0.10	0.20	0.20	0.20	0.20	0.20
3.24	Jam, jellies, preserves and other spreads	0.10	0.20	0.30	0.30	0.30	0.30
3.25	Sweets and chocolates	1.50	2.40	2.10	1.60	1.30	2.00
3.26	Ice cream and sorbets	0.40	0.60	0.50	0.40	0.30	0.50
3.27	Tea	0.20	0.50	0.60	0.50	0.50	0.50
3.28	Coffee	0.30	0.50	0.70	0.50	0.40	0.50
3.29	Drinking chocolate, other food drinks	0.10	0.20	0.20	0.20	0.10	0.20
3.30	Fruit juice, squashes, bottled water	1.10	1.80	1.40	0.90	0.70	1.40
3.31	Fizzy drinks	1.10	1.40	1.00	0.50	0.40	1.00
3.32	Soup	0.20	0.30	0.30	0.30	0.30	0.30
3.33	Pizzas, vegetarian pies, quiches	0.90	1.00	0.70	0.40	0.20	0.80
3.34	Other convenience foods	2.10	2.70	2.20	1.50	1.30	2.20
3.35	Potato crisps and savoury snacks	1.00	1.50	0.90	0.50	0.30	1.00
3.36	Restaurant and café meals	10.40	11.70	12.60	7.30	4.40	10.40
3.37	Take-away meals eaten at home	5.90	5.00	2.90	1.10	0.90	3.60
3.38	Other take-away food and snack food	6.30	6.90	3.80	1.00	0.50	4.50
3.39	State school meals and meals at work	2.60	3.30	1.60	0.20	[0.10]	2.00
3.40	Other foods	1.40	1.90	1.70	1.20	0.80	1.60
4	**Alcoholic drink**	**18.70**	**17.90**	**17.40**	**7.90**	**4.90**	**15.00**
	Percentage standard error	*5*	*3*	*4*	*6*	*8*	*2*
4.1	Beer, cider	10.50	9.40	9.10	3.20	1.60	7.70
4.2	Wines, fortified wines	3.10	4.30	4.20	2.70	1.70	3.60
4.3	Spirits, liqueurs	2.80	2.20	2.70	1.60	1.50	2.20
4.4	Other drinks	2.20	2.00	1.30	0.30	[0.10]	1.40
5	**Tobacco**	**7.50**	**6.90**	**7.20**	**3.90**	**1.80**	**6.10**
	Percentage standard error	*6*	*4*	*5*	*8*	*13*	*3*
5.1	Cigarettes	6.90	6.20	6.20	3.40	1.70	5.40
5.2	Tobacco and other tobacco products	0.60	0.70	1.10	0.50	[0.10]	0.70
6	**Clothing and footwear**	**25.00**	**29.80**	**21.10**	**12.20**	**5.80**	**22.00**
	Percentage standard error	*6*	*3*	*4*	*6*	*8*	*2*
6.1	Men's outerwear	6.00	5.90	4.40	2.00	0.80	4.40
6.2	Men's underwear and hosiery	0.40	0.60	0.50	0.50	0.20	0.50
6.3	Women's outerwear	8.80	9.00	8.40	5.40	2.40	7.60
6.4	Women's underwear and hosiery	1.20	1.40	1.40	0.90	0.70	1.20
6.5	Boys' outerwear	0.50	1.50	0.60	..	..	0.80
6.6	Girls' outerwear	0.50	2.30	0.70	0.20	..	1.20
6.7	Babies' outerwear	1.20	1.00	0.50	0.20	..	0.70
6.8	Boys', girls' and babies' underwear	0.50	0.70	0.20	0.10	..	0.40
6.9	Ties, belts, hats, gloves, etc	0.80	0.70	0.50	0.30	0.10	0.60
6.10	Haberdashery, textiles and clothes hire	0.30	0.60	0.40	0.30	0.20	0.40
6.11	Footwear	4.90	6.00	3.40	2.20	1.30	4.20

2.3 Detailed household expenditure by age of head of household (cont.)

based on weighted data and including children's expenditure

	Under 30	30 and under 50	50 and under 65	65 and under 75	75 or over	All house-holds
Commodity or service	Average weekly household expenditure (£)					
7 **Household goods**	**28.20**	**37.30**	**37.80**	**28.90**	**14.40**	**32.60**
Percentage standard error	*7*	*4*	*5*	*10*	*9*	*3*
7.1 Furniture	9.10	12.30	8.90	7.10	2.90	9.30
7.2 Floor coverings	3.10	3.50	4.20	3.20	1.30	3.30
7.3 Soft furnishings and bedding	1.20	2.10	2.30	1.80	1.20	1.90
7.4 Gas and electric appliances, inc repairs	4.30	4.30	6.00	4.40	2.90	4.60
7.5 Kitchen/garden equipment, household hardware	4.20	5.10	6.40	5.20	2.00	5.00
7.6 Kitchen and electrical consumables	0.60	1.20	1.20	1.00	0.70	1.00
7.7 Greetings cards, stationery and paper goods	1.50	2.20	2.00	1.30	0.90	1.80
7.8 Detergents and other cleaning materials	1.50	2.30	2.30	1.80	1.10	2.00
7.9 Toilet paper	0.60	0.80	0.80	0.60	0.40	0.70
7.10 Pets and pet food	2.10	3.40	3.80	2.50	1.10	3.00
8 **Household services**	**20.80**	**26.90**	**21.70**	**17.60**	**11.80**	**22.00**
Percentage standard error	*9*	*3*	*4*	*11*	*6*	*2*
8.1 Insurance of contents of dwelling	1.40	2.30	2.30	1.90	1.50	2.00
8.2 Postage	0.30	0.40	0.60	0.70	0.60	0.50
8.3 Telephone	9.60	10.00	8.90	5.20	4.00	8.40
8.4 Domestic help and childcare	1.50	5.30	1.70	2.50	3.10	3.40
8.5 Repairs to footwear, watches, etc	..	0.20	..	0.90	0.20	0.30
8.6 Laundry, cleaning and dyeing	0.30	0.40	0.60	0.30	0.30	0.40
8.7 Subscriptions	0.60	1.50	1.30	0.60	0.20	1.10
8.8 Professional fees	1.80	2.30	2.90	1.70	[1.10]	2.20
8.9 Other services	5.20	4.50	3.10	3.70	0.90	3.70
9 **Personal goods and services**	**16.30**	**17.00**	**15.70**	**11.20**	**7.50**	**14.70**
Percentage standard error	*8*	*3*	*4*	*7*	*7*	*2*
9.1 Leather and travel goods, jewellery, watches etc	3.40	2.80	1.90	1.20	0.50	2.10
9.2 Baby toiletries and equipment	2.10	1.10	0.30	0.10	0.00	0.80
9.3 Medicines, prescriptions, spectacles	3.00	3.20	4.00	2.80	1.70	3.10
9.4 Medical, dental, optical and nursing fees	1.20	1.40	2.00	2.20	1.40	1.60
9.5 Toiletries and soap	1.80	2.40	2.00	1.20	0.90	1.90
9.6 Cosmetics and hair products	2.70	3.10	2.70	1.40	0.70	2.50
9.7 Hairdressing, beauty treatment	2.20	3.00	2.80	2.30	2.20	2.70
10 **Motoring**	**52.00**	**67.30**	**67.60**	**32.70**	**15.40**	**55.10**
Percentage standard error	*6*	*3*	*4*	*5*	*9*	*2*
10.1 Cars, vans and motorcycles purchase	23.70	28.30	28.60	11.20	5.50	23.00
10.2 Spares and accessories	1.50	2.30	1.80	1.30	[0.40]	1.70
10.3 Car and van repairs and servicing	3.10	5.10	5.90	3.50	1.90	4.50
10.4 Motor vehicle insurance and taxation	8.00	9.80	9.70	5.50	3.30	8.20
10.5 Petrol, diesel and other motor oils	14.00	19.80	19.20	9.90	3.70	15.80
10.6 Other motoring costs	1.70	2.10	2.30	1.30	0.70	1.80
11 **Fares and other travel costs**	**12.00**	**11.80**	**10.10**	**5.40**	**2.50**	**9.50**
Percentage standard error	*12*	*6*	*10*	*21*	*20*	*5*
11.1 Rail and tube fares	3.70	2.50	1.90	0.70	0.40	2.00
11.2 Bus and coach fares	1.60	1.80	1.50	0.80	0.50	1.40
11.3 Taxis, air and other travel	6.40	6.30	5.90	2.70	1.60	5.20
11.4 Bicycles, boats, purchase and repair	0.40	1.10	0.80	..	..	0.80

ONS, Family Spending 2000-01, © Crown copyright 2002

2.3 Detailed household expenditure by age of head of household (cont.)

2000-01

based on weighted data and including children's expenditure

	Under 30	30 and under 50	50 and under 65	65 and under 75	75 or over	All house-holds
Commodity or service	**Average weekly household expenditure (£)**					
12 Leisure goods	**18.80**	**25.60**	**19.60**	**14.20**	**7.30**	**19.70**
Percentage standard error	*10*	*4*	*5*	*11*	*8*	*3*
12.1 Books, maps, diaries	1.60	2.00	1.90	1.10	0.50	1.70
12.2 Newspapers	0.80	1.60	2.50	2.80	2.60	2.00
12.3 Magazines and periodicals	0.90	1.30	1.00	0.90	0.60	1.00
12.4 TVs, videos, computers and audio equipment	11.40	12.40	7.60	4.70	1.70	8.80
12.5 Sports and camping equipment	0.60	1.40	0.90	0.30	..	0.90
12.6 Toys and hobbies	1.90	3.30	1.50	1.00	0.30	2.10
12.7 Photography and camcorders	0.70	1.50	1.10	0.70	0.20	1.10
12.8 Horticultural goods, plants, flowers	0.80	2.10	3.10	2.60	1.30	2.20
13 Leisure services	**38.30**	**61.20**	**60.80**	**34.90**	**22.40**	**50.60**
Percentage standard error	*7*	*4*	*5*	*5*	*10*	*2*
13.1 Cinema and theatre	1.30	1.50	1.40	0.70	0.20	1.20
13.2 Sports admissions and subscriptions	3.70	4.40	3.40	1.60	..	3.30
13.3 TV, video and satellite rental, television licences and Internet	4.50	5.20	4.80	3.50	2.30	4.40
13.4 Miscellaneous entertainments	1.70	2.00	1.20	0.70	0.30	1.40
13.5 Educational and training expenses	5.10	9.30	8.50	1.10	0.50	6.50
13.6 Holiday in UK	1.20	2.60	2.60	3.60	2.30	2.50
13.7 Holiday abroad	9.60	14.40	15.40	11.70	3.40	12.50
13.8 Other incidental holiday expenses	6.60	8.80	9.00	1.60	[1.30]	6.80
13.9 Gambling payments	2.10	4.00	5.10	4.10	2.40	3.90
13.10 Cash gifts, donations	2.60	9.00	9.40	6.50	9.00	8.10
14 Miscellaneous	**0.60**	**1.20**	**0.60**	**0.20**	**0.10**	**0.70**
Percentage standard error	*15*	*8*	*11*	*16*	*26*	*6*
1-14 All expenditure groups	**381.70**	**472.80**	**416.40**	**262.60**	**169.10**	**385.70**
Percentage standard error	*3*	*1*	*2*	*3*	*3*	*1*
15 Other payments recorded						
15.1 Life assurance, contributions to pension funds	12.70	30.90	27.50	4.10	1.80	21.20
15.2 Medical insurance premiums	0.40	0.90	1.80	1.90	1.30	1.30
15.3 Other insurance premiums	0.60	1.40	1.30	0.60	0.40	1.00
15.4 Income tax, payments less refunds	62.00	98.10	76.90	29.60	16.00	70.40
15.5 National insurance contributions	23.20	27.80	18.60	1.20	0.80	18.40
15.6 Purchase or alteration of dwellings, mortgages	15.60	33.30	28.50	11.50	9.00	24.50
15.7 Savings and investments	5.50	12.30	15.20	..	1.10	10.40
15.8 Repayment of loans to clear other debts	5.00	4.50	2.70	[0.60]	..	3.10

2.4 Household expenditure by gross income quintile group where the head of household is aged under 30
1998-99 - 2000-01
based on weighted data and including children's expenditure

	Lowest twenty per cent	Second quintile group	Third quintile group	Fourth quintile group	Highest twenty per cent	All house-holds
Lower boundary of group (£ per week)[1]		163	310	489	739	
Average number of grossed households (thousands)	690	470	670	580	450	2,850
Total number of households in sample (over 3 years)	632	401	522	430	287	2,272
Total number of persons in sample (over 3 years)	1,323	938	1,210	1,063	689	5,223
Total number of adults in sample (over 3 years)	724	598	885	832	607	3,646
Weighted average number of persons per household	2.0	2.2	2.2	2.4	2.4	2.2

Commodity or service	Average weekly household expenditure (£)					
1 **Housing (Net)**	22.50	56.10	69.70	92.30	136.30	71.30
Percentage standard error	6	4	2	3	3	2
2 **Fuel and power**	7.90	9.90	9.10	10.00	10.60	9.40
"	3	14	3	3	6	3
3 **Food and non-alcoholic drinks**	30.80	41.20	49.90	63.90	85.90	52.40
"	3	3	2	2	3	1
4 **Alcoholic drink**	7.50	11.80	17.30	22.30	33.50	17.70
"	8	8	6	5	6	3
5 **Tobacco**	6.20	7.10	7.80	6.40	5.70	6.70
"	6	7	7	9	14	3
6 **Clothing and footwear**	10.70	16.60	20.20	30.10	45.70	23.40
"	6	7	6	6	8	3
7 **Household goods**	11.60	16.90	23.20	40.30	49.00	26.90
"	7	7	8	11	10	5
8 **Household services**	7.40	13.60	17.80	24.50	34.90	18.70
"	5	5	4	5	15	5
9 **Personal goods and services**	5.20	8.20	12.70	16.30	31.20	13.90
"	6	7	6	8	16	6
10 **Motoring**	7.40	23.70	47.00	75.60	99.00	47.70
"	11	8	5	5	8	3
11 **Fares and other travel costs**	5.90	7.60	10.70	10.90	28.20	11.80
"	13	11	16	13	10	6
12 **Leisure goods**	10.20	12.60	18.60	25.90	26.90	18.40
"	12	8	12	14	12	6
13 **Leisure services**	14.00	19.90	27.10	38.20	80.80	33.50
"	14	12	8	7	9	5
14 **Miscellaneous**	0.30	0.40	1.10	1.40	1.80	0.90
"	24	19	14	15	17	8
1-14 **All expenditure groups**	147.60	245.50	332.20	458.10	669.40	352.60
Percentage standard error	3	3	2	2	3	2

Average weekly expenditure per person (£)						
All expenditure groups	75.10	112.30	151.70	191.30	276.20	159.30

1 Boundaries divide the complete set of UK households into five equal groups. Reports before 1999-2000, for this table, divided just the households where the head was aged under 30 into equal groups.

ONS, Family Spending 2000-01, © Crown copyright 2002

2.5 Household expenditure by gross income quintile group where the head of household is aged 30 to 49

1998-99 - 2000-01

based on weighted data and including children's expenditure

	Lowest twenty per cent	Second quintile group	Third quintile group	Fourth quintile group	Highest twenty per cent	All house-holds
Lower boundary of group (£ per week)[1]		163	310	489	739	
Average number of grossed households (thousands)	1,050	1,290	2,040	2,650	2,830	9,860
Total number of households in sample (over 3 years)	921	1,137	1,690	2,124	2,192	8,064
Total number of persons in sample (over 3 years)	2,153	3,381	4,973	6,965	7,425	24,897
Total number of adults in sample (over 3 years)	1,130	1,734	2,916	4,245	4,811	14,836
Weighted average number of persons per household	2.2	2.8	2.8	3.1	3.3	2.9

Commodity or service	Average weekly household expenditure (£)					
1 **Housing (Net)**	24.40	43.40	64.80	80.20	121.60	78.20
Percentage standard error	5	3	1	1	2	1
2 **Fuel and power**	9.90	11.10	11.20	12.60	14.60	12.40
"	2	2	2	1	1	1
3 **Food and non-alcoholic drinks**	36.70	50.00	60.50	77.10	98.50	72.00
"	2	2	1	1	1	1
4 **Alcoholic drink**	5.80	9.00	14.10	18.80	27.00	17.50
"	6	5	3	2	3	2
5 **Tobacco**	6.20	9.00	8.00	7.40	5.90	7.20
"	5	4	4	4	5	2
6 **Clothing and footwear**	9.90	16.80	20.40	29.70	45.30	28.50
"	7	5	4	3	3	2
7 **Household goods**	13.60	20.30	25.80	36.20	60.80	36.70
"	6	6	4	3	3	2
8 **Household services**	9.80	13.20	18.10	24.40	39.20	24.30
"	5	5	3	3	3	2
9 **Personal goods and services**	5.10	7.40	11.60	17.40	25.70	16.00
"	5	5	4	3	3	2
10 **Motoring**	15.30	31.00	49.80	71.20	106.40	65.70
"	7	5	3	2	3	2
11 **Fares and other travel costs**	4.20	5.60	6.80	9.60	20.00	10.90
"	7	6	6	5	5	3
12 **Leisure goods**	8.10	13.20	18.40	26.20	35.80	23.70
"	7	5	4	4	4	2
13 **Leisure services**	13.20	20.80	33.50	51.60	101.30	54.10
"	8	5	4	3	3	2
14 **Miscellaneous**	0.50	0.70	1.50	1.70	2.40	1.60
"	14	12	13	8	8	5
1-14 **All expenditure groups**	162.60	251.50	344.60	464.20	704.50	448.80
Percentage standard error	2	2	1	1	1	1

Average weekly expenditure per person (£)

All expenditure groups	74.00	90.20	125.10	147.70	216.10	152.10

1 Boundaries divide the complete set of UK households into five equal groups. Reports before 1999-2000, for this table, divided just the households where the head was aged 30 to 49 into equal groups.

2.6 Household expenditure by gross income quintile group where the head of household is aged 50 to 64
1998-99 - 2000-01

based on weighted data and including children's expenditure

	Lowest twenty per cent	Second quintile group	Third quintile group	Fourth quintile group	Highest twenty per cent	All house-holds
Lower boundary of group (£ per week)[1]		163	310	489	739	
Average number of grossed households (thousands)	930	1,040	1,250	1,290	1,450	5,960
Total number of households in sample (over 3 years)	804	895	1,033	1,052	1,080	4,864
Total number of persons in sample (over 3 years)	1,103	1,645	2,226	2,531	3,149	10,654
Total number of adults in sample (over 3 years)	1,033	1,503	2,001	2,315	2,769	9,621
Weighted average number of persons per household	1.4	1.8	2.1	2.4	2.9	2.2

Commodity or service	Average weekly household expenditure (£)					
1 Housing (Net)	**23.40**	**36.50**	**46.00**	**60.00**	**85.80**	**53.60**
Percentage standard error	*5*	*3*	*2*	*3*	*3*	*1*
2 Fuel and power	**9.10**	**10.70**	**12.00**	**13.30**	**16.40**	**12.70**
"	*2*	*2*	*2*	*2*	*2*	*1*
3 Food and non-alcoholic drinks	**29.80**	**45.90**	**59.10**	**73.80**	**101.20**	**65.70**
"	*2*	*2*	*2*	*1*	*1*	*1*
4 Alcoholic drink	**6.30**	**10.00**	**15.00**	**19.20**	**29.90**	**17.30**
"	*8*	*5*	*4*	*4*	*3*	*2*
5 Tobacco	**5.70**	**7.40**	**7.60**	**7.00**	**6.70**	**6.90**
"	*6*	*6*	*6*	*6*	*7*	*3*
6 Clothing and footwear	**6.70**	**13.80**	**19.80**	**24.40**	**37.90**	**22.10**
"	*8*	*10*	*6*	*4*	*4*	*3*
7 Household goods	**15.70**	**24.40**	**29.60**	**38.90**	**58.70**	**35.60**
"	*10*	*7*	*5*	*5*	*4*	*3*
8 Household services	**9.00**	**13.00**	**16.50**	**20.20**	**36.80**	**20.50**
"	*8*	*5*	*8*	*4*	*6*	*3*
9 Personal goods and services	**6.10**	**8.50**	**13.50**	**17.00**	**26.90**	**15.50**
"	*17*	*5*	*6*	*4*	*4*	*3*
10 Motoring	**16.60**	**30.50**	**56.40**	**76.30**	**122.10**	**66.10**
"	*10*	*6*	*5*	*3*	*4*	*2*
11 Fares and other travel costs	**3.30**	**5.20**	**7.90**	**11.20**	**19.20**	**10.20**
"	*22*	*9*	*19*	*15*	*9*	*7*
12 Leisure goods	**5.20**	**10.20**	**18.00**	**23.60**	**34.40**	**19.90**
"	*6*	*6*	*5*	*5*	*5*	*3*
13 Leisure services	**16.50**	**25.50**	**38.40**	**59.60**	**110.70**	**54.90**
"	*10*	*7*	*4*	*4*	*4*	*3*
14 Miscellaneous	**0.20**	**0.70**	**0.80**	**1.10**	**2.20**	**1.10**
"	*25*	*18*	*15*	*13*	*12*	*7*
1-14 All expenditure groups	**153.70**	**242.10**	**340.50**	**445.80**	**688.80**	**401.90**
Percentage standard error	*4*	*2*	*2*	*1*	*2*	*1*
Average weekly expenditure per person (£)						
All expenditure groups	**112.70**	**131.60**	**158.50**	**183.40**	**233.50**	**180.40**

1 Boundaries divide the complete set of UK households into five equal groups. Reports before 1999-2000, for this table, divided just the households where the head was aged 50 to 64 into equal groups.

ONS, Family Spending 2000-01, © Crown copyright 2002

2.7 Household expenditure by gross income quintile group where the head of household is aged 65 to 74

1998-99 - 2000-01

based on weighted data and including children's expenditure

	Lowest twenty per cent	Second quintile group	Third quintile group	Fourth quintile group	Highest twenty per cent	All house-holds
Lower boundary of group (£ per week)[1]		163	310	489	739	
Average number of grossed households (thousands)	920	1,210	660	320	200	3,310
Total number of households in sample (over 3 years)	807	1,053	567	263	155	2,845
Total number of persons in sample (over 3 years)	970	1,772	1,124	589	353	4,808
Total number of adults in sample (over 3 years)	963	1,759	1,093	574	343	4,732
Weighted average number of persons per household	1.2	1.7	2.0	2.3	2.4	1.7

Commodity or service	Average weekly household expenditure (£)					
1 **Housing (Net)**	**22.30**	**32.50**	**36.40**	**43.10**	**56.70**	**33.00**
Percentage standard error	3	3	3	4	8	2
2 **Fuel and power**	**9.00**	**10.60**	**12.20**	**14.30**	**17.30**	**11.30**
"	3	2	2	3	5	1
3 **Food and non-alcoholic drinks**	**26.50**	**42.10**	**56.20**	**72.40**	**89.40**	**46.40**
"	2	2	2	3	4	1
4 **Alcoholic drink**	**3.00**	**6.70**	**11.30**	**14.90**	**25.80**	**8.60**
"	8	5	5	8	9	3
5 **Tobacco**	**3.00**	**3.90**	**4.00**	**4.60**	**4.30**	**3.80**
"	8	7	12	15	23	5
6 **Clothing and footwear**	**4.50**	**10.30**	**16.70**	**25.80**	**25.60**	**12.40**
"	8	5	7	9	12	4
7 **Household goods**	**11.50**	**21.20**	**31.50**	**41.90**	**66.10**	**25.30**
"	8	6	7	10	25	5
8 **Household services**	**7.90**	**10.10**	**14.80**	**24.80**	**50.10**	**14.20**
"	6	4	7	20	19	6
9 **Personal goods and services**	**5.40**	**8.60**	**14.60**	**18.30**	**26.50**	**11.00**
"	9	6	6	10	12	4
10 **Motoring**	**10.40**	**24.60**	**46.60**	**64.50**	**96.60**	**33.40**
"	11	5	8	9	11	4
11 **Fares and other travel costs**	**1.60**	**3.40**	**5.90**	**7.20**	**16.30**	**4.50**
"	9	10	24	16	32	9
12 **Leisure goods**	**5.20**	**9.40**	**18.80**	**23.20**	**29.40**	**12.70**
"	7	5	13	9	19	5
13 **Leisure services**	**10.80**	**28.40**	**48.10**	**72.40**	**110.80**	**36.70**
"	6	6	6	8	12	4
14 **Miscellaneous**	**0.10**	**0.40**	**0.70**	**..**	**1.00**	**0.70**
"	28	26	25	..	37	29
1-14 **All expenditure groups**	**121.30**	**212.20**	**317.90**	**430.30**	**616.20**	**254.00**
Percentage standard error	2	2	2	3	5	2

Average weekly expenditure per person (£)

All expenditure groups	**103.20**	**126.90**	**159.20**	**187.10**	**255.80**	**149.00**

1 Boundaries divide the complete set of UK households into five equal groups. Reports before 1999-2000, for this table, divided just the households where the head was aged 65 to 74 into equal groups.

2.8 Household expenditure by gross income quintile group where the head of household is aged 75 or over

1998-99 - 2000-01

based on weighted data and including children's expenditure

	Lowest twenty per cent	Second quintile group	Third quintile group	Fourth quintile group	Highest twenty per cent	All house-holds
Lower boundary of group (£ per week)[1]		163	310	489	739	
Average number of grossed households (thousands)	1,410	1,000	380	160	60	3,020
Total number of households in sample (over 3 years)	1,051	790	297	130	51	2,319
Total number of persons in sample (over 3 years)	1,196	1,237	550	261	103	3,347
Total number of adults in sample (over 3 years)	1,194	1,233	549	258	101	3,335
Weighted average number of persons per household	1.1	1.5	1.9	2.0	2.1	1.4

Commodity or service	Average weekly household expenditure (£)					
1 Housing (Net)	**20.10**	**29.20**	**34.60**	**49.10**	**51.80**	**27.10**
Percentage standard error	3	4	4	14	11	2
2 Fuel and power	**8.20**	**10.10**	**11.60**	**13.20**	**16.60**	**9.70**
"	3	2	4	5	8	2
3 Food and non-alcoholic drinks	**23.40**	**34.60**	**49.60**	**57.80**	**66.60**	**33.10**
"	2	2	3	4	7	1
4 Alcoholic drink	**2.30**	**5.00**	**8.90**	**12.70**	**13.70**	**4.80**
"	7	7	10	13	18	4
5 Tobacco	**1.10**	**2.10**	**3.20**	**2.80**	**2.40**	**1.80**
"	11	11	19	35	43	7
6 Clothing and footwear	**3.70**	**6.60**	**9.00**	**15.60**	**15.10**	**6.20**
"	8	8	11	18	22	5
7 Household goods	**7.70**	**14.10**	**21.60**	**36.10**	**34.70**	**13.70**
"	7	9	11	15	21	5
8 Household services	**8.10**	**11.80**	**15.80**	**30.10**	**35.30**	**12.00**
"	12	7	8	22	11	5
9 Personal goods and services	**5.40**	**7.90**	**12.10**	**13.70**	**15.40**	**7.80**
"	10	6	8	11	22	4
10 Motoring	**3.60**	**12.90**	**29.30**	**44.00**	**60.60**	**13.30**
"	9	8	10	13	14	5
11 Fares and other travel costs	**1.50**	**2.30**	**4.60**	**4.50**	**7.40**	**2.40**
"	9	9	29	24	36	9
12 Leisure goods	**3.60**	**6.40**	**13.90**	**17.60**	**24.00**	**7.00**
"	5	7	13	15	20	5
13 Leisure services	**9.20**	**19.30**	**35.90**	**59.90**	**72.00**	**19.80**
"	6	9	11	16	19	5
14 Miscellaneous	**0.10**	**0.20**	**0.30**	**..**	**0.20**	**0.20**
"	34	41	35	..	37	21
1-14 All expenditure groups	**98.10**	**162.40**	**250.50**	**358.00**	**415.70**	**158.80**
Percentage standard error	2	2	3	5	7	2

Average weekly expenditure per person (£)

	Lowest twenty per cent	Second quintile group	Third quintile group	Fourth quintile group	Highest twenty per cent	All house-holds
All expenditure groups	**87.20**	**105.50**	**135.10**	**178.70**	**200.90**	**111.70**

1 Boundaries divide the complete set of UK households into five equal groups. Reports before 1999-2000, for this table, divided just the households where the head was aged 75 or over into equal groups.

ONS, Family Spending 2000-01, © Crown copyright 2002

2.9 Household expenditure by by age of household reference person

based on weighted data and including children's expenditure

2000-01

Commodity or service		Under 30	30 and under 50	50 and under 65	65 and under 75	75 or over	All house-holds
Grossed number of households (thousands)		2,760	10,070	6,140	3,120	2,950	25,030
Total number of households in sample		708	2,635	1,624	937	733	6,637
Total number of persons in sample		1,694	8,100	3,513	1,580	1,038	15,925
Total number of adults in sample		1,181	4,890	3,186	1,560	1,035	11,852
Weighted average number of persons per household		2.3	3.0	2.2	1.7	1.4	2.4
Commodity or service		**Average weekly household expenditure (£)**					
1	**Housing (Net)**	**78.30**	**83.70**	**56.90**	**33.70**	**29.70**	**63.90**
	Percentage standard error	3	2	3	3	5	1
2	**Fuel and power**	**10.10**	**12.30**	**13.00**	**11.80**	**9.90**	**11.90**
	"	7	1	2	2	2	1
3	**Food and non-alcoholic drinks**	**55.70**	**73.70**	**66.60**	**46.70**	**33.90**	**61.90**
	"	2	1	2	2	2	1
4	**Alcoholic drink**	**18.90**	**18.00**	**16.80**	**8.20**	**4.70**	**15.00**
	"	5	3	4	6	8	2
5	**Tobacco**	**7.80**	**6.90**	**7.10**	**4.00**	**1.70**	**6.10**
	"	6	4	5	8	14	3
6	**Clothing and footwear**	**25.10**	**29.60**	**20.80**	**12.30**	**5.60**	**22.00**
	"	5	3	4	6	7	2
7	**Household goods**	**26.20**	**38.00**	**38.30**	**27.30**	**14.00**	**32.60**
	"	6	4	5	10	9	3
8	**Household services**	**20.30**	**27.10**	**21.70**	**17.20**	**11.50**	**22.00**
	"	9	3	4	11	6	2
9	**Personal goods and services**	**16.40**	**16.90**	**16.00**	**10.60**	**7.40**	**14.70**
	"	8	3	4	6	7	2
10	**Motoring**	**51.80**	**67.60**	**67.50**	**32.40**	**13.60**	**55.10**
	"	6	3	4	5	9	2
11	**Fares and other travel costs**	**11.90**	**12.30**	**9.40**	**4.90**	**2.50**	**9.50**
	"	12	7	8	22	21	5
12	**Leisure goods**	**18.10**	**25.80**	**19.50**	**14.10**	**7.00**	**19.70**
	"	9	4	5	11	8	3
13	**Leisure services**	**36.40**	**61.70**	**61.10**	**34.10**	**21.90**	**50.60**
	"	7	4	5	5	10	2
14	**Miscellaneous**	**0.60**	**1.20**	**0.60**	**0.20**	**0.10**	**0.70**
	"	14	8	11	16	27	6
1-14	**All expenditure groups**	**377.50**	**474.80**	**415.20**	**257.60**	**163.60**	**385.70**
	Percentage standard error	3	1	2	3	3	1
Average weekly expenditure per person (£)							
All expenditure groups		**162.40**	**160.90**	**190.10**	**152.80**	**116.50**	**163.90**

ONS, Family Spending 2000-01, © Crown copyright 2002

Chapter 3

Expenditure by socio-economic characteristics

- Households headed by **self-employed** people had the highest average expenditure, £570 a week, over two and a half times that of households with a **retired** head (£210 a week). Households with a head employed **full-time** spent on average of £500 a week, compared with £360 for households with a head employed **part-time**.

- Households with a head in a **professional occupation** on average spent £640 a week, while those with a head in an **unskilled occupation** spent £230 a week. There were especially large differences in spending on leisure goods and services and on motoring.

- Leisure goods and services were the largest item of spending for households with **professional** and with **managerial or technical** heads. Housing was the largest item for those with a **skilled non-manual** head, while food and non-alcoholic drink was the largest item in households with heads in **skilled manual, partially skilled** and **unskilled occupations**.

- Spending on tobacco was higher in the **skilled manual, partially skilled** and **unskilled occupations** than in the **non-manual occupations**.

- Total expenditure increased by age at which the head of household completed continuous full-time education from just under **£200** a week for those who were aged 14 or under, to about **£580** a week for those aged 22 or over. Those who completed education at a young age tend to be older and many are now retired.

- Expenditure on **leisure services** showed a large increase with age of completing continuous full-time education, from £24 a week in households who left at age 14 or less, to £97 a week where the age was 22 or higher. Households with a head who completed continuous education at age 15 spent the most on **tobacco**.

Expenditure by socio-economic characteristics

This chapter contains tables showing household expenditure analysed by some socio-economic characteristics of the head of household. **Tables 3.3** and **3.4** also include a further breakdown by income. Definitions for all categories are in Appendix D. Next year these tables will be based on the characteristics of the household reference person, as explained in Appendix D. **Tables 3.8** and **3.9** show expenditure by economic activity status and occupation of the household reference person.

Economic activity status

Table 3.1 and **Figure 3.1** show household expenditure by the economic activity status of the head of household. Households headed by self-employed people had the highest total expenditure, £570 a week, compared with £500 a week for full-time employees and £360 for part-time employees. Households with an unemployed head spent £220 a week, though households with a retired head had the lowest figure, £210 a week.

Social class

Table 3.5 shows average spending by the social class of the head of household. It covers all currently in paid work, unemployed heads who have ever worked and recently retired heads. Households headed by professionals spent an average of £640 a week, compared with the £230 a week spent by households headed by unskilled workers, the lowest spending group. Spending fell progressively from professional through to unskilled classes, except that the skilled manual class had a slightly higher expenditure than the skilled non-manual subdivision, £410 a week compared with £390 a week. Spending on food and non-alcoholic drink varied relatively little with social class, from £87 a week for households with a professional head to £49 a week for those with a head in an unskilled occupation. The largest variation was on leisure goods and services, where spending by households with a professional head was four and a half times as high as for households with a head in an unskilled occupation, £146 a week compared with £32 a week. The ratio was also high for motoring, at four to one. Leisure spending was the largest item for households with professional and also with managerial and technical heads, followed in both cases by housing. Housing was the largest item for heads in a skilled non-manual job but food and non-alcoholic drink was the largest item when the head was in a skilled manual job. This is associated with larger average household size for the skilled

3.1 **Expenditure by economic activity status**

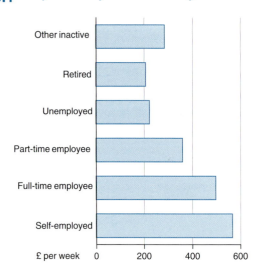

ONS, Family Spending 2000-01, © Crown copyright 2002

manuals, 2.9 persons compared with 2.3 persons for the skilled non-manuals. Food and non-alcoholic drink was the largest item for the partly skilled and unskilled occupations. Spending on tobacco was highest in households with a head in a partly skilled occupation.

Table 3.7 shows expenditure by the age at which the head of household left continuous full-time education. Total expenditure is shown to increase with the time spent in continuous full-time education by the head of household. The figures show that households with heads who had been 22 or over spent almost three times as much a week (£580 a week) as those whose head left continuous full-time education aged 14 or under (£200 a week). Much of the difference at the low ages of completing continuous full-time education is related to age. The table shows that the average age of heads who completed at 14 or less was 72 at the time of interview. The three groups completing at 16 or under spent more on food and non-alcoholic drinks than any other item of expenditure, while the remaining groups spent more on housing.

Figure 3.2 looks at expenditure on tobacco. Households with heads who left aged 15 spent the most on tobacco, £8.60 a week, and thereafter expenditure on tobacco decreases the later the head of household completed full-time education. In contrast, **Figure 3.3** shows that expenditure on leisure goods and services increased the longer the head of household stayed in continuous full-time education. For leisure services spending ranged from £24 a week in households whose head left aged 14 or under to £97 a week among households whose head continued to age 22 and beyond.

Expenditure by characteristics of the household reference person

Table 3.8 shows expenditure by the economic activity status of the household reference person. The distribution of reference persons is fairly different from the distribution of household heads. Two per cent more reference persons are in employment overall, but 9 per cent fewer are self-employed. Four per cent more are employees, including two per cent more working full-time and 20 per cent more working part-time. A comparison with **Table 3.1** shows that average expenditures are very similar whether the reference person or the head is used, even for those in part-time employment. The same is true for occupation, comparing **Table 3.9** with **Table 3.2**.

3.2 **Expenditure on tobacco by age at which the head of household left continuous full-time education**

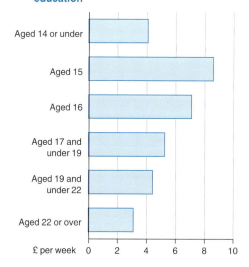

3.3 **Leisure goods and services by age at which the head of household left continuous full-time education**

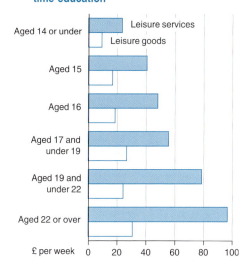

3.1 Household expenditure by economic activity status of head of household
based on weighted data and including children's expenditure

2000-01

	Employees			Self-employed	All in employ-ment[1]
	Full-time	Part-time	All		
Grossed number of households (thousands)	11,150	1,460	12,610	2,020	14,700
Total number of households in sample	2,835	397	3,232	537	3,788
Total number of persons in sample	7,818	931	8,749	1,648	10,438
Total number of adults in sample	5,489	641	6,130	1,141	7,300
Weighted average number of persons per household	2.7	2.3	2.6	3.0	2.7

Commodity or service	Average weekly household expenditure (£)				
1 **Housing (Net)**	**90.10**	**57.30**	**86.30**	**85.90**	**86.00**
Percentage standard error	*1*	*5*	*1*	*4*	*1*
2 **Fuel and power**	**12.30**	**11.00**	**12.10**	**14.80**	**12.50**
"	*2*	*3*	*2*	*3*	*1*
3 **Food and non-alcoholic drinks**	**74.20**	**61.20**	**72.70**	**85.90**	**74.30**
"	*1*	*3*	*1*	*2*	*1*
4 **Alcoholic drink**	**19.80**	**15.30**	**19.30**	**21.30**	**19.50**
"	*3*	*8*	*2*	*6*	*2*
5 **Tobacco**	**6.90**	**5.80**	**6.80**	**6.00**	**6.70**
"	*4*	*10*	*3*	*10*	*3*
6 **Clothing and footwear**	**29.70**	**20.90**	**28.70**	**32.50**	**29.10**
"	*3*	*7*	*3*	*6*	*2*
7 **Household goods**	**38.90**	**26.90**	**37.50**	**47.90**	**38.80**
"	*3*	*9*	*3*	*9*	*3*
8 **Household services**	**27.30**	**19.70**	**26.40**	**32.70**	**27.20**
"	*3*	*8*	*3*	*8*	*3*
9 **Personal goods and services**	**19.00**	**13.00**	**18.30**	**19.30**	**18.30**
"	*3*	*8*	*3*	*6*	*2*
10 **Motoring**	**74.90**	**48.70**	**71.90**	**94.90**	**74.80**
"	*2*	*10*	*2*	*5*	*2*
11 **Fares and other travel costs**	**13.40**	**9.10**	**12.90**	**11.90**	**12.70**
"	*6*	*10*	*5*	*20*	*5*
12 **Leisure goods**	**25.50**	**17.30**	**24.50**	**28.90**	**25.00**
"	*4*	*8*	*4*	*10*	*3*
13 **Leisure services**	**64.30**	**51.50**	**62.80**	**84.70**	**65.60**
"	*3*	*12*	*3*	*7*	*3*
14 **Miscellaneous**	**1.10**	**0.50**	**1.00**	**1.30**	**1.00**
"	*8*	*22*	*7*	*16*	*7*
1-14 **All expenditure groups**	**497.30**	**358.00**	**481.20**	**567.80**	**491.60**
Percentage standard error	*1*	*4*	*1*	*3*	*1*

Average weekly expenditure per person (£)					
All expenditure groups	**185.80**	**154.50**	**182.60**	**190.30**	**183.40**

1 Includes 19 households where the head was on a Government-supported training scheme.

ONS, Family Spending 2000-01, © Crown copyright 2002

3.1 Household expenditure
by economic activity status of head of household (cont.)
based on weighted data and including children's expenditure

2000-01

| | ILO unem- ployed | All economi- cally active[1] | Economically inactive | | | All house- holds |
			Retired	Other	All	
Grossed number of households (thousands)	760	15,460	6,170	3,390	9,570	25,030
Total number of households in sample	199	3,987	1,700	950	2,650	6,637
Total number of persons in sample	527	10,965	2,627	2,333	4,960	15,925
Total number of adults in sample	337	7,637	2,607	1,608	4,215	11,852
Weighted average number of persons per household	2.6	2.7	1.5	2.4	1.8	2.4

Commodity or service — Average weekly household expenditure (£)

		ILO	All econ	Retired	Other	All	All hh
1	Housing (Net)	30.70	83.20	31.30	35.20	32.70	63.90
	Percentage standard error	9	1	3	5	2	1
2	Fuel and power	10.90	12.40	10.70	11.60	11.00	11.90
	"	5	1	2	2	1	1
3	Food and non-alcoholic drinks	48.80	73.00	39.50	52.10	44.00	61.90
	"	5	1	1	2	1	1
4	Alcoholic drink	11.00	19.10	6.10	12.80	8.50	15.00
	"	11	2	5	6	4	2
5	Tobacco	8.60	6.80	2.90	8.40	4.90	6.10
	"	10	3	7	5	4	3
6	Clothing and footwear	13.70	28.30	8.60	17.40	11.70	22.00
	"	13	2	5	6	4	2
7	Household goods	14.20	37.60	21.70	30.00	24.60	32.60
	"	11	3	8	7	5	3
8	Household services	12.30	26.50	13.80	16.20	14.70	22.00
	"	10	3	7	7	5	2
9	Personal goods and services	7.00	17.80	9.40	10.40	9.70	14.70
	"	15	2	5	6	4	2
10	Motoring	24.50	72.30	22.50	36.00	27.30	55.10
	"	13	2	5	7	4	2
11	Fares and other travel costs	6.10	12.40	3.40	7.00	4.70	9.50
	"	12	5	15	13	10	5
12	Leisure goods	15.20	24.50	10.30	15.00	12.00	19.70
	"	23	3	8	6	5	3
13	Leisure services	18.20	63.30	27.40	35.00	30.10	50.60
	"	16	3	5	7	4	2
14	Miscellaneous	0.40	1.00	0.10	0.50	0.30	0.70
	"	30	7	14	13	10	6
1-14	All expenditure groups	221.40	478.20	208.00	287.60	236.20	385.70
	Percentage standard error	6	1	2	3	2	1

Average weekly expenditure per person (£)

| All expenditure groups | 85.10 | 178.60 | 136.10 | 120.70 | 129.00 | 163.90 |

1 Includes 19 households where the head was on a Government-supported training scheme.

3.2 Household expenditure by occupation of head of household[1]

2000-01

based on weighted data and including children's expenditure

	Profes-sional	Employ-ers and managers	Interme-diate non manual	Junior non manual	Skilled manual	Semi-skilled manual	Unskilled manual
Grossed number of households (thousands)	1,050	3,070	1,850	1,590	2,920	2,170	600
Total number of households in sample	251	796	464	416	749	560	160
Total number of persons in sample	677	2,270	1,128	921	2,267	1,460	431
Total number of adults in sample	493	1,572	811	664	1,555	1,022	280
Weighted average number of persons per household	2.6	2.8	2.4	2.2	2.9	2.5	2.6

Commodity or service	Average weekly household expenditure (£)						
1 Housing (Net)	**101.40**	**111.80**	**93.00**	**74.90**	**72.40**	**56.90**	**46.80**
Percentage standard error	*4*	*3*	*3*	*2*	*3*	*3*	*6*
2 Fuel and power	**13.60**	**14.10**	**11.60**	**10.20**	**12.30**	**10.70**	**9.20**
"	*4*	*2*	*3*	*3*	*5*	*3*	*5*
3 Food and non-alcoholic drinks	**84.00**	**86.00**	**69.70**	**58.10**	**73.70**	**57.70**	**52.90**
"	*3*	*2*	*3*	*3*	*2*	*2*	*5*
4 Alcoholic drink	**21.50**	**22.30**	**20.70**	**15.10**	**18.40**	**15.70**	**13.50**
"	*7*	*4*	*9*	*7*	*4*	*6*	*11*
5 Tobacco	**4.00**	**6.20**	**5.00**	**5.60**	**8.70**	**9.20**	**8.40**
"	*16*	*8*	*12*	*9*	*6*	*7*	*11*
6 Clothing and footwear	**32.50**	**34.20**	**26.20**	**26.20**	**27.90**	**21.70**	**15.90**
"	*9*	*5*	*6*	*8*	*6*	*6*	*15*
7 Household goods	**45.50**	**50.60**	**36.00**	**30.80**	**28.50**	**30.00**	**19.90**
"	*10*	*5*	*8*	*8*	*5*	*8*	*13*
8 Household services	**34.40**	**33.10**	**29.00**	**21.40**	**22.00**	**19.00**	**12.00**
"	*8*	*5*	*9*	*6*	*8*	*0*	*8*
9 Personal goods and services	**21.10**	**24.00**	**19.30**	**17.70**	**15.20**	**11.40**	**8.80**
"	*7*	*5*	*6*	*10*	*5*	*6*	*11*
10 Motoring	**83.50**	**95.30**	**73.10**	**52.00**	**66.40**	**49.90**	**25.30**
"	*6*	*5*	*5*	*7*	*3*	*5*	*11*
11 Fares and other travel costs	**17.90**	**16.30**	**14.80**	**14.90**	**8.60**	**7.80**	**7.20**
"	*15*	*9*	*10*	*24*	*11*	*11*	*14*
12 Leisure goods	**31.10**	**29.60**	**28.10**	**19.00**	**22.90**	**18.00**	**11.00**
"	*12*	*6*	*11*	*9*	*8*	*9*	*12*
13 Leisure services	**109.20**	**93.40**	**61.90**	**40.20**	**46.80**	**31.50**	**24.20**
"	*11*	*6*	*8*	*7*	*5*	*6*	*12*
14 Miscellaneous	**0.80**	**1.40**	**0.80**	**1.00**	**0.80**	**0.90**	**0.20**
"	*24*	*14*	*18*	*21*	*13*	*22*	*35*
1-14 All expenditure groups	**600.60**	**618.30**	**489.20**	**387.00**	**424.60**	**340.40**	**255.20**
Percentage standard error	*3*	*2*	*3*	*3*	*2*	*2*	*5*
Average weekly expenditure per person (£)							
All expenditure groups	**230.50**	**222.20**	**206.00**	**174.30**	**145.20**	**134.90**	**96.70**

1 Excludes households where the head is retired, unoccupied, self employed,
in the armed forces or with an inadequately described occupation.

ONS, Family Spending 2000-01, © Crown copyright 2002

3.3 Household expenditure by gross income: the head of household is a full-time employee

2000-01

based on weighted data and including children's expenditure

	Lowest twenty per cent	Second quintile group	Third quintile group	Fourth quintile group	Highest twenty per cent	All house-holds
Lower boundary of group (£ per week)[1]		163	310	489	739	
Grossed number of households (thousands)	110	1,070	2,700	3,430	3,830	11,150
Total number of households in sample	31	288	706	875	935	2,835
Total number of persons in sample	48	497	1,747	2,552	2,974	7,818
Total number of adults in sample	37	382	1,188	1,746	2,136	5,489
Weighted average number of persons per household	1.5	1.7	2.3	2.8	3.1	2.7

Commodity or service	Average weekly household expenditure (£)					
1 Housing (Net)	**57.20**	**56.80**	**67.80**	**83.90**	**121.70**	**90.10**
Percentage standard error	*12*	*3*	*2*	*2*	*2*	*1*
2 Fuel and power	**7.80**	**11.00**	**10.30**	**12.20**	**14.30**	**12.30**
"	*16*	*15*	*2*	*2*	*2*	*2*
3 Food and non-alcoholic drinks	**37.60**	**37.40**	**55.50**	**74.70**	**98.30**	**74.20**
"	*15*	*4*	*2*	*2*	*1*	*1*
4 Alcoholic drink	**13.20**	**9.40**	**14.50**	**17.80**	**28.30**	**19.80**
"	*29*	*9*	*5*	*4*	*4*	*3*
5 Tobacco	**4.50**	**6.10**	**7.60**	**7.50**	**6.30**	**6.90**
"	*31*	*11*	*6*	*6*	*8*	*4*
6 Clothing and footwear	**19.30**	**13.20**	**20.20**	**28.00**	**42.70**	**29.70**
"	*30*	*10*	*6*	*4*	*4*	*3*
7 Household goods	**8.60**	**21.80**	**25.50**	**34.70**	**57.70**	**38.90**
"	*19*	*15*	*6*	*5*	*5*	*3*
8 Household services	**12.40**	**15.90**	**16.70**	**25.50**	**40.00**	**27.30**
"	*21*	*8*	*4*	*4*	*5*	*3*
9 Personal goods and services	**8.30**	**8.00**	**12.40**	**17.90**	**28.00**	**19.00**
"	*31*	*9*	*5*	*5*	*4*	*3*
10 Motoring	**29.70**	**30.40**	**51.90**	**77.70**	**102.60**	**74.90**
"	*32*	*7*	*4*	*3*	*3*	*2*
11 Fares and other travel costs	**5.80**	**5.40**	**8.50**	**9.50**	**22.90**	**13.40**
"	*31*	*14*	*14*	*9*	*8*	*6*
12 Leisure goods	**10.00**	**10.30**	**17.00**	**25.40**	**36.20**	**25.50**
"	*26*	*11*	*6*	*7*	*6*	*4*
13 Leisure services	**23.90**	**26.20**	**34.30**	**50.90**	**109.30**	**64.30**
"	*28*	*11*	*7*	*4*	*5*	*3*
14 Miscellaneous	**[0.50]**	**0.40**	**0.90**	**1.10**	**1.40**	**1.10**
"	*49*	*24*	*18*	*12*	*13*	*8*
1-14 All expenditure groups	**238.90**	**252.30**	**343.00**	**466.60**	**709.70**	**497.30**
Percentage standard error	*14*	*3*	*2*	*1*	*2*	*1*
Average weekly expenditure per person (£)						
All expenditure groups	**158.30**	**150.80**	**146.50**	**164.80**	**229.50**	**185.80**

1 Boundaries divide the complete set of UK households into five equal groups. Reports up to 1999-2000, for this table, divided just the households where the head was a full-time employee into equal groups.

3.4 Household expenditure by gross income: head of household is self-employed
based on weighted data and including children's expenditure

2000-01

	Lowest twenty per cent	Second quintile group	Third quintile group	Fourth quintile group	Highest twenty per cent	All house- holds
Lower boundary of group (£ per week)[1]		163	310	489	739	
Grossed number of households (thousands)	110	320	440	530	630	2,020
Total number of households in sample	33	86	121	144	153	537
Total number of persons in sample	93	224	371	454	506	1,648
Total number of adults in sample	53	154	239	326	369	1,141
Weighted average number of persons per household	2.5	2.5	3.0	3.1	3.2	3.0

Commodity or service	Average weekly household expenditure (£)					
1 Housing (Net)	**84.60**	**61.00**	**67.10**	**82.60**	**114.70**	**85.90**
Percentage standard error	*27*	*8*	*6*	*4*	*9*	*4*
2 Fuel and power	**13.00**	**12.00**	**12.80**	**14.20**	**18.50**	**14.80**
"	*11*	*7*	*7*	*6*	*5*	*3*
3 Food and non-alcoholic drinks	**55.60**	**61.80**	**75.90**	**84.40**	**111.80**	**85.90**
"	*11*	*6*	*5*	*4*	*4*	*2*
4 Alcoholic drink	**[7.40]**	**13.10**	**17.00**	**20.60**	**31.40**	**21.30**
"	*23*	*16*	*11*	*8*	*10*	*6*
5 Tobacco	**..**	**5.20**	**5.40**	**5.70**	**7.20**	**6.00**
"	*..*	*32*	*17*	*16*	*19*	*10*
6 Clothing and footwear	**20.90**	**21.70**	**27.50**	**31.70**	**44.10**	**32.50**
"	*31*	*20*	*10*	*10*	*10*	*6*
7 Household goods	**22.60**	**24.10**	**33.10**	**41.30**	**80.30**	**47.90**
"	*18*	*14*	*10*	*17*	*16*	*9*
8 Household services	**19.60**	**21.50**	**18.40**	**35.50**	**48.40**	**32.70**
"	*20*	*25*	*8*	*19*	*11*	*8*
9 Personal goods and services	**6.70**	**10.20**	**16.80**	**20.50**	**26.80**	**19.30**
"	*21*	*14*	*13*	*11*	*9*	*6*
10 Motoring	**45.40**	**63.90**	**81.30**	**85.90**	**136.40**	**94.90**
"	*22*	*14*	*11*	*8*	*9*	*5*
11 Fares and other travel costs	**[3.30]**	**4.70**	**6.50**	**10.40**	**22.00**	**11.90**
"	*48*	*26*	*21*	*18*	*32*	*20*
12 Leisure goods	**19.70**	**15.00**	**19.60**	**25.90**	**46.40**	**28.90**
"	*28*	*13*	*12*	*17*	*18*	*10*
13 Leisure services	**28.80**	**47.30**	**47.60**	**67.70**	**153.90**	**84.70**
"	*25*	*22*	*10*	*10*	*10*	*7*
14 Miscellaneous	**..**	**0.60**	**1.10**	**1.10**	**2.00**	**1.30**
"	*..*	*36*	*36*	*25*	*28*	*16*
1-14 All expenditure groups	**332.90**	**362.10**	**430.10**	**527.30**	**844.00**	**567.80**
Percentage standard error	*11*	*6*	*4*	*4*	*5*	*3*

Average weekly expenditure per person (£)

All expenditure groups	**131.10**	**143.80**	**145.60**	**170.80**	**261.30**	**190.30**

1 Boundaries divide the complete set of UK households into five equal groups. Reports up to 1999-2000, for this table, divided just the households where the head was self-employed into equal groups.

ONS, Family Spending 2000-01, © Crown copyright 2002

3.5 Household expenditure by social class[1] of head of household

2000-01

based on weighted data and including children's expenditure

	I	II	III N	III M	IV	V
	Profes-sional etc.	Manage-rial and technical	Skilled non-manual	Skilled manual	Partly skilled occupa-tions	Unskilled occupa-tions
Grossed number of households (thousands)	1,370	5,490	2,380	4,610	2,900	910
Total number of households in sample	332	1,425	625	1,201	771	252
Total number of persons in sample	917	3,857	1,464	3,576	2,039	634
Total number of adults in sample	664	2,694	1,020	2,464	1,391	425
Weighted average number of persons per household	2.7	2.6	2.3	2.9	2.6	2.5

Commodity or service	Average weekly household expenditure (£)					
1 Housing (Net)	112.40	100.50	69.50	65.40	50.90	38.50
Percentage standard error	*5*	*3*	*2*	*3*	*6*	*6*
2 Fuel and power	14.70	13.40	10.70	12.10	10.90	9.60
"	*4*	*2*	*2*	*3*	*2*	*4*
3 Food and non-alcoholic drinks	87.20	79.50	59.80	70.40	57.90	48.60
"	*3*	*1*	*2*	*2*	*2*	*4*
4 Alcoholic drink	23.90	20.80	15.80	17.90	14.50	11.30
"	*6*	*4*	*6*	*4*	*5*	*9*
5 Tobacco	4.20	5.40	6.80	8.60	9.40	8.70
"	*13*	*6*	*8*	*5*	*6*	*9*
6 Clothing and footwear	34.20	30.90	24.70	26.70	20.50	14.70
"	*7*	*4*	*6*	*4*	*6*	*12*
7 Household goods	47.80	47.00	32.30	29.80	28.40	19.40
"	*9*	*4*	*7*	*6*	*6*	*10*
8 Household services	38.90	32.20	20.90	20.50	18.20	10.10
"	*8*	*4*	*4*	*6*	*6*	*6*
9 Personal goods and services	22.50	21.40	16.80	13.90	11.00	7.90
"	*7*	*4*	*7*	*4*	*5*	*9*
10 Motoring	92.00	84.50	56.00	64.40	43.10	23.10
"	*6*	*3*	*6*	*3*	*5*	*9*
11 Fares and other travel costs	17.50	14.90	14.20	8.60	7.10	6.70
"	*12*	*7*	*17*	*14*	*10*	*15*
12 Leisure goods	30.70	30.10	19.50	20.70	17.50	11.10
"	*10*	*6*	*8*	*6*	*8*	*10*
13 Leisure services	115.20	81.70	45.30	46.30	29.70	21.40
"	*9*	*4*	*7*	*5*	*5*	*10*
14 Miscellaneous	1.10	1.20	0.80	0.80	1.00	0.20
"	*23*	*10*	*18*	*11*	*17*	*28*
1-14 All expenditure groups	642.40	563.50	393.10	406.10	320.40	231.50
Percentage standard error	*3*	*2*	*3*	*2*	*2*	*4*
Average weekly expenditure per person (£)						
All expenditure groups	238.60	213.80	169.70	140.80	125.30	94.00

1 See Appendix D

3.6 Household expenditure by number of persons working
based on weighted data and including children's expenditure

2000-01

	Number of persons working					All house-holds
	None	One	Two	Three	Four or more	
Grossed number of households (thousands)	8,780	7,110	7,290	1,410	440	25,030
Total number of households in sample	2,450	1,871	1,896	322	98	6,637
Total number of persons in sample	4,312	4,179	5,750	1,212	472	15,925
Total number of adults in sample	3,575	2,946	4,012	933	386	11,852
Weighted average number of persons per household	1.7	2.1	2.9	3.7	4.7	2.4
Weighted average age of head of household	65	45	41	48	46	51
Employment status of head[1]:						
- % working full-time or self-employed	*0*	*68*	*91*	*92*	*94*	*51*
- % working part-time	*0*	*14*	*6*	*7*	*4*	*6*
- % not working	*100*	*18*	*3*	*1*	*2*	*43*

Commodity or service	Average weekly household expenditure (£)					
1 Housing (Net)	**28.90**	**69.70**	**93.70**	**84.50**	**108.60**	**63.90**
Percentage standard error	*3*	*2*	*2*	*4*	*10*	*1*
2 Fuel and power	**10.50**	**11.60**	**12.90**	**15.00**	**17.20**	**11.90**
"	*1*	*3*	*1*	*3*	*6*	*1*
3 Food and non-alcoholic drinks	**38.90**	**56.70**	**81.40**	**111.00**	**126.70**	**61.90**
"	*1*	*1*	*1*	*2*	*4*	*1*
4 Alcoholic drink	**6.60**	**13.30**	**20.80**	**35.20**	**48.80**	**15.00**
"	*4*	*3*	*3*	*5*	*9*	*2*
5 Tobacco	**4.40**	**6.20**	**6.30**	**12.30**	**13.30**	**6.10**
"	*5*	*5*	*5*	*9*	*16*	*3*
6 Clothing and footwear	**9.50**	**20.10**	**32.10**	**46.50**	**54.70**	**22.00**
"	*4*	*4*	*3*	*6*	*10*	*£*
7 Household goods	**21.20**	**30.90**	**43.90**	**46.10**	**58.60**	**32.60**
"	*6*	*5*	*4*	*7*	*18*	*3*
8 Household services	**13.10**	**20.80**	**31.70**	**29.10**	**32.70**	**22.00**
"	*5*	*3*	*4*	*9*	*12*	*2*
9 Personal goods and services	**8.30**	**13.20**	**20.80**	**26.10**	**30.10**	**14.70**
"	*4*	*4*	*3*	*6*	*12*	*2*
10 Motoring	**21.60**	**54.10**	**84.40**	**98.10**	**116.50**	**55.10**
"	*4*	*4*	*2*	*5*	*8*	*2*
11 Fares and other travel costs	**3.70**	**9.40**	**12.80**	**21.90**	**29.70**	**9.50**
"	*13*	*7*	*7*	*12*	*36*	*5*
12 Leisure goods	**10.00**	**18.90**	**28.10**	**32.90**	**47.20**	**19.70**
"	*4*	*6*	*5*	*8*	*15*	*3*
13 Leisure services	**26.00**	**50.20**	**72.90**	**77.10**	**94.20**	**50.60**
"	*5*	*5*	*4*	*8*	*20*	*2*
14 Miscellaneous	**0.20**	**0.80**	**1.10**	**1.20**	**1.70**	**0.70**
"	*11*	*11*	*9*	*24*	*33*	*6*
1-14 All expenditure groups	**202.90**	**375.80**	**542.90**	**636.90**	**780.10**	**385.70**
Percentage standard error	*2*	*2*	*1*	*2*	*5*	*1*

Average weekly expenditure per person (£)						
All expenditure groups	**119.40**	**175.30**	**184.40**	**172.90**	**164.30**	**163.90**

1 Excludes19 households where the head was on a Government-supported training scheme.

ONS, Family Spending 2000-01, © Crown copyright 2002

3.7 Household expenditure by age at which the head of household completed continuous full-time education

2000-01

based on weighted data and including children's expenditure

	Aged 14 and under	Aged 15	Aged 16	Aged 17 and under 19	Aged 19 and under 22	Aged 22 or over
Grossed number of households (thousands)	4,040	5,520	7,030	4,040	2,100	2,300
Total number of households in sample	1,104	1,458	1,901	1,073	536	565
Total number of persons in sample	1,864	3,391	5,239	2,702	1,343	1,386
Total number of adults in sample	1,774	2,776	3,418	1,900	953	1,031
Weighted average number of persons per household	1.7	2.3	2.7	2.4	2.4	2.4
Weighted average age of head of household	72	55	43	46	43	43

Commodity or service	Average weekly household expenditure (£)					
1 Housing (Net)	**30.90**	**47.80**	**63.50**	**73.80**	**104.60**	**107.40**
Percentage standard error	*3*	*2*	*2*	*2*	*5*	*3*
2 Fuel and power	**10.30**	**11.60**	**12.20**	**12.60**	**12.70**	**12.40**
"	*2*	*2*	*2*	*2*	*3*	*3*
3 Food and non-alcoholic drinks	**39.60**	**59.80**	**64.80**	**68.20**	**72.10**	**77.20**
"	*2*	*2*	*1*	*2*	*3*	*3*
4 Alcoholic drink	**6.50**	**15.50**	**15.40**	**17.10**	**17.60**	**21.60**
"	*7*	*4*	*4*	*4*	*6*	*6*
5 Tobacco	**4.10**	**8.60**	**7.10**	**5.30**	**4.50**	**3.20**
"	*8*	*5*	*4*	*7*	*11*	*11*
6 Clothing and footwear	**10.90**	**19.30**	**24.80**	**24.30**	**27.90**	**29.80**
"	*8*	*4*	*3*	*5*	*6*	*6*
7 Household goods	**17.90**	**31.50**	**31.90**	**36.10**	**46.80**	**44.40**
"	*7*	*5*	*4*	*5*	*10*	*9*
8 Household services	**10.40**	**16.70**	**21.80**	**26.60**	**32.50**	**37.50**
"	*6*	*4*	*5*	*4*	*8*	*8*
9 Personal goods and services	**7.30**	**12.50**	**15.10**	**17.20**	**22.70**	**20.30**
"	*5*	*4*	*4*	*5*	*6*	*6*
10 Motoring	**20.50**	**49.30**	**59.40**	**64.10**	**79.20**	**78.70**
"	*6*	*4*	*3*	*4*	*6*	*6*
11 Fares and other travel costs	**4.90**	**7.00**	**8.20**	**12.80**	**12.70**	**18.40**
"	*26*	*8*	*10*	*9*	*10*	*11*
12 Leisure goods	**9.40**	**17.20**	**18.90**	**26.60**	**24.50**	**30.30**
"	*6*	*7*	*4*	*7*	*8*	*10*
13 Leisure services	**23.70**	**40.30**	**47.90**	**55.50**	**77.90**	**97.50**
"	*7*	*4*	*4*	*5*	*7*	*8*
14 Miscellaneous	**0.20**	**0.50**	**0.80**	**1.10**	**0.90**	**1.10**
"	*22*	*13*	*10*	*13*	*16*	*17*
1-14 All expenditure groups	**196.50**	**337.60**	**391.90**	**441.20**	**536.50**	**579.90**
Percentage standard error	*3*	*2*	*2*	*2*	*3*	*3*

Average weekly expenditure per person (£)						
All expenditure groups	**117.20**	**144.80**	**146.10**	**181.50**	**222.60**	**241.00**

3.8 Household expenditure by economic activity status of household reference person
based on weighted data and including children's expenditure

2000-01

	Employees			Self-employed	All in employ-ment[1]
	Full-time	Part-time	All		
Grossed number of households (thousands)	11,390	1,770	13,150	1,840	15,050
Total number of households in sample	2,888	481	3,369	492	3,876
Total number of persons in sample	7,880	1,233	9,113	1,510	10,657
Total number of adults in sample	5,620	828	6,448	1,042	7,512
Weighted average number of persons per household	41	46	42	46	42

Commodity or service	Average weekly household expenditure (£)				
1 **Housing (Net)**	**89.60**	**59.40**	**85.60**	**86.40**	**85.40**
Percentage standard error	*1*	*4*	*1*	*5*	*1*
2 **Fuel and power**	**12.30**	**11.30**	**12.10**	**14.70**	**12.40**
"	*2*	*3*	*1*	*3*	*1*
3 **Food and non-alcoholic drinks**	**74.10**	**62.80**	**72.60**	**86.40**	**74.10**
"	*1*	*3*	*1*	*2*	*1*
4 **Alcoholic drink**	**19.90**	**15.60**	**19.40**	**20.60**	**19.50**
"	*2*	*7*	*2*	*6*	*2*
5 **Tobacco**	**7.00**	**6.30**	**6.90**	**5.90**	**6.80**
"	*4*	*9*	*3*	*10*	*3*
6 **Clothing and footwear**	**29.50**	**20.70**	**28.30**	**33.70**	**28.90**
"	*3*	*6*	*2*	*6*	*2*
7 **Household goods**	**40.00**	**24.90**	**38.00**	**45.70**	**38.80**
"	*3*	*8*	*3*	*7*	*3*
8 **Household services**	**27.20**	**19.70**	**26.20**	**33.00**	**27.00**
"	*3*	*6*	*3*	*9*	*3*
9 **Personal goods and services**	**19.10**	**12.20**	**18.10**	**20.00**	**18.30**
"	*3*	*7*	*3*	*6*	*2*
10 **Motoring**	**75.10**	**51.40**	**71.90**	**92.80**	**74.30**
"	*2*	*8*	*2*	*5*	*2*
11 **Fares and other travel costs**	**13.50**	**9.60**	**13.00**	**11.90**	**12.80**
"	*6*	*10*	*5*	*21*	*5*
12 **Leisure goods**	**25.20**	**18.20**	**24.30**	**30.10**	**24.90**
"	*4*	*7*	*3*	*12*	*3*
13 **Leisure services**	**64.70**	**48.50**	**62.60**	**82.60**	**64.90**
"	*3*	*11*	*3*	*7*	*3*
14 **Miscellaneous**	**1.10**	**0.70**	**1.00**	**1.20**	**1.00**
"	*8*	*17*	*7*	*17*	*7*
1-14 **All expenditure groups**	**498.40**	**361.30**	**480.00**	**565.00**	**489.20**
Percentage standard error	*1*	*3*	*1*	*3*	*1*
Average weekly expenditure per person (£)					
All expenditure groups	**12.10**	**7.80**	**11.40**	**12.20**	**11.50**

1 Includes 19 households where the head was on a Government-supported training scheme.

ONS, Family Spending 2000-01, © Crown copyright 2002

3.8 Household expenditure
by economic activity status of household reference person (cont.)
2000-01
based on weighted data and including children's expenditure

	ILO unem- ployed	All economi- cally active[1]	Economically inactive			All house- holds
			Retired	Other	All	
Grossed number of households (thousands)	610	15,660	6,130	3,240	9,370	25,030
Total number of households in sample	160	4,036	1,685	916	2,601	6,637
Total number of persons in sample	380	11,037	2,592	2,296	4,888	15,925
Total number of adults in sample	242	7,754	2,571	1,527	4,098	11,852
Weighted average number of persons per household	43	42	75	47	65	51

Commodity or service	Average weekly household expenditure (£)					
1 **Housing (Net)**	25.00	83.10	30.60	34.50	31.90	63.90
Percentage standard error	11	1	3	5	2	1
2 **Fuel and power**	10.80	12.40	10.70	11.60	11.00	11.90
"	6	1	2	2	1	1
3 **Food and non-alcoholic drinks**	44.20	73.00	39.20	51.60	43.50	61.90
"	6	1	1	2	1	1
4 **Alcoholic drink**	9.50	19.10	6.20	12.20	8.30	15.00
"	13	2	5	6	4	2
5 **Tobacco**	6.10	6.80	3.00	8.50	4.90	6.10
"	12	3	7	5	4	3
6 **Clothing and footwear**	13.50	28.30	8.60	16.90	11.50	22.00
"	16	2	5	6	4	2
7 **Household goods**	13.00	37.80	20.80	30.20	24.00	32.60
"	12	3	8	8	6	3
8 **Household services**	12.30	26.40	13.50	16.40	14.50	22.00
"	11	3	7	7	5	2
9 **Personal goods and services**	7.30	17.90	9.10	10.00	9.40	14.70
"	17	2	5	6	4	2
10 **Motoring**	21.60	72.20	21.90	35.10	26.50	55.10
"	14	2	5	7	4	2
11 **Fares and other travel costs**	6.10	12.60	3.20	6.30	4.30	9.50
"	14	5	16	14	11	5
12 **Leisure goods**	9.50	24.30	10.20	15.70	12.10	19.70
"	11	3	8	7	6	3
13 **Leisure services**	18.40	63.00	26.90	35.50	29.90	50.60
"	19	3	5	8	4	2
14 **Miscellaneous**	0.40	1.00	0.10	0.50	0.30	0.70
"	33	7	15	14	11	6
1-14 **All expenditure groups**	197.60	477.80	203.90	284.90	231.90	385.70
Percentage standard error	7	1	2	3	2	1

Average weekly expenditure per person (£)

All expenditure groups	4.60	11.30	2.70	6.10	3.60	7.60

1 Includes 19 households where the head was on a Government-supported training scheme.

3.9 Household expenditure by occupation of household reference person

based on weighted data and including children's expenditure

2000-01

	Profes-sional	Employ-ers and managers	Interme-diate non manual	Junior non manual	Skilled manual	Semi-skilled manual	Unskilled manual
Grossed number of households (thousands)	1,070	3,200	2,130	1,920	2,620	2,140	570
Total number of households in sample	257	831	535	492	670	554	156
Total number of persons in sample	705	2,370	1,329	1,130	1,989	1,437	415
Total number of adults in sample	505	1,653	972	832	1,378	1,013	271
Weighted average number of persons per household	2.7	2.8	2.4	2.3	2.9	2.5	2.6

Commodity or service	Average weekly household expenditure (£)						
1 **Housing (Net)**	102.40	110.50	91.50	72.30	70.90	58.00	47.30
Percentage standard error	4	3	3	3	3	3	6
2 **Fuel and power**	13.50	14.00	11.80	10.50	12.20	10.80	9.30
"	4	2	2	3	6	3	5
3 **Food and non-alcoholic drinks**	83.60	85.50	72.00	60.80	71.50	58.30	51.20
"	3	2	2	3	2	2	5
4 **Alcoholic drink**	20.30	22.00	21.00	17.10	18.60	15.60	12.40
"	7	4	8	6	5	6	11
5 **Tobacco**	4.00	6.30	5.30	5.70	8.30	9.50	8.40
"	16	7	11	8	7	7	12
6 **Clothing and footwear**	31.80	33.60	27.10	26.80	26.50	22.00	16.50
"	9	5	6	7	6	6	15
7 **Household goods**	45.30	53.90	34.20	31.80	27.70	30.00	20.10
"	9	6	7	8	5	8	14
8 **Household services**	36.10	33.10	28.40	21.70	21.30	18.70	10.90
"	7	5	8	5	9	6	8
9 **Personal goods and services**	20.70	24.20	21.00	15.70	14.30	11.50	8.40
"	7	5	7	7	5	6	11
10 **Motoring**	83.30	95.80	76.90	55.30	63.40	49.10	24.40
"	6	4	5	6	3	5	12
11 **Fares and other travel costs**	17.30	17.60	14.50	12.90	8.50	8.00	6.10
"	15	11	10	15	12	11	15
12 **Leisure goods**	30.80	29.70	27.70	20.50	20.50	17.50	9.60
"	12	6	10	9	7	8	11
13 **Leisure services**	105.20	92.50	65.20	44.30	44.50	31.40	24.60
"	11	6	9	8	5	6	12
14 **Miscellaneous**	1.00	1.30	1.00	0.80	0.90	0.90	0.40
"	24	14	16	20	14	23	35
1-14 **All expenditure groups**	595.30	620.10	497.60	396.20	409.10	341.30	249.60
Percentage standard error	3	2	3	3	2	2	5
Average weekly expenditure per person (£)							
All expenditure groups	224.30	222.90	203.70	171.10	142.60	135.80	96.00

1 Excludes households where the household reference person is retired, unoccupied, self employed,
in the armed forces or with an inadequately described occupation.

ONS, Family Spending 2000-01, © Crown copyright 2002

Chapter *4*

Expenditure by household composition, income & tenure

- Average weekly expenditure was highest for households consisting of three or more adults with children, at £640 a week, followed by households with three or more adults and no children, at £580 a week.

- Expenditure was lowest for one person households mainly dependent on a state pension, at £101 a week, 40 per cent lower than the next group which was couples mainly dependent on the state pension.

- **Leisure** spending, goods and services combined, was the largest item of expenditure for retired couples with income besides the state pension and for couples below retirement age, for couples with one or two children and for households with three or more adults.

- **Food and non-alcoholic drink** was the largest item of spending for households mainly dependent on the state pension, both singles and couples, and for one parent households with two or more children.

Households with the lowest fifth of incomes
- Among households with the lowest fifth of incomes, one person households who were not retired spent the highest proportion on **alcohol**, 5 per cent, followed by couples below retirement age without children at 4 per cent.

- Within the income group the highest proportion of spending going on **tobacco** was among one parent households, couples with children and one person households who were not retired, around 4 per cent. Retired households of all kinds spent the least.

- Couples and single people without children and below retirement age, and single retired people with income in addition to the state pension, were the types in the low income group who spent the highest proportion on **leisure services**, 10 to 12 per cent. Couples with children and lone parents spent the lowest proportion, at 7 or 8 per cent.

4 Expenditure by household composition, income and tenure

4.1 Households by household type

Per cent

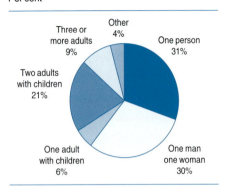

This chapter contains tables exploring expenditure analysed by household composition and income. **Table 4.1** shows spending patterns for a selection of household types. The breakdowns by income are in **Tables 4.2 to 4.9**. The way incomes are shown changed last year. The same income groups are now used in every table, so that comparisons can be made between spending of households of different types but with the same income. This year, for the first time, **Tables 4.2 to 4.9** are based on data from the last three years, 1998-99 – 2000-01. This increases sample size and reliability.

Household composition

Figure 4.1 shows a breakdown by household type. It can be seen that 31 per cent of households contained only one person. Similarly, 30 per cent accounted for one man and one woman households. Two adults with children made up 21 per cent of households. The change to the harmonised definition of the household in the 2000-01 survey reduced the proportion of one person households slightly. There is a fuller discussion in Chapter 9.

Table 4.1 shows that the group who spent the smallest weekly amount at £101 was households with one person, retired and mainly dependent on state pension. Their average expenditure was over 40 per cent less than the next lowest spender, namely one man and one woman, mainly dependent on state pension. Three or more adults with children, on average, spent the largest amount at £640 a week and the next highest spenders were households of three or more adults and no children, at £580 a week.

Leisure spending, on goods and services, when combined, was the largest item for retired couples with income besides the state pension and for non-retired couples, for two adults with one or two children and for households with three or more adults.

4.2 Expenditure on leisure services between 1995-96 and 2000-01 by household type

£ per week 2000-01 prices

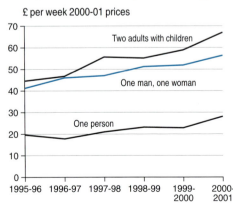

Food and non-alcoholic drinks accounted for the largest amount spent for retired households mainly dependent on a state pension, and for one adult households with two or more children. One person, retired and not mainly dependent on state pension, along with one person, non-retired households, both spent the largest proportion of their total spending on housing.

ONS, Family Spending 2000-01, © Crown copyright 2002

Figure 4.2 is an illustration of how expenditure on leisure services has changed between 1995-96 and 2000-01. In general, the trend shows that more was spent on leisure services each year. Of the three groups compared, two adults with children consistently spent the most on leisure services. In 2000-01, two adults with children spent an average of £67 a week, which was nearly 20 per cent more than the amount spent by one man and one woman households, at £56 a week. Over the five years since 1995-96, they were also the group with the largest proportionate increase in spending. The household group to spend the least each year was one person households.

Expenditure by income

Tables 4.2 to 4.9 show expenditure by income group for different household compositions. Many of the differences in spending between different types of household are the result of difference in income. These tables allow households in the same income groups to be compared. The analysis in this section concentrates on households with the lowest fifth of incomes.

Variations between different household types in the lowest and middle income quintiles

To aid comparisons between different items, the household types have been ordered in the same way, by total expenditure of the lowest income group. The order is from the highest total spending at the top to the lowest at the bottom.

In the middle income group figures are not shown for retired households mainly dependent on the state pension and in the lowest income group they are not shown for retired couples with income in addition to the state pension. In both cases there are no or very few such households.

Alcoholic drink

Figure 4.3a shows that, among households with the lowest fifth of incomes, one person non-retired households had the highest proportion of spending going on alcohol, 5 per cent, followed by non-retired couples at 4 per cent. **Figure 4.3b** shows a comparison between expenditure on alcohol by the lowest and third quintiles.

4.3a Proportion spent on alcoholic drink by household type: lowest income quintile group

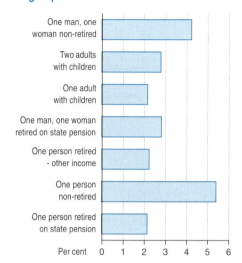

4.3b Spending on alcohol by household type: lowest and third income quintiles

	Lowest quintile	Third quintile
	£ per week	
One man, one woman non-retired	10	15
Two adults with children	6	12
One adult with children	3	9
One man, one woman retired on state pension	4	..
One person retired - other income	3	6
One person non-retired	7	15
One person retired on state pension	2	..
One man, one woman retired - other income	..	11

4.4a Proportion spent on tobacco by household type: lowest income quintile group

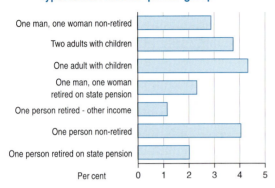

Tobacco

Within the lowest income quintile, **Figure 4.4a** shows that lone parents, couples with children and one person, non-retired households spent the highest proportion on tobacco, around 4 per cent.

Retired households in the lowest quintile spent the smallest amount on tobacco, paying less than £4 each week. There were no great differences in expenditure on tobacco between the lowest and the third income groups for all household types, as can be seen from **Figure 4.4b**.

Leisure services

Figure 4.5a shows that non-retired couples, one person non-retired and one person retired with extra income beside the state pension, spent the highest proportion on leisure services, at 10 to 12 per cent. Couples with children and lone parents spent the lowest proportion at 7 or 8 per cent. In money terms the table in **Figure 4.5b** shows that the difference in expenditure between the lowest and middle income groups was quite pronounced for adults with children, one person non-retired and one person with an income other than a state pension. In the middle income group retired couples with other income beside the state pension spent the most on leisure services, £46 a week.

4.4b Spending on tobacco by household type: lowest and third income quintiles

	Lowest quintile	Third quintile
	£ per week	
One man, one woman non-retired	7	7
Two adults with children	9	9
One adult with children	6	6
One man, one woman retired on state pension	0	..
One person retired - other income	1	2
One person non-retired	5	5
One person retired on state pension	2	..
One man, one woman retired - other income	..	3

4.5a Proportion spent on leisure services by household type: lowest income quintile group

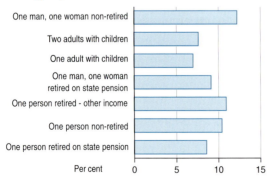

ONS, Family Spending 2000-01, © Crown copyright 2002

Tenure

Table 4.10 shows total spending by housing tenure and **Figure 4.6** show the average spent on housing. The most was spent on housing by private renters of furnished accommodation and by people buying with a mortgage. Both groups spent over £90 a week, with the renters spending almost one quarter of their total weekly expenditure at £470.

Other than rent free tenants, the groups to spend the lowest amount on housing costs, at about £32 a week, were council tenants and outright owners. However, outright owners used only 10 per cent of their total expenditure on housing, whereas council tenants spent 16 per cent.

Figure 4.7 shows the expenditure on selected commodities by tenure. Households in the owners sector spent the same amount each week on food and non-alcoholic drink and motoring at £68. They also spent the most on food and motoring, comparing their expenditure with that of the private rented sector and the social rented group.

The private rented sector spent the second largest amount on each observed commodity, except for fares and other travel costs where they spent the most at £14 per week. The social rented sector spent the least on fares and other travel costs, motoring and food, but spent the most, out of the three groups, on tobacco.

4.5b Spending on leisure services by household type: lowest and third income quintiles

	Lowest quintile	Third quintile
	£ per week	
One man, one woman non-retired	29	37
Two adults with children	17	32
One adult with children	10	38
One man, one woman retired on state pension	13	..
One person retired - other income	14	42
One person non-retired	13	30
One person retired on state pension	8	..
One man, one woman retired - other income	..	46

4.6 Housing by tenure

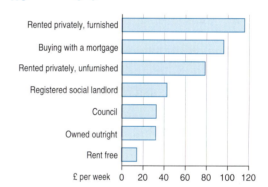

4.7 Expenditure on selected commodities by tenure

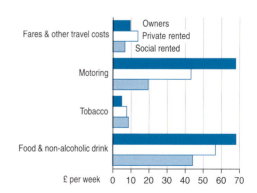

4.1 Expenditure by household composition

based on weighted data and including children's expenditure

2000-01

	Retired households				Non-retired	
	State pension[1]		Other retired		One person	One man and one woman
	One person	One man and one woman	One person	One man and one woman		
Grossed number of households (thousands)	1,770	610	1,510	1,840	4,190	4,930
Total number of households in sample	457	178	404	548	1,039	1,243
Total number of persons in sample	457	356	404	1,096	1,039	2,486
Total number of adults in sample	457	356	404	1,096	1,039	2,486
Weighted average number of persons per household	1.0	2.0	1.0	2.0	1.0	2.0

Commodity or service	Average weekly household expenditure (£)					
1 **Housing (Net)**	**18.10**	**28.90**	**35.90**	**39.90**	**56.50**	**77.40**
Percentage standard error	5	8	6	3	3	2
2 **Fuel and power**	**8.80**	**10.80**	**10.00**	**12.40**	**8.30**	**11.90**
"	4	6	4	2	2	2
3 **Food and non-alcoholic drinks**	**23.60**	**40.80**	**29.70**	**55.60**	**32.00**	**66.50**
"	2	3	3	2	2	1
4 **Alcoholic drink**	**1.90**	**5.40**	**3.90**	**10.70**	**11.30**	**20.40**
"	12	15	11	6	5	4
5 **Tobacco**	**1.90**	**3.60**	**2.00**	**3.10**	**4.90**	**6.10**
"	13	15	16	13	6	6
6 **Clothing and footwear**	**4.50**	**6.60**	**6.90**	**12.60**	**9.90**	**22.50**
"	10	13	11	7	6	5
7 **Household goods**	**9.70**	**18.20**	**16.70**	**36.90**	**19.70**	**41.80**
"	10	14	13	13	8	5
8 **Household services**	**9.10**	**10.00**	**14.50**	**19.10**	**14.30**	**24.60**
"	7	17	9	14	4	7
9 **Personal goods and services**	**4.90**	**6.30**	**8.50**	**14.50**	**7.50**	**18.90**
"	15	11	11	8	7	5
10 **Motoring**	**3.60**	**19.50**	**17.10**	**42.80**	**35.30**	**75.60**
"	14	13	13	6	6	4
11 **Fares and other travel costs**	**1.20**	**2.30**	**2.70**	**5.10**	**7.10**	**11.00**
"	10	19	14	30	12	12
12 **Leisure goods**	**3.90**	**8.50**	**7.60**	**17.40**	**11.20**	**22.10**
"	7	15	9	14	6	7
13 **Leisure services**	**9.60**	**17.80**	**27.10**	**46.10**	**36.30**	**65.00**
"	8	14	13	7	8	5
14 **Miscellaneous**	**0.10**	**0.10**	**0.10**	**0.20**	**0.60**	**0.70**
"	47	35	28	20	20	11
1-14 **All expenditure groups**	**101.00**	**178.90**	**182.90**	**316.40**	**255.00**	**464.40**
Percentage standard error	3	4	4	3	2	2
Average weekly expenditure per person (£)						
All expenditure groups	**101.00**	**89.50**	**182.90**	**158.20**	**255.00**	**232.20**

1 Mainly dependent on state pension and not economically active - see appendix D.

4.1 Expenditure by household composition (cont.)
based on weighted data and including children's expenditure

2000-01

| | Retired and non-retired households | | | | | | |
| | One adult | | Two adults | | | Three or more adults | |
Commodity or service	with one child	with two or more children	with one child	with two children	with three or more children	without children	with children
Grossed number of households (thousands)	680	690	1,810	2,270	970	2,230	1,000
Total number of households in sample	208	241	494	656	310	462	262
Total number of persons in sample	416	845	1,482	2,624	1,645	1,528	1,277
Total number of adults in sample	208	241	988	1,312	620	1,528	847
Weighted average number of persons per household	2.0	3.5	3.0	4.0	5.3	3.3	4.8

Commodity or service	Average weekly household expenditure (£)						
1 Housing (Net)	**38.80**	**38.50**	**84.70**	**98.60**	**83.80**	**78.40**	**79.30**
Percentage standard error	*8*	*8*	*3*	*4*	*4*	*6*	*5*
2 Fuel and power	**10.70**	**11.70**	**13.50**	**15.00**	**15.40**	**14.90**	**16.30**
"	*4*	*4*	*2*	*5*	*4*	*3*	*4*
3 Food and non-alcoholic drinks	**44.60**	**56.90**	**73.50**	**91.70**	**98.40**	**98.50**	**114.80**
"	*4*	*3*	*2*	*2*	*2*	*2*	*3*
4 Alcoholic drink	**6.10**	**5.20**	**14.80**	**15.70**	**11.70**	**33.20**	**28.70**
"	*11*	*12*	*6*	*5*	*8*	*5*	*7*
5 Tobacco	**5.00**	**6.70**	**7.10**	**6.40**	**8.50**	**12.90**	**11.10**
"	*12*	*10*	*8*	*7*	*10*	*7*	*10*
6 Clothing and footwear	**22.20**	**22.10**	**31.40**	**38.30**	**30.90**	**37.50**	**51.90**
"	*11*	*8*	*6*	*5*	*6*	*5*	*7*
7 Household goods	**20.70**	**23.80**	**44.40**	**40.70**	**37.20**	**43.20**	**55.10**
"	*14*	*9*	*10*	*6*	*7*	*7*	*10*
8 Household services	**19.40**	**20.60**	**31.40**	**33.20**	**27.90**	**28.30**	**28.20**
"	*13*	*9*	*5*	*6*	*7*	*9*	*6*
9 Personal goods and services	**10.40**	**10.00**	**18.50**	**19.40**	**16.80**	**23.10**	**24.00**
"	*11*	*9*	*5*	*5*	*6*	*6*	*7*
10 Motoring	**24.60**	**23.60**	**76.90**	**79.20**	**75.50**	**89.20**	**85.90**
"	*13*	*9*	*5*	*5*	*8*	*5*	*6*
11 Fares and other travel costs	**6.60**	**5.90**	**10.50**	**12.30**	**8.40**	**18.10**	**23.20**
"	*18*	*11*	*12*	*11*	*12*	*10*	*21*
12 Leisure goods	**14.10**	**17.70**	**22.60**	**31.50**	**34.70**	**29.60**	**35.80**
"	*15*	*14*	*6*	*8*	*10*	*8*	*10*
13 Leisure services	**30.60**	**23.60**	**65.20**	**70.00**	**63.30**	**71.10**	**82.10**
"	*15*	*10*	*7*	*6*	*9*	*9*	*10*
14 Miscellaneous	**0.30**	**1.80**	**0.90**	**1.30**	**1.40**	**0.70**	**1.90**
"	*39*	*22*	*14*	*13*	*14*	*19*	*26*
1-14 All expenditure groups	**253.90**	**268.30**	**495.50**	**553.40**	**513.90**	**578.70**	**638.30**
Percentage standard error	*6*	*4*	*3*	*2*	*3*	*3*	*3*
Average weekly expenditure per person (£)							
All expenditure groups	**127.00**	**77.20**	**165.20**	**138.30**	**97.20**	**173.50**	**132.60**

4.2 Expenditure of one person retired households mainly dependent on state pensions[1] by gross income group   1998-99 - 2000-01
based on weighted data and including children's expenditure

	Lowest twenty per cent	Second quintile group	Third quintile group	Fourth quintile group	Highest twenty per cent	All house-holds
Lower boundary of group (£ per week)[2]		163	310	489	739	
Average number of grossed households (thousands)	1,550	240	0	0	0	1,790
Total number of households in sample (over 3 years)	1,208	183	1	0	0	1,392
Total number of persons in sample (over 3 years)	1,208	183	1	0	0	1,392
Total number of adults in sample (over 3 years)	1,208	183	1	0	0	1,392
Weighted average number of persons per household	1.0	1.0	1.0	0	0	1.0

Commodity or service	Average weekly household expenditure (£)					
1 **Housing (Net)**	**16.70**	**14.00**	..	..	..	**16.30**
Percentage standard error	*3*	*11*	*..*	*..*	*..*	*3*
2 **Fuel and power**	**8.10**	**8.90**	..	..	..	**8.20**
"	*3*	*5*	*..*	*..*	*..*	*2*
3 **Food and non-alcoholic drinks**	**22.30**	**27.40**	..	..	..	**23.00**
"	*1*	*4*	*..*	*..*	*..*	*1*
4 **Alcoholic drink**	**2.00**	**2.80**	..	..	..	**2.10**
"	*7*	*17*	*..*	*..*	*..*	*7*
5 **Tobacco**	**1.90**	**2.80**	..	..	..	**2.00**
"	*8*	*17*	*..*	*..*	*..*	*7*
6 **Clothing and footwear**	**3.70**	**7.30**	..	..	..	**4.20**
"	*7*	*23*	*..*	*..*	*..*	*8*
7 **Household goods**	**9.50**	**10.40**	..	..	..	**9.60**
"	*8*	*16*	*..*	*..*	*..*	*7*
8 **Household services**	**8.10**	**13.50**	..	..	..	**8.80**
"	*11*	*10*	*..*	*..*	*..*	*9*
9 **Personal goods and services**	**5.00**	**5.20**	..	..	..	**5.00**
"	*11*	*12*	*..*	*..*	*..*	*10*
10 **Motoring**	**3.70**	**3.30**	..	..	..	**3.60**
"	*12*	*21*	*..*	*..*	*..*	*10*
11 **Fares and other travel costs**	**1.30**	**2.10**	..	..	..	**1.40**
"	*7*	*16*	*..*	*..*	*..*	*6*
12 **Leisure goods**	**3.70**	**3.90**	..	..	..	**3.70**
"	*5*	*9*	*..*	*..*	*..*	*5*
13 **Leisure services**	**8.10**	**10.20**	..	..	..	**8.40**
"	*5*	*11*	*..*	*..*	*..*	*4*
14 **Miscellaneous**	**0.10**	..	..	..	..	**0.10**
"	*35*	*..*	*..*	*..*	*..*	*32*
1-14 **All expenditure groups**	**94.10**	**111.90**	..	..	..	**96.40**
Percentage standard error	*2*	*4*	*..*	*..*	*..*	*2*

Average weekly expenditure per person (£)

All expenditure groups	**94.10**	**111.90**	..	..	..	**96.40**

1 Mainly dependent on state pension and not economically active - see appendix D.

2 Boundaries divide the complete set of UK households into 5 equal groups.

   Reports up to 1999-2000, for this table, divided just the one person retired households into equal groups

4.3 Expenditure of one person retired households not mainly dependent on state pensions by gross income quintile group

1998-99 - 2000-01

based on weighted data and including children's expenditure

	Lowest twenty per cent	Second quintile group	Third quintile group	Fourth quintile group	Highest twenty per cent	All house-holds
Lower boundary of group (£ per week)[1]		163	310	489	739	
Average number of grossed households (thousands)	570	730	220	50	30	1,600
Total number of households in sample (over 3 years)	458	576	176	42	22	1,274
Total number of persons in sample (over 3 years)	458	576	176	42	22	1,274
Total number of adults in sample (over 3 years)	458	576	176	42	22	1,274
Weighted average number of persons per household	1.0	1.0	1.0	1.0	1.0	1.0

Commodity or service	Average weekly household expenditure (£)					
1 Housing (Net)	**30.50**	**33.20**	**33.70**	..	**36.00**	**33.40**
Percentage standard error	*4*	*4*	*5*	*..*	*10*	*3*
2 Fuel and power	**8.50**	**9.40**	**11.50**	**13.10**	**13.80**	**9.60**
"	*3*	*3*	*6*	*12*	*10*	*2*
3 Food and non-alcoholic drinks	**23.70**	**29.00**	**35.60**	**41.60**	**43.00**	**28.70**
"	*2*	*2*	*4*	*9*	*12*	*2*
4 Alcoholic drink	**2.80**	**4.20**	**6.40**	**10.30**	**9.40**	**4.30**
"	*10*	*9*	*11*	*29*	*32*	*6*
5 Tobacco	**1.40**	**2.40**	**2.20**	..	..	**2.00**
"	*16*	*12*	*29*	*..*	*..*	*9*
6 Clothing and footwear	**4.20**	**7.70**	**12.10**	..	..	**7.50**
"	*10*	*9*	*15*	*..*	*..*	*6*
7 Household goods	**9.00**	**16.70**	**23.00**	..	**23.20**	**15.90**
"	*10*	*10*	*15*	*..*	*29*	*7*
8 Household services	**7.40**	**13.20**	**21.20**	..	**35.30**	**13.70**
"	*5*	*6*	*13*	*..*	*21*	*6*
9 Personal goods and services	**6.90**	**7.30**	**9.90**	**9.90**	..	**8.00**
"	*11*	*8*	*16*	*19*	*..*	*6*
10 Motoring	**9.10**	**14.30**	**33.40**	**32.00**	..	**17.10**
"	*18*	*9*	*13*	*22*	*..*	*7*
11 Fares and other travel costs	**1.80**	**2.90**	**3.90**	**4.40**	..	**2.80**
"	*12*	*11*	*26*	*32*	*..*	*9*
12 Leisure goods	**5.20**	**7.10**	**10.90**	**16.40**	**21.80**	**7.40**
"	*10*	*6*	*11*	*20*	*36*	*5*
13 Leisure services	**13.60**	**24.50**	**42.10**	**72.80**	**76.30**	**25.60**
"	*9*	*12*	*15*	*30*	*38*	*7*
14 Miscellaneous	**0.20**	**0.30**	..	..	..	**0.30**
"	*35*	*41*	*..*	*..*	*..*	*27*
1-14 All expenditure groups	**124.20**	**172.20**	**246.60**	**375.90**	**393.00**	**176.30**
Percentage standard error	*3*	*3*	*5*	*11*	*16*	*2*
Average weekly expenditure per person (£)						
All expenditure groups	**124.20**	**172.20**	**246.60**	**375.90**	**393.00**	**176.30**

1 Boundaries divide the complete set of UK households into 5 equal groups.

4.4 Expenditure of one person non-retired households by gross income quintile group
1998-99 - 2000-01

based on weighted data and including children's expenditure

	Lowest twenty per cent	Second quintile group	Third quintile group	Fourth quintile group	Highest twenty per cent	All house-holds
Lower boundary of group (£ per week)[1]		163	310	489	739	
Average number of grossed households (thousands)	1,220	1,000	1,090	560	270	4,140
Total number of households in sample (over 3 years)	976	796	799	410	177	3,158
Total number of persons in sample (over 3 years)	976	796	799	410	177	3,158
Total number of adults in sample (over 3 years)	976	796	799	410	177	3,158
Weighted average number of persons per household	1.0	1.0	1.0	1.0	1.0	1.0
Commodity or service	**Average weekly household expenditure (£)**					
1 **Housing (Net)**	25.10	47.10	61.80	78.20	111.40	52.80
Percentage standard error	5	2	2	3	5	2
2 **Fuel and power**	7.20	7.50	8.30	9.00	9.90	8.00
"	3	2	2	3	4	1
3 **Food and non-alcoholic drinks**	22.00	28.40	35.30	45.30	54.70	32.30
"	2	2	2	3	4	1
4 **Alcoholic drink**	6.70	9.80	15.20	15.50	23.00	11.90
"	6	6	4	6	8	3
5 **Tobacco**	5.00	5.80	5.00	3.70	2.10	4.80
"	5	7	7	12	25	3
6 **Clothing and footwear**	4.70	10.00	11.50	19.30	25.70	11.10
"	8	7	6	8	17	4
7 **Household goods**	9.70	16.40	18.90	26.80	50.10	18.70
"	9	8	7	9	17	4
8 **Household services**	7.60	11.50	14.90	19.60	27.50	13.40
"	6	5	4	5	11	0
9 **Personal goods and services**	2.90	6.10	8.20	14.50	20.20	7.70
"	7	7	8	15	42	8
10 **Motoring**	11.00	23.90	42.80	61.50	108.10	35.50
"	8	6	5	8	16	4
11 **Fares and other travel costs**	3.70	5.30	7.80	10.10	23.20	7.30
"	11	8	14	12	20	6
12 **Leisure goods**	4.80	9.00	15.10	16.60	21.20	11.20
"	7	6	8	9	16	4
13 **Leisure services**	12.90	19.00	29.80	45.60	121.60	30.40
"	9	6	8	6	12	4
14 **Miscellaneous**	0.30	0.50	1.60	1.80	0.80	0.90
"	24	23	26	26	28	14
1-14 **All expenditure groups**	123.40	200.30	276.20	367.30	599.30	246.00
Percentage standard error	2	2	2	2	5	1
Average weekly expenditure per person (£)						
All expenditure groups	123.40	200.30	276.20	367.30	599.30	246.00

1 Boundaries divide the complete set of UK households into 5 equal groups.

ONS, Family Spending 2000-01, © Crown copyright 2002

4.5 Expenditure of one adult households with children by gross income quintile group

1998-99 - 2000-01

based on weighted data and including children's expenditure

	Lowest twenty per cent	Second quintile group	Third quintile group	Fourth quintile group	Highest twenty per cent	All house- holds
Lower boundary of group (£ per week)[1]		163	310	489	739	
Average number of grossed households (thousands)	740	370	220	100	30	1,460
Total number of households in sample (over 3 years)	767	385	200	92	30	1,474
Total number of persons in sample (over 3 years)	2,078	1,218	536	257	77	4,166
Total number of adults in sample (over 3 years)	767	385	200	92	30	1,474
Weighted average number of persons per household	2.7	3.1	2.7	2.8	2.5	2.8

Commodity or service	Average weekly household expenditure (£)					
1 Housing (Net)	15.30	36.30	61.20	84.60	..	34.50
Percentage standard error	6	5	4	7	..	3
2 Fuel and power	10.80	11.80	11.60	13.30	..	11.50
"	2	3	4	5	..	2
3 Food and non-alcoholic drinks	38.10	52.50	60.70	64.60	..	47.90
"	2	3	3	5	..	1
4 Alcoholic drink	3.20	4.50	9.40	10.00	..	5.10
"	7	10	10	13	..	5
5 Tobacco	6.40	6.90	5.80	5.50	..	6.30
"	5	7	14	18	..	4
6 Clothing and footwear	12.10	24.10	22.90	33.00	..	18.80
"	5	7	9	13	..	4
7 Household goods	15.30	21.80	22.90	30.00	..	20.00
"	7	6	11	13	..	4
8 Household services	9.10	14.70	24.20	50.20	..	16.50
"	4	7	8	12	..	4
9 Personal goods and services	6.10	8.80	12.80	14.80	..	8.80
"	5	7	9	14	..	4
10 Motoring	7.80	17.90	40.10	50.90	..	20.50
"	8	8	9	14	..	6
11 Fares and other travel costs	3.70	5.50	6.90	7.20	..	5.30
"	7	8	12	18	..	5
12 Leisure goods	8.10	13.20	20.20	25.40	..	13.40
"	7	8	12	22	..	6
13 Leisure services	10.30	20.00	37.50	54.70	..	22.90
"	7	7	12	13	..	6
14 Miscellaneous	0.50	0.80	1.20	2.10	..	0.80
"	15	19	26	37	..	11
1-14 All expenditure groups	146.70	238.90	337.10	446.40	..	232.10
Percentage standard error	2	2	3	5	..	2

Average weekly expenditure per person (£)

	Lowest twenty per cent	Second quintile group	Third quintile group	Fourth quintile group	Highest twenty per cent	All house- holds
All expenditure groups	55.00	77.40	127.20	161.50	..	83.70

1 Boundaries divide the complete set of UK households into 5 equal groups.

4.6 Expenditure of two adult households with children by gross income quintile group
1998-99 - 2000-01
based on weighted data and including children's expenditure

	Lowest twenty per cent	Second quintile group	Third quintile group	Fourth quintile group	Highest twenty per cent	All house-holds
Lower boundary of group (£ per week)[1]		163	310	489	739	
Average number of grossed households (thousands)	210	590	1,140	1,530	1,530	4,990
Total number of households in sample (over 3 years)	199	567	1,047	1,373	1,336	4,522
Total number of persons in sample (over 3 years)	756	2,352	4,181	5,407	5,205	17,901
Total number of adults in sample (over 3 years)	398	1,134	2,094	2,746	2,672	9,044
Weighted average number of persons per household	3.7	4.1	3.9	3.9	3.8	3.9

Commodity or service	Average weekly household expenditure (£)					
1 **Housing (Net)**	26.00	41.30	65.20	84.10	128.10	85.80
Percentage standard error	*9*	*4*	*2*	*2*	*2*	*1*
2 **Fuel and power**	12.70	14.10	12.60	13.30	16.10	14.10
"	*5*	*6*	*2*	*1*	*1*	*1*
3 **Food and non-alcoholic drinks**	57.20	63.70	75.00	85.10	104.60	85.10
"	*4*	*2*	*1*	*1*	*1*	*1*
4 **Alcoholic drink**	6.30	7.70	11.80	15.60	19.40	14.60
"	*10*	*8*	*4*	*3*	*3*	*2*
5 **Tobacco**	8.60	11.20	8.70	6.40	4.20	6.90
"	*9*	*5*	*5*	*5*	*7*	*3*
6 **Clothing and footwear**	16.30	18.00	25.30	31.50	44.20	31.80
"	*12*	*6*	*4*	*3*	*3*	*2*
7 **Household goods**	18.20	23.00	27.60	38.90	62.90	41.00
"	*10*	*9*	*4*	*4*	*4*	*3*
8 **Household services**	11.50	13.30	18.90	25.80	47.20	28.70
"	*8*	*4*	*3*	*3*	*4*	*3*
9 **Personal goods and services**	8.90	8.50	14.20	17.00	26.80	18.00
"	*9*	*5*	*4*	*3*	*3*	*2*
10 **Motoring**	27.50	37.20	54.20	74.20	103.20	72.30
"	*11*	*7*	*3*	*3*	*3*	*2*
11 **Fares and other travel costs**	4.40	5.30	7.80	8.50	16.90	10.40
"	*13*	*8*	*19*	*6*	*6*	*5*
12 **Leisure goods**	12.10	14.30	20.50	29.40	38.40	27.70
"	*12*	*7*	*5*	*5*	*4*	*3*
13 **Leisure services**	17.40	20.70	32.50	53.40	104.60	59.00
"	*17*	*7*	*5*	*4*	*4*	*2*
14 **Miscellaneous**	0.50	1.00	1.10	1.80	2.70	1.80
"	*22*	*14*	*10*	*8*	*10*	*6*
1-14 **All expenditure groups**	227.60	279.20	375.50	485.00	719.30	497.00
Percentage standard error	*5*	*2*	*1*	*1*	*1*	*1*
Average weekly expenditure per person (£)						
All expenditure groups	60.70	68.50	95.70	124.40	187.10	127.30

1 Boundaries divide the complete set of UK households into 5 equal groups.

ONS, Family Spending 2000-01, © Crown copyright 2002

4.7 Expenditure of one man one woman non-retired households by gross income quintile group
1998-99 - 2000-01
based on weighted data and including children's expenditure

	Lowest twenty per cent	Second quintile group	Third quintile group	Fourth quintile group	Highest twenty per cent	All house-holds
Lower boundary of group (£ per week)[1]		163	310	489	739	
Average number of grossed households (thousands)	280	620	1,110	1,460	1,470	4,950
Total number of households in sample (over 3 years)	237	520	909	1,127	1,072	3,865
Total number of persons in sample (over 3 years)	474	1,040	1,818	2,254	2,144	7,730
Total number of adults in sample (over 3 years)	474	1,040	1,818	2,254	2,144	7,730
Weighted average number of persons per household	2.0	2.0	2.0	2.0	2.0	2.0

Commodity or service	Average weekly household expenditure (£)					
1 Housing (Net)	**31.20**	**41.00**	**54.00**	**75.10**	**110.90**	**74.20**
Percentage standard error	*9*	*4*	*2*	*2*	*2*	*1*
2 Fuel and power	**10.60**	**12.00**	**11.40**	**11.60**	**13.30**	**12.10**
"	*4*	*3*	*2*	*2*	*2*	*1*
3 Food and non-alcoholic drinks	**42.40**	**50.80**	**56.80**	**64.80**	**81.50**	**64.90**
"	*4*	*2*	*1*	*1*	*1*	*1*
4 Alcoholic drink	**10.10**	**11.50**	**14.90**	**19.80**	**26.30**	**19.00**
"	*13*	*6*	*4*	*3*	*4*	*2*
5 Tobacco	**6.90**	**7.40**	**7.00**	**6.50**	**4.10**	**6.00**
"	*11*	*8*	*6*	*6*	*8*	*3*
6 Clothing and footwear	**10.30**	**12.80**	**18.60**	**23.70**	**37.40**	**24.50**
"	*12*	*9*	*6*	*4*	*5*	*3*
7 Household goods	**22.80**	**26.20**	**32.30**	**39.90**	**60.40**	**41.60**
"	*17*	*8*	*5*	*5*	*5*	*3*
8 Household services	**12.80**	**13.90**	**15.90**	**22.40**	**34.50**	**23.00**
"	*17*	*8*	*5*	*7*	*6*	*4*
9 Personal goods and services	**10.70**	**9.10**	**13.40**	**18.20**	**25.40**	**17.70**
"	*28*	*7*	*6*	*5*	*4*	*3*
10 Motoring	**33.60**	**38.00**	**60.50**	**72.00**	**104.20**	**72.60**
"	*15*	*8*	*5*	*3*	*4*	*2*
11 Fares and other travel costs	**7.80**	**5.30**	**6.10**	**9.70**	**18.60**	**10.80**
"	*35*	*16*	*11*	*16*	*9*	*6*
12 Leisure goods	**10.00**	**11.40**	**17.60**	**21.00**	**29.50**	**20.90**
"	*21*	*7*	*7*	*6*	*7*	*4*
13 Leisure services	**29.30**	**28.10**	**37.40**	**52.50**	**97.70**	**58.10**
"	*17*	*9*	*5*	*4*	*5*	*3*
14 Miscellaneous	**0.20**	**0.80**	**1.10**	**1.10**	**1.80**	**1.20**
"	*39*	*27*	*14*	*11*	*11*	*7*
1-14 All expenditure groups	**238.70**	**268.20**	**346.90**	**438.30**	**645.70**	**446.70**
Percentage standard error	*8*	*2*	*2*	*1*	*2*	*1*

Average weekly expenditure per person (£)

All expenditure groups	**119.40**	**134.10**	**173.40**	**219.20**	**322.90**	**223.30**

1 Boundaries divide the complete set of UK households into 5 equal groups.

4.8 Expenditure of one man one woman retired households mainly dependent on state pensions[1] by gross income quintile group

1998-99 - 2000-01

based on weighted data and including children's expenditure

	Lowest twenty per cent	Second quintile group	Third quintile group	Fourth quintile group	Highest twenty per cent	All house-holds
Lower boundary of group (£ per week)[2]		163	310	489	739	
Average number of grossed households (thousands)	290	360	10	0	0	670
Total number of households in sample (over 3 years)	261	320	13	1	0	595
Total number of persons in sample (over 3 years)	522	640	26	2	0	1,190
Total number of adults in sample (over 3 years)	522	640	26	2	0	1,190
Weighted average number of persons per household	2.0	2.0	2.0	2.0	0	2.0

Commodity or service	Average weekly household expenditure (£)					
1 Housing (Net)	22.60	30.40	..	..	..	27.10
Percentage standard error	5	6	..	..	..	4
2 Fuel and power	10.00	11.10	..	..	..	10.50
"	4	4	..	..	..	3
3 Food and non-alcoholic drinks	37.60	41.40	..	..	..	39.80
"	3	2	..	..	..	2
4 Alcoholic drink	4.10	6.60	..	..	..	5.50
"	11	10	..	..	..	7
5 Tobacco	3.30	3.50	..	..	..	3.40
"	14	12	..	..	..	9
6 Clothing and footwear	5.80	7.90	..	..	..	7.00
"	12	9	..	..	..	7
7 Household goods	12.40	21.30	..	..	..	17.50
"	10	10	..	..	..	8
8 Household services	8.00	8.10	..	..	..	8.30
"	13	6	..	..	..	8
9 Personal goods and services	5.80	8.50	..	..	..	7.40
"	10	10	..	..	..	7
10 Motoring	13.80	21.30	..	..	..	17.50
"	9	11	..	..	..	7
11 Fares and other travel costs	2.10	2.60	..	..	..	2.40
"	23	13	..	..	..	11
12 Leisure goods	5.40	9.00	..	..	..	7.20
"	9	10	..	..	..	7
13 Leisure services	13.20	19.70	..	..	..	17.10
"	11	10	..	..	..	8
14 Miscellaneous	0.20	0.20	..	..	..	0.20
"	37	42	..	..	..	30
1-14 All expenditure groups	144.30	191.70	..	..	..	170.90
Percentage standard error	3	3	..	..	..	2

Average weekly expenditure per person (£)						
All expenditure groups	72.10	95.80	..	..	..	85.40

1 Mainly dependent on state pension and not economically active - see appendix D.

2 Boundaries divide the complete set of UK households into 5 equal groups.

ONS, Family Spending 2000-01, © Crown copyright 2002

4.9 Expenditure of one man one woman retired households not mainly dependent on state pensions by gross income quintile group

1998-99 - 2000-01

based on weighted data and including children's expenditure

	Lowest twenty per cent	Second quintile group	Third quintile group	Fourth quintile group	Highest twenty per cent	All house-holds
Lower boundary of group (£ per week)[1]		163	310	489	739	
Average number of grossed households (thousands)	30	740	590	260	130	1,740
Total number of households in sample (over 3 years)	23	656	510	231	105	1,525
Total number of persons in sample (over 3 years)	46	1,312	1,020	462	210	3,050
Total number of adults in sample (over 3 years)	46	1,312	1,020	462	210	3,050
Weighted average number of persons per household	2.0	2.0	2.0	2.0	2.0	2.0

Commodity or service	Average weekly household expenditure (£)					
1 **Housing (Net)**	..	34.10	35.60	44.50	56.40	37.70
Percentage standard error	..	3	3	4	10	2
2 **Fuel and power**	..	11.00	11.90	14.40	16.90	12.20
"	..	2	3	3	4	1
3 **Food and non-alcoholic drinks**	..	46.80	55.80	64.10	79.40	54.70
"	..	2	2	3	5	1
4 **Alcoholic drink**	..	7.70	10.50	12.50	17.40	10.20
"	..	6	6	8	10	4
5 **Tobacco**	..	3.20	2.50	2.40	1.80	2.80
"	..	10	16	20	30	7
6 **Clothing and footwear**	..	9.30	14.70	18.70	19.40	13.20
"	..	6	8	11	17	5
7 **Household goods**	..	20.50	30.30	40.50	77.20	30.60
"	..	9	8	11	31	7
8 **Household services**	..	9.80	14.00	20.10	55.90	15.90
"	..	7	6	7	24	6
9 **Personal goods and services**	..	9.60	15.20	16.80	27.40	13.90
"	..	6	6	11	16	4
10 **Motoring**	..	27.00	44.10	62.30	78.90	41.90
"	..	6	9	11	14	5
11 **Fares and other travel costs**	..	3.10	5.90	4.10	10.10	4.70
"	..	16	27	21	34	13
12 **Leisure goods**	..	9.60	18.50	20.80	34.70	16.10
"	..	7	15	12	25	7
13 **Leisure services**	..	30.80	46.30	74.80	107.60	48.20
"	..	6	6	9	16	4
14 **Miscellaneous**	..	0.30	0.40	..	0.40	..
"	..	38	22	..	31	..
1-14 **All expenditure groups**	..	222.80	305.60	399.50	583.60	302.70
Percentage standard error	..	2	3	3	8	2
Average weekly expenditure per person (£)						
All expenditure groups	..	111.40	152.80	199.70	291.80	151.30

1 Boundaries divide the complete set of UK households into 5 equal groups.

4.10 Household expenditure by tenure

based on weighted data and including children's expenditure

2000-01

	Owners			Social rented from		
	Owned outright	Buying with a mortgage [1]	All	Council [2]	Registered Social Landlord [3]	All
Grossed number of households (thousands)	6,870	10,210	17,080	3,870	1,470	5,340
Total number of households in sample	1,873	2,665	4,538	1,075	395	1,470
Total number of persons in sample	3,605	7,598	11,203	2,401	915	3,316
Total number of adults in sample	3,313	5,233	8,546	1,649	585	2,234
Weighted average number of persons per household	1.9	2.8	2.4	2.2	2.2	2.2

Commodity or service	Average weekly household expenditure (£)					
1 Housing (Net)	**32.30**	**96.30**	**70.60**	**32.70**	**42.70**	**35.50**
Percentage standard error	*3*	*1*	*1*	*3*	*4*	*2*
2 Fuel and power	**12.80**	**13.00**	**12.90**	**9.40**	**10.00**	**9.60**
"	*2*	*1*	*1*	*2*	*12*	*4*
3 Food and non-alcoholic drinks	**56.30**	**76.20**	**68.20**	**44.40**	**44.10**	**44.30**
"	*2*	*1*	*1*	*2*	*4*	*2*
4 Alcoholic drink	**12.30**	**19.70**	**16.70**	**8.80**	**7.10**	**8.40**
"	*5*	*2*	*2*	*6*	*9*	*5*
5 Tobacco	**3.40**	**6.10**	**5.00**	**8.90**	**8.10**	**8.70**
"	*7*	*4*	*3*	*5*	*8*	*4*
6 Clothing and footwear	**17.00**	**29.40**	**24.40**	**13.40**	**15.40**	**14.00**
"	*4*	*3*	*2*	*6*	*11*	*5*
7 Household goods	**32.80**	**43.00**	**38.90**	**18.90**	**16.50**	**18.20**
"	*6*	*3*	*3*	*6*	*0*	*5*
8 Household services	**21.00**	**29.60**	**26.20**	**10.20**	**12.80**	**10.90**
"	*6*	*3*	*3*	*4*	*8*	*4*
9 Personal goods and services	**14.40**	**19.30**	**17.30**	**6.40**	**8.90**	**7.10**
"	*4*	*3*	*2*	*5*	*9*	*4*
10 Motoring	**50.20**	**79.90**	**68.00**	**18.20**	**23.60**	**19.70**
"	*4*	*2*	*2*	*6*	*11*	*5*
11 Fares and other travel costs	**6.00**	**12.10**	**9.70**	**6.30**	**7.70**	**6.70**
"	*10*	*7*	*6*	*9*	*28*	*11*
12 Leisure goods	**16.20**	**26.90**	**22.60**	**10.70**	**12.00**	**11.00**
"	*4*	*4*	*3*	*7*	*8*	*5*
13 Leisure services	**51.40**	**68.50**	**61.60**	**18.10**	**21.20**	**18.90**
"	*4*	*3*	*3*	*5*	*10*	*5*
14 Miscellaneous	**0.30**	**1.20**	**0.80**	**0.40**	**0.70**	**0.50**
"	*16*	*8*	*7*	*15*	*25*	*13*
1-14 All above expenditure	**326.20**	**521.20**	**442.70**	**206.80**	**230.80**	**213.40**
Percentage standard error	*2*	*1*	*1*	*2*	*4*	*2*
Average weekly expenditure per person (£)						
All expenditure groups	**169.30**	**188.40**	**182.30**	**95.00**	**104.10**	**97.50**

1 Including shared owners (who own part of the equity and pay mortgage, part rent).

2 "Council" includes local authorities, New Towns and Scottish Homes, but see note 3 below.

3 Formerly Housing Associations

ONS, Family Spending 2000-01, © Crown copyright 2002

4.10 Household expenditure by tenure (cont.)
based on weighted data and including children's expenditure

2000-01

	Private rented [4]				All tenures
	Rent free	Rent paid, unfurn- ished [5]	Rent paid, furnished	All	
Grossed number of households (thousands)	380	1,580	650	2,600	25,030
Total number of households in sample	100	389	140	629	6,637
Total number of persons in sample	211	894	301	1,406	15,925
Total number of adults in sample	164	640	268	1,072	11,852
Weighted average number of persons per household	2.0	2.2	2.3	2.2	2.4

Commodity or service	Average weekly household expenditure (£)				
1 Housing (Net)	**14.30**	**78.80**	**115.80**	**78.60**	**63.90**
Percentage standard error	*13*	*4*	*8*	*4*	*1*
2 Fuel and power	**12.00**	**10.30**	**7.80**	**9.90**	**11.90**
"	*7*	*4*	*7*	*3*	*1*
3 Food and non-alcoholic drinks	**57.70**	**52.60**	**67.10**	**56.90**	**61.90**
"	*8*	*3*	*7*	*3*	*1*
4 Alcoholic drink	**10.20**	**15.00**	**28.50**	**17.70**	**15.00**
"	*23*	*7*	*11*	*6*	*2*
5 Tobacco	**4.60**	**8.20**	**8.40**	**7.70**	**6.10**
"	*22*	*8*	*17*	*7*	*3*
6 Clothing and footwear	**22.90**	**17.70**	**34.00**	**22.50**	**22.00**
"	*22*	*8*	*15*	*7*	*2*
7 Household goods	**23.00**	**22.50**	**17.60**	**21.40**	**32.60**
"	*15*	*10*	*19*	*8*	*3*
8 Household services	**19.60**	**15.80**	**18.50**	**17.00**	**22.00**
"	*17*	*6*	*8*	*5*	*2*
9 Personal goods and services	**10.50**	**12.40**	**16.20**	**13.00**	**14.70**
"	*12*	*12*	*13*	*8*	*2*
10 Motoring	**36.00**	**49.50**	**32.40**	**43.30**	**55.10**
"	*15*	*8*	*16*	*6*	*2*
11 Fares and other travel costs	**9.60**	**11.70**	**21.70**	**13.90**	**9.50**
"	*42*	*19*	*13*	*12*	*5*
12 Leisure goods	**16.10**	**15.70**	**29.30**	**19.20**	**19.70**
"	*15*	*11*	*23*	*10*	*3*
13 Leisure services	**38.70**	**31.40**	**75.40**	**43.40**	**50.60**
"	*19*	*10*	*20*	*9*	*2*
14 Miscellaneous	**[0.50]**	**0.60**	**0.60**	**0.60**	**0.70**
"	*48*	*21*	*27*	*16*	*6*
1-14 All above expenditure	**275.70**	**342.30**	**473.20**	**365.20**	**385.70**
Percentage standard error	*8*	*4*	*7*	*3*	*1*
Average weekly expenditure per person (£)					
All expenditure groups	**135.40**	**154.60**	**207.60**	**165.70**	**163.90**

4 All tenants whose accommodation goes with the job of someone in the household are allocated to "rented privately", even if the landlord is a local authority or housing association or Housing Action Trust, or if the accommodation is rent free. Squatters are also included in this category.

5 "Unfurnished" includes the answers: "partly furnished".

Statistical Regions of the United Kingdom

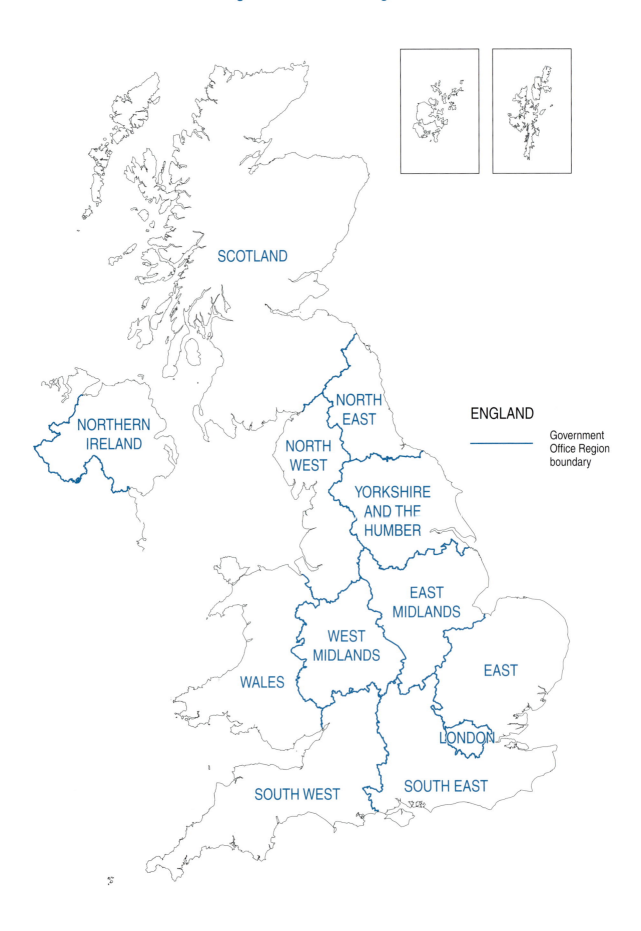

SCOTLAND

NORTHERN
IRELAND

NORTH
EAST

NORTH
WEST

YORKSHIRE
AND THE
HUMBER

ENGLAND

Government
Office Region
boundary

EAST
MIDLANDS

WEST
MIDLANDS

WALES

EAST

LONDON

SOUTH WEST

SOUTH EAST

ONS, Family Spending 2000-01, © Crown copyright 2002

Chapter 5

Expenditure by region

- Averaged over the last three years, **total expenditure** varied from £440 a week in London to £300 in the North East. Average expenditure was above the UK average in the South East and the East of England as well as in London. Expenditure was below the UK average by 10 per cent or more in Northern Ireland, Wales and the North East.

- In London a high share of average spending went on **housing**, 19 per cent compared with the UK proportion of 16 per cent, but a low share went on **motoring**, 11 per cent compared with 15 per cent.

- In Northern Ireland **housing** accounted for only 10 per cent of expenditure, but spending on **food and non-alcoholic drink** was 20 per cent of expenditure, compared with the UK average of 16 per cent.

Urban and rural areas
Classification based on the population of the continuous built-up areas, irrespective of administrative boundaries.

- Averaged over the last two years, **total expenditure** was highest in the London built-up area at £460 a week. It was lowest in other metropolitan built-up areas at £320 a week and increased as the size of settlement became smaller, so that it was highest, apart from London, in rural areas at £420 a week.

- **Motoring** expenditure was much the highest in rural areas, averaging £74 a week. It was also relatively high in small urban areas with populations under 10,000, where it was £58 a week. Spending on **motoring** in the London built-up area was higher than in the other urban areas, £55 a week compared with the lowest, £44 a week in other metropolitan built-up areas.

- Expenditure on **fares and other travel costs** was high in the London built-up area, nearly £18 a week. Elsewhere it varied between about £7 and £9 a week.

- Rural areas had the highest average spending on **fuel and power**, £13.70 a week compared with the next highest of £11.90 in small towns, on **household goods**, £42 a week compared with the next highest of £35 a week in the London built-up area, and on **leisure goods**, £21.90 with London again the next highest at £20.40.

- Spending on **tobacco** was lowest in rural areas along with medium-sized towns (10,000 to 25,000 population) at £5.00 a week. It was highest in other metropolitan built-up areas, where it averaged £7.10 a week.

5   Expenditure by region

5.1   Total expenditure in relation to the UK average

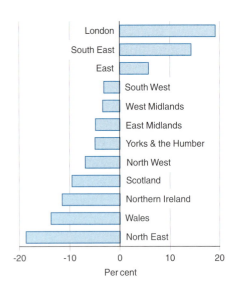

Per cent

This chapter illustrates the household expenditure patterns between the countries and regions of the United Kingdom and between types of area.

The regional breakdowns are based on Government Office Regions (GORs) in England, and Wales, Scotland and Northern Ireland. A map can be found on page 80. This year a new table shows a breakdown between urban and rural areas.

As in last year's edition of Family Spending, the tables and analyses in this chapter are based mostly on data from the last three years, now 1998-99–2000-2001. This increases sample size and reliability.

Overview of national and regional differences

Both the level and the composition of expenditure vary across the countries and regions of the UK.

Table 5.1 shows the average weekly expenditure of households by UK countries and Government Office Regions. **Figure 5.1** compares the total average weekly expenditure in each region with that for the UK. Over the last three years the UK average was £370. It can be seen that the South East, London and the East of England all had a weekly expenditure greater than the UK average. Households in London spent an average of £440 a week, which is almost 20 per cent higher than the UK average. Northern Ireland, Wales and the North East had an average expenditure that was over 10 per cent below the UK average. The North East had the lowest average weekly expenditure of £300.

5.2   Expenditure on uncooked meat in relation to the UK average

Per cent

Table 5.2 shows household expenditure on the main commodity headings as a percentage of total expenditure. It can be seen that patterns of expenditure were very similar across the regions for the majority of commodity headings. Exceptions included the proportion spent on housing in London at 19 per cent compared to the UK average of 16 per cent. In contrast, London spent a small percentage on motoring, at 11 per cent, compared to the national average of 15 per cent. Northern Ireland also showed some differences in percentage of total expenditure compared with other regions. Net housing was only 10 per cent of total expenditure compared with 16 per cent in the UK as a whole. The share of spending on food and non-alcoholic drink was more in Northern Ireland than the in the UK by 4 percentage points, that is 20 per cent compared with 16 per cent.

82   ONS, Family Spending 2000-01, © Crown copyright 2002

Detailed expenditure patterns

Table 5.3 shows detailed household expenditure on the full range of commodities and services by UK countries and GORs.

Meat

Figure 5.2 illustrates expenditure on uncooked meat by region in relation to the UK average amount spent. Northern Ireland had much the largest expenditure. At an amount of £7.70, Northern Ireland spent 40 per cent more than the national average. **Table 5.3** also shows that Northern Ireland spent an especially large amount on beef and veal at £2.90 a week, substantially more than the figure for Scotland, the next highest spender at £1.80. Apart from Northern Ireland, only the West Midlands, the East and the South East spent more than the national average on uncooked meat. Households in the North East had the lowest expenditure on uncooked meat at £4.90 a week which is 10 per cent less than the UK average.

Restaurant and Café meals

Figure 5.3 shows the percentage difference in spending on restaurant and café meals in relation to the UK average. London households were much the greatest spenders in this category. Expenditure on restaurant and café meals was £14.50 a week which was almost 50 per cent above the national average of £9.90 a week. Apart from London, the South East and the East, all other regions were below the UK average for expenditure. Wales and the North East spent the least on restaurants at £7.30 a week, about 25 per cent less than the national average. Households in London spent £7.20 a week more than households in Wales and the North East.

Medical, dental, optical and nursing fees

Figure 5.4 shows a comparison between regions for expenditure on medical, dental, optical and nursing fees. The South East and London both spent over £2 a week. South Eastern households spent £2.50 a week which is two thirds as much again as the UK average of £1.50. Wales, Scotland, Northern Ireland and the North East all paid £1 or less. The North East paid just 60p. This is less than half of the national average.

Payments for NHS services accounted for 56 per cent of UK expenditure on medical, dental, optical and nursing fees in 2000-01. The rest was due to private fees. This is illustrated in Chapter 7, **Table 7.1**.

5.3 **Expenditure on restaurant and café meals in relation to the UK average**

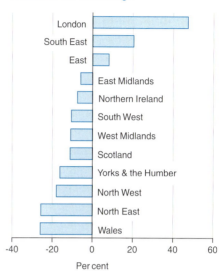

5.4 **Expenditure on medical, dental, optical and nursing fees**

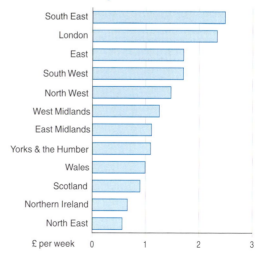

5.5 **Expenditure on domestic help and child-care in relation to the UK average**

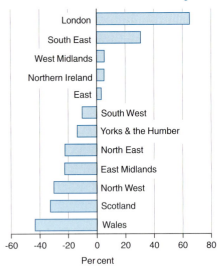

Domestic help and childcare

Figure 5.5 shows some large differences between average regional and average UK expenditure on domestic help and child-care. London spent £4.70 which is 60 per cent higher than the UK average of £2.90. The South East spent £3.70 which was 30 per cent greater than UK average. Other than those places already mentioned along with the West Midlands, Northern Ireland and the East, expenditure was below the national average for all other regions.

Chapter 7, **Table 7.1** shows that just under half of expenditure on domestic help and child-care in 2000-01 was on domestic help only. The rest was split between payments for child-care, and for nursery, creche and playschools.

Type of area

For several years Family Spending has included a table showing how spending varies between types of administrative area, **Table 5.4** in this report. A limitation is that the classification is based on local authority districts, which are fairly large and may include both urban and rural areas. A more refined classification of settlement size has been derived by the Department for Transport, Local Government and the Regions (DTLR) based on the 1991 Census. **Table 5.5** shows expenditure by this classification. Data from the two years 1999-2000 and 2000-01 have been combined to reduce sampling variability. Note that the metropolitan built-up areas are not the same as the metropolitan administrative districts. They exclude any rural areas within the metropolitan districts and include any built up areas adjoining them.

Figure 5.6 is a summary of how total spending varied by type of area. Total expenditure was highest in the London built-up area at £457 a week. It was lowest in other metropolitan built-up areas, at £320 a week, and generally increased as the size of settlement grew smaller so that average spending was highest, after London, in rural areas, at £415 a week.

Spending on many items, such as housing and food, followed the same pattern as total spending. Two items where this was not so were motoring and fares, shown in **Figure 5.7**. Motoring expenditure was much the highest in rural areas, averaging £74 a week. It was also relatively high in small urban areas with

5.6 **Expenditure by urban and rural areas**

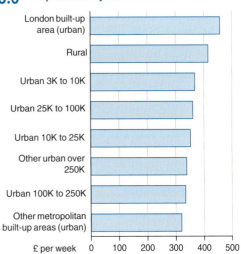

ONS, Family Spending 2000-01, © Crown copyright 2002

populations of under 10,000, where it was £58 a week. Spending on motoring in the London built-up area was higher than in other urban areas, £55 a week compared with the lowest, £44 a week in other metropolitan built-up areas. Expenditure on fares and other travel costs was high in the London built-up area, nearly £18 a week. Elsewhere it varied between about £7 and £9 a week without any clear pattern.

There were a number of items as well as motoring where spending was highest in rural areas. They were: fuel and power, with average expenditure of £13.70 a week compared with the next highest, £11.90 in small urban areas; household goods, £42 a week compared with the next highest of £35 a week in the London built-up areas; and leisure goods, £21.90 with London again the next highest at £20.40. Spending on tobacco, however, was lowest in rural areas along with medium-sized towns (10,000 to 25,000 population), both £5.00 a week and was also low in London, £5.50 a week. It was highest in other metropolitan built-up areas, where it averaged £7.10 a week.

5.7 **Expenditure on motoring and fares and other travel costs by urban and rural areas**

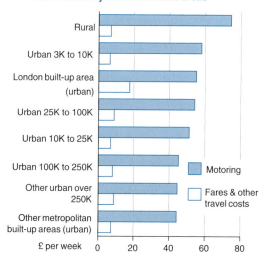

5.1 Household expenditure by UK Countries and Government Office Regions

1998-99 - 2000-01

based on weighted data and including children's expenditure

	North East	North West	Yorks and the Humber	East Midlands	West Midlands	East	London
Average number of grossed households (thousands)	1,160	2,840	2,100	1,760	2,160	2,290	3,060
Total number of households in sample (over 3 years)	886	2,181	1,657	1,356	1,658	1,799	1,980
Total number of persons in sample (over 3 years)	2,044	5,219	4,033	3,236	4,138	4,372	4,568
Total number of adults in sample (over 3 years)	1,510	3,830	2,976	2,439	3,052	3,282	3,342
Weighted average number of persons per household	2.3	2.4	2.4	2.4	2.4	2.3	2.3

Commodity or service	Average weekly household expenditure (£)						
1 Housing (Net)	**46.60**	**51.50**	**53.60**	**53.50**	**54.80**	**63.50**	**83.00**
Percentage standard error	3	2	2	2	2	2	2
2 Fuel and power	**11.30**	**11.90**	**11.50**	**11.60**	**12.00**	**11.00**	**10.90**
"	2	1	2	2	2	1	3
3 Food and non-alcoholic drinks	**52.20**	**56.20**	**56.30**	**58.90**	**58.70**	**62.50**	**68.50**
"	2	1	2	2	2	1	2
4 Alcoholic drink	**16.50**	**15.50**	**15.60**	**14.40**	**14.70**	**13.00**	**16.40**
"	7	3	3	4	3	4	4
5 Tobacco	**6.10**	**6.90**	**6.60**	**6.10**	**5.90**	**4.50**	**5.40**
"	6	4	5	6	5	5	5
6 Clothing and footwear	**20.20**	**22.20**	**21.10**	**18.70**	**20.40**	**20.60**	**26.00**
"	6	4	5	4	4	4	4
7 Household goods	**26.40**	**28.10**	**29.50**	**31.20**	**31.00**	**35.00**	**31.60**
"	7	4	5	5	4	4	5
8 Household services	**15.20**	**16.20**	**17.50**	**16.80**	**18.00**	**21.10**	**27.00**
"	8	4	4	3	4	4	5
9 Personal goods and services	**9.90**	**12.50**	**13.40**	**12.80**	**12.70**	**15.90**	**16.60**
"	5	4	5	4	4	4	4
10 Motoring	**36.80**	**51.40**	**52.80**	**54.50**	**56.10**	**63.80**	**48.40**
"	5	4	4	4	4	4	4
11 Fares and other travel costs	**6.60**	**6.50**	**8.10**	**6.80**	**6.60**	**10.20**	**17.60**
"	8	6	14	10	10	9	5
12 Leisure goods	**14.40**	**16.80**	**18.60**	**18.30**	**19.20**	**20.20**	**20.10**
"	7	5	6	7	6	4	5
13 Leisure services	**34.10**	**43.80**	**41.90**	**43.30**	**42.00**	**44.50**	**62.40**
"	6	4	4	5	4	4	5
14 Miscellaneous	**1.00**	**0.90**	**0.90**	**1.00**	**1.20**	**1.10**	**1.80**
"	15	10	16	14	18	11	16
1-14 All expenditure groups	**297.20**	**340.40**	**347.50**	**347.90**	**353.20**	**386.60**	**435.70**
Percentage standard error	3	2	2	2	2	2	2
Average weekly expenditure per person (£)							
All expenditure groups	**129.50**	**144.70**	**146.20**	**147.80**	**144.40**	**165.50**	**186.80**

ONS, Family Spending 2000-01, © Crown copyright 2002

5.1 Household expenditure
by UK Countries and Government Office Regions (cont.)
based on weighted data and including children's expenditure

1998-99 - 2000-01

	South East	South West	England	Wales	Scotland	Northern Ireland	United Kingdom
Average number of grossed households (thousands)	3,480	2,090	20,940	1,220	2,200	640	25,010
Total number of households in sample (over 3 years)	2,613	1,770	15,900	976	1,779	1,709	20,364
Total number of persons in sample (over 3 years)	6,244	4,237	38,091	2,358	4,050	4,430	48,929
Total number of adults in sample (over 3 years)	4,666	3,196	28,293	1,718	3,052	3,107	36,170
Weighted average number of persons per household	2.3	2.3	2.3	2.4	2.3	2.6	2.3

Commodity or service	Average weekly household expenditure (£)						
1 Housing (Net)	73.30	57.60	62.10	45.30	49.60	31.50	59.40
Percentage standard error	2	2	1	3	2	3	1
2 Fuel and power	11.30	11.30	11.40	12.00	12.40	15.70	11.60
"	1	2	1	2	1	2	0
3 Food and non-alcoholic drinks	64.20	57.60	60.40	55.10	59.00	65.60	60.20
"	1	1	1	2	2	2	0
4 Alcoholic drink	14.10	14.20	14.90	13.40	15.10	13.20	14.80
"	3	4	1	5	3	4	1
5 Tobacco	4.80	4.70	5.60	6.40	8.10	9.20	6.00
"	4	5	2	6	4	4	1
6 Clothing and footwear	21.70	17.70	21.40	20.50	22.40	27.10	21.60
"	3	4	1	5	4	4	1
7 Household goods	36.80	29.40	31.60	28.40	27.70	29.40	31.00
"	4	4	2	6	5	4	1
8 Household services	25.20	21.60	20.60	16.10	16.10	17.10	19.90
"	4	6	2	8	4	6	1
9 Personal goods and services	17.10	14.60	14.40	11.60	11.40	12.00	14.00
"	3	6	2	5	4	4	1
10 Motoring	62.00	56.60	54.60	44.30	46.20	44.50	53.10
"	3	4	1	5	4	6	1
11 Fares and other travel costs	10.90	5.90	9.40	5.30	7.90	5.90	9.00
"	7	10	3	10	10	7	3
12 Leisure goods	20.90	20.30	19.10	16.10	17.90	13.80	18.70
"	4	6	2	6	6	5	2
13 Leisure services	54.00	41.60	47.10	39.80	36.10	36.70	45.50
"	4	5	2	7	4	6	1
14 Miscellaneous	1.30	0.90	1.20	1.00	0.80	1.70	1.10
"	9	12	5	14	11	9	4
1-14 All expenditure groups	417.80	354.10	373.80	315.40	330.70	323.50	365.80
Percentage standard error	1	2	1	2	2	2	1

Average weekly expenditure per person (£)

	South East	South West	England	Wales	Scotland	Northern Ireland	United Kingdom
All expenditure groups	183.70	152.60	159.70	132.70	144.80	123.70	156.00

5.2 Household expenditure as a percentage of total expenditure by UK Countries and Government Office Regions

1998-99 - 2000-01

based on weighted data and including children's expenditure

	North East	North West	Yorks and the Humber	East Midlands	West Midlands	East	London
Average number of grossed households (thousands)	1,160	2,840	2,100	1,760	2,160	2,290	3,060
Total number of households in sample (over 3 years)	886	2,181	1,657	1,356	1,658	1,799	1,980
Total number of persons in sample (over 3 years)	2,044	5,219	4,033	3,236	4,138	4,372	4,568
Total number of adults in sample (over 3 years)	1,510	3,830	2,976	2,439	3,052	3,282	3,342
Weighted average number of persons per household	2.3	2.4	2.4	2.4	2.4	2.3	2.3

Commodity or service	Percentage of total expenditure						
1 **Housing (Net)**	16	15	15	15	16	16	19
2 **Fuel and power**	4	4	3	3	3	3	3
3 **Food and non-alcoholic drinks**	18	17	16	17	17	16	16
4 **Alcoholic drink**	6	5	4	4	4	3	4
5 **Tobacco**	2	2	2	2	2	1	1
6 **Clothing and footwear**	7	7	6	5	6	5	6
7 **Household goods**	9	8	8	9	9	9	7
8 **Household services**	5	5	5	5	5	5	6
9 **Personal goods and services**	3	4	4	4	4	4	4
10 **Motoring**	12	15	15	16	16	16	11
11 **Fares and other travel costs**	2	2	2	2	2	3	4
12 **Leisure goods**	5	5	5	5	5	5	5
13 **Leisure services**	11	13	12	12	12	11	14
14 **Miscellaneous**	0	0	0	0	0	0	0
1-14 **All expenditure groups**	100	100	100	100	100	100	100

ONS, Family Spending 2000-01, © Crown copyright 2002

5.2 Household expenditure as a percentage of total expenditure by UK Countries and Government Office Regions (cont.)
1998-99 - 2000-01
based on weighted data and including children's expenditure

	South East	South West	England	Wales	Scotland	Northern Ireland	United Kingdom
Average number of grossed households (thousands)	3,480	2,090	20,940	1,220	2,200	640	25,010
Total number of households in sample (over 3 years)	2,613	1,770	15,900	976	1,779	1,709	20,364
Total number of persons in sample (over 3 years)	6,244	4,237	38,091	2,358	4,050	4,430	48,929
Total number of adults in sample (over 3 years)	4,666	3,196	28,293	1,718	3,052	3,107	36,170
Weighted average number of persons per household	2.3	2.3	2.3	2.4	2.3	2.6	2.3

Commodity or service	Percentage of total expenditure						
1 Housing (Net)	18	16	17	14	15	10	16
2 Fuel and power	3	3	3	4	4	5	3
3 Food and non-alcoholic drinks	15	16	16	17	18	20	16
4 Alcoholic drink	3	4	4	4	5	4	4
5 Tobacco	1	1	2	2	2	3	2
6 Clothing and footwear	5	5	6	7	7	8	6
7 Household goods	9	8	8	9	8	9	8
8 Household services	6	6	6	5	5	5	5
9 Personal goods and services	4	4	4	4	3	4	4
10 Motoring	15	16	15	14	14	14	15
11 Fares and other travel costs	3	2	3	2	2	2	2
12 Leisure goods	5	6	5	5	5	4	5
13 Leisure services	13	12	13	13	11	11	12
14 Miscellaneous	0	0	0	0	0	1	0
1-14 All expenditure groups	100	100	100	100	100	100	100

5.3 Detailed household expenditure by UK Countries and Government Office Regions

1998-99 - 2000-01

based on weighted data and including children's expenditure

	North East	North West	Yorks and the Humber	East Midlands	West Midlands	East	London
Average number of grossed households (thousands)	1,160	2,840	2,100	1,760	2,160	2,290	3,060
Total number of households in sample (over 3 years)	886	2,181	1,657	1,356	1,658	1,799	1,980
Total number of persons in sample (over 3 years)	2,044	5,219	4,033	3,236	4,138	4,372	4,568
Total number of adults in sample (over 3 years)	1,510	3,830	2,976	2,439	3,052	3,282	3,342
Weighted average number of persons per household	2.3	2.4	2.4	2.4	2.4	2.3	2.3

Commodity or service	Average weekly household expenditure (£)						
1 Housing (Net)	**46.60**	**51.50**	**53.60**	**53.50**	**54.80**	**63.50**	**83.00**
Percentage standard error	*3*	*2*	*2*	*2*	*2*	*2*	*2*
1.1 Gross rent, mortgage interest payments, water charges, council tax, etc	53.50	55.20	52.60	52.50	56.00	62.80	88.30
1.2 *less* housing benefit, rebates and allowances received	13.20	11.50	8.00	7.20	9.30	7.80	13.70
1.3 Net rent, mortgage interest payments, water charges, council tax, etc	40.30	43.70	44.60	45.30	46.60	55.00	74.70
1.4 Repairs, maintenance and decorations	6.30	7.80	9.10	8.20	8.10	8.50	8.40
2 Fuel and power	**11.30**	**11.90**	**11.50**	**11.60**	**12.00**	**11.00**	**10.90**
Percentage standard error	*2*	*1*	*2*	*2*	*2*	*1*	*3*
2.1 Gas	5.20	5.60	5.50	5.20	5.10	4.60	5.20
2.2 Electricity	5.40	5.80	5.50	5.60	6.00	5.70	5.60
2.3 Other fuels	0.70	0.50	0.60	0.80	0.90	0.70	0.10
3 Food and non-alcoholic drinks	**52.20**	**56.20**	**56.30**	**58.90**	**58.70**	**62.50**	**68.50**
Percentage standard error	*2*	*1*	*2*	*2*	*2*	*1*	*2*
3.1 Bread, rolls etc	1.70	1.90	1.80	1.80	1.80	1.70	1.70
3.2 Pasta, rice, flour and other cereals	0.30	0.40	0.40	0.40	0.40	0.50	0.80
3.3 Biscuits, cakes etc	2.70	2.70	2.80	2.90	2.90	3.10	2.30
3.4 Breakfast cereals	0.70	0.80	0.90	0.90	0.80	0.90	0.80
3.5 Beef and veal (uncooked)	1.40	1.50	1.40	1.50	1.50	1.50	1.20
3.6 Mutton and lamb (uncooked)	0.40	0.70	0.50	0.60	0.70	0.60	0.90
3.7 Pork (uncooked)	0.60	0.60	0.70	0.70	0.70	0.70	0.50
3.8 Bacon and ham (uncooked)	0.80	0.90	0.80	0.80	0.90	0.80	0.60
3.9 Poultry (uncooked)	1.70	1.80	1.80	1.70	2.00	2.10	2.10
3.10 Cold meats, ready to eat meats	1.30	1.50	1.40	1.50	1.40	1.40	1.20
3.11 Meat pies, sausages and other meats	1.40	1.30	1.30	1.30	1.30	1.30	1.00
3.12 Fish, shellfish and fish products	1.20	1.40	1.40	1.40	1.40	1.60	1.90
3.13 Butter	0.30	0.30	0.30	0.30	0.30	0.30	0.30
3.14 Margarine	0.30	0.40	0.40	0.40	0.40	0.40	0.30
3.15 Cooking oils and fats	0.10	0.20	0.20	0.20	0.20	0.20	0.30
3.16 Fresh milk	2.00	2.20	2.20	2.20	2.20	2.10	1.80
3.17 Milk products including cream	1.10	1.30	1.30	1.40	1.30	1.50	1.30
3.18 Cheese	1.00	1.10	1.10	1.40	1.30	1.50	1.30
3.19 Eggs	0.40	0.40	0.30	0.40	0.40	0.40	0.50
3.20 Potatoes, potato products (excluding crisps)	1.20	1.20	1.20	1.20	1.30	1.30	1.10
3.21 Other vegetables	2.50	2.60	3.00	3.30	3.10	3.50	3.90
3.22 Fruit, nuts	2.00	2.30	2.40	2.60	2.50	3.00	3.40

ONS, Family Spending 2000-01, © Crown copyright 2002

5.3 Detailed household expenditure by UK Countries and Government Office Regions (cont.)
based on weighted data and including children's expenditure

1998-99 - 2000-01

	South East	South West	England	Wales	Scotland	Northern Ireland	United Kingdom
Average number of grossed households (thousands)	3,480	2,090	20,940	1,220	2,200	640	25,010
Total number of households in sample (over 3 years)	2,613	1,770	15,900	976	1,779	1,709	20,364
Total number of persons in sample (over 3 years)	6,244	4,237	38,091	2,358	4,050	4,430	48,929
Total number of adults in sample (over 3 years)	4,666	3,196	28,293	1,718	3,052	3,107	36,170
Weighted average number of persons per household	2.3	2.3	2.3	2.4	2.3	2.6	2.3

Commodity or service	Average weekly household expenditure (£)						
1 Housing (Net)	**73.30**	**57.60**	**62.10**	**45.30**	**49.60**	**31.50**	**59.40**
Percentage standard error	*2*	*2*	*1*	*3*	*2*	*3*	*1*
1.1 Gross rent, mortgage interest payments, water charges, council tax, etc	72.40	58.40	63.50	49.10	54.40	34.00	61.30
1.2 *less* housing benefit, rebates and allowances received	7.60	8.90	9.70	10.50	11.60	9.80	9.90
1.3 Net rent, mortgage interest payments, water charges, council tax, etc	64.80	49.50	53.90	38.60	42.80	24.30	51.40
1.4 Repairs, maintenance and decorations	8.40	8.10	8.20	6.80	6.80	7.20	8.00
2 Fuel and power	**11.30**	**11.30**	**11.40**	**12.00**	**12.40**	**15.70**	**11.60**
Percentage standard error	*1*	*2*	*1*	*2*	*1*	*2*	*0*
2.1 Gas	5.00	3.70	5.00	4.80	4.40	0.20	4.80
2.2 Electricity	5.70	6.30	5.70	6.20	7.20	7.20	5.90
2.3 Other fuels	0.70	1.30	0.70	1.00	0.80	8.30	0.90
3 Food and non-alcoholic drinks	**64.20**	**57.60**	**60.40**	**55.10**	**59.00**	**65.60**	**60.20**
Percentage standard error	*1*	*1*	*1*	*2*	*2*	*2*	*0*
3.1 Bread, rolls etc	1.70	1.70	1.70	1.80	2.00	2.90	1.80
3.2 Pasta, rice, flour and other cereals	0.50	0.40	0.50	0.30	0.40	0.30	0.50
3.3 Biscuits, cakes etc	3.00	2.90	2.80	3.00	2.80	3.80	2.90
3.4 Breakfast cereals	0.90	0.90	0.90	0.80	0.80	1.10	0.90
3.5 Beef and veal (uncooked)	1.40	1.40	1.40	1.40	1.80	2.90	1.50
3.6 Mutton and lamb (uncooked)	0.60	0.60	0.60	0.60	0.30	0.40	0.60
3.7 Pork (uncooked)	0.70	0.70	0.60	0.70	0.50	0.80	0.60
3.8 Bacon and ham (uncooked)	0.80	0.80	0.80	1.00	0.90	1.30	0.80
3.9 Poultry (uncooked)	2.20	1.90	2.00	1.80	1.90	2.30	2.00
3.10 Cold meats, ready to eat meats	1.40	1.30	1.40	1.50	1.60	1.70	1.40
3.11 Meat pies, sausages and other meats	1.30	1.30	1.30	1.30	1.40	1.50	1.30
3.12 Fish, shellfish and fish products	1.60	1.30	1.50	1.20	1.30	1.20	1.50
3.13 Butter	0.30	0.30	0.30	0.30	0.30	0.50	0.30
3.14 Margarine	0.40	0.40	0.40	0.40	0.30	0.50	0.40
3.15 Cooking oils and fats	0.20	0.20	0.20	0.10	0.20	0.20	0.20
3.16 Fresh milk	2.00	2.20	2.10	2.20	1.90	2.90	2.10
3.17 Milk products including cream	1.50	1.50	1.40	1.20	1.20	1.30	1.30
3.18 Cheese	1.50	1.40	1.30	1.10	1.20	1.00	1.30
3.19 Eggs	0.40	0.40	0.40	0.30	0.40	0.40	0.40
3.20 Potatoes, potato products (excluding crisps)	1.30	1.20	1.20	1.30	1.30	1.80	1.20
3.21 Other vegetables	3.60	3.20	3.30	2.60	2.40	2.80	3.10
3.22 Fruit, nuts	3.10	3.00	2.80	2.30	2.40	2.70	2.70

5.3 Detailed household expenditure by UK Countries and Government Office Regions (cont.)

1998-99 - 2000-01

based on weighted data and including children's expenditure

Commodity or service	North East	North West	Yorks and the Humber	East Midlands	West Midlands	East	London
	Average weekly household expenditure (£)						
3 Food and non-alcoholic drinks (continued)							
3.23 Sugar	0.20	0.20	0.20	0.20	0.20	0.20	0.20
3.24 Jam, jellies, preserves and other spreads	0.20	0.20	0.20	0.30	0.20	0.30	0.30
3.25 Sweets and chocolates	2.00	1.90	1.90	2.00	1.90	2.10	1.60
3.26 Ice cream and sorbets	0.40	0.40	0.40	0.40	0.50	0.60	0.50
3.27 Tea	0.40	0.50	0.50	0.50	0.60	0.50	0.40
3.28 Coffee	0.60	0.60	0.70	0.60	0.60	0.60	0.50
3.29 Drinking chocolate, other food drinks	0.10	0.20	0.10	0.20	0.20	0.20	0.20
3.30 Fruit juice, squashes, bottled water	0.90	1.10	1.00	1.20	1.20	1.50	1.90
3.31 Fizzy drinks	0.90	1.10	0.90	1.00	1.00	0.90	1.00
3.32 Soup	0.30	0.30	0.30	0.30	0.30	0.30	0.30
3.33 Pizzas, vegetarian pies, quiches	0.80	0.70	0.90	0.70	0.70	0.70	0.70
3.34 Other convenience foods	1.90	2.10	1.80	1.90	1.90	1.90	2.20
3.35 Potato crisps and savoury snacks	0.90	1.00	0.90	1.10	1.10	1.10	0.80
3.36 Restaurant and café meals	7.30	8.10	8.30	9.30	8.80	10.70	14.50
3.37 Take-away meals eaten at home	3.40	3.10	3.30	3.30	3.50	3.20	4.10
3.38 Other take-away food and snack food	3.40	4.00	3.90	3.50	3.60	3.70	5.90
3.39 State school meals and meals at work	1.90	1.80	2.00	2.00	2.10	2.00	2.50
3.40 Other foods	1.20	1.30	1.50	1.50	1.50	1.60	1.70
4 Alcoholic drink	**16.50**	**15.50**	**15.60**	**14.40**	**14.70**	**13.00**	**16.40**
Percentage standard error	*7*	*3*	*3*	*4*	*3*	*4*	*4*
4.1 Beer, cider	10.20	9.30	10.30	8.20	9.20	7.10	7.80
4.2 Wines, fortified wines	2.60	3.20	2.90	3.30	2.80	3.10	5.00
4.3 Spirits, liqueurs	2.10	2.30	1.60	2.00	1.80	1.90	2.50
4.4 Other drinks	1.60	0.70	0.70	0.90	0.80	0.80	1.00
5 Tobacco	**6.10**	**6.90**	**6.60**	**6.10**	**5.90**	**4.50**	**5.40**
Percentage standard error	*6*	*4*	*5*	*6*	*5*	*5*	*5*
5.1 Cigarettes	5.60	6.30	5.90	5.60	5.30	3.90	4.90
5.2 Tobacco and other tobacco products	0.50	0.50	0.70	0.50	0.50	0.60	0.50
6 Clothing and footwear	**20.20**	**22.20**	**21.10**	**18.70**	**20.40**	**20.60**	**26.00**
Percentage standard error	*6*	*4*	*5*	*4*	*4*	*4*	*4*
6.1 Men's outerwear	4.20	4.50	4.20	4.00	4.20	4.40	5.50
6.2 Men's underwear and hosiery	0.40	0.40	0.40	0.40	0.40	0.50	0.60
6.3 Women's outerwear	6.80	7.50	7.50	6.50	7.00	7.40	9.20
6.4 Women's underwear and hosiery	1.30	1.20	1.20	1.20	1.20	1.30	1.40
6.5 Boys' outerwear	1.00	0.80	0.80	0.70	0.70	0.70	0.80
6.6 Girls' outerwear	1.10	1.20	0.90	0.90	1.10	1.00	0.90
6.7 Babies' outerwear	0.70	0.70	0.60	0.50	0.70	0.60	0.70
6.8 Boys', girls' and babies' underwear	0.50	0.50	0.40	0.40	0.40	0.40	0.40
6.9 Ties, belts, hats, gloves, etc	0.60	0.50	0.60	0.60	0.60	0.50	1.00
6.10 Haberdashery, textiles and clothes hire	0.50	0.30	0.30	0.30	0.50	0.40	0.40
6.11 Footwear	3.10	4.70	4.10	3.30	3.70	3.30	5.00

5.3 Detailed household expenditure by UK Countries and Government Office Regions (cont.)

1998-99 - 2000-01

based on weighted data and including children's expenditure

Commodity or service	South East	South West	England	Wales	Scotland	Northern Ireland	United Kingdom
	\multicolumn{7}{c}{Average weekly household expenditure (£)}						
3 Food and non-alcoholic drinks (continued)							
3.23 Sugar	0.20	0.20	0.20	0.20	0.20	0.20	0.20
3.24 Jam, jellies, preserves and other spreads	0.30	0.30	0.30	0.20	0.30	0.30	0.30
3.25 Sweets and chocolates	2.00	1.90	1.90	2.20	2.00	1.80	1.90
3.26 Ice cream and sorbets	0.60	0.50	0.50	0.50	0.50	0.50	0.50
3.27 Tea	0.50	0.50	0.50	0.50	0.40	0.50	0.50
3.28 Coffee	0.60	0.60	0.60	0.50	0.60	0.50	0.60
3.29 Drinking chocolate, other food drinks	0.20	0.20	0.20	0.20	0.10	0.10	0.20
3.30 Fruit juice, squashes, bottled water	1.50	1.30	1.40	1.00	1.20	1.30	1.30
3.31 Fizzy drinks	1.00	0.80	1.00	1.20	1.70	1.60	1.10
3.32 Soup	0.30	0.20	0.30	0.30	0.40	0.40	0.30
3.33 Pizzas, vegetarian pies, quiches	0.80	0.70	0.70	0.60	0.70	0.70	0.70
3.34 Other convenience foods	2.30	1.90	2.00	2.00	2.10	1.70	2.00
3.35 Potato crisps and savoury snacks	1.10	1.10	1.00	1.00	1.10	1.00	1.00
3.36 Restaurant and café meals	11.90	8.80	10.20	7.30	8.80	9.10	9.90
3.37 Take-away meals eaten at home	3.20	2.80	3.30	3.00	3.70	4.50	3.40
3.38 Other take-away food and snack food	3.70	3.30	4.00	3.70	4.50	3.20	4.00
3.39 State school meals and meals at work	2.10	1.70	2.00	2.10	2.00	2.60	2.10
3.40 Other foods	1.70	1.60	1.50	1.30	1.40	1.30	1.50
4 Alcoholic drink	**14.10**	**14.20**	**14.90**	**13.40**	**15.10**	**13.20**	**14.80**
Percentage standard error	*3*	*4*	*1*	*5*	*3*	*4*	*1*
4.1 Beer, cider	7.00	7.90	8.40	8.20	7.10	6.10	8.20
4.2 Wines, fortified wines	4.30	3.80	3.60	2.10	2.80	2.60	3.40
4.3 Spirits, liqueurs	2.00	1.80	2.00	2.00	3.90	3.00	2.20
4.4 Other drinks	0.80	0.70	0.90	1.10	1.40	1.50	0.90
5 Tobacco	**4.80**	**4.70**	**5.60**	**6.40**	**8.10**	**9.20**	**6.00**
Percentage standard error	*4*	*5*	*2*	*6*	*4*	*4*	*1*
5.1 Cigarettes	4.20	3.80	5.00	5.60	7.30	8.80	5.30
5.2 Tobacco and other tobacco products	0.60	0.90	0.60	0.90	0.80	0.40	0.60
6 Clothing and footwear	**21.70**	**17.70**	**21.40**	**20.50**	**22.40**	**27.10**	**21.60**
Percentage standard error	*3*	*4*	*1*	*5*	*4*	*4*	*1*
6.1 Men's outerwear	4.70	3.50	4.50	4.20	5.00	6.10	4.50
6.2 Men's underwear and hosiery	0.50	0.50	0.50	0.40	0.50	0.50	0.50
6.3 Women's outerwear	7.70	6.00	7.40	7.20	7.10	8.80	7.40
6.4 Women's underwear and hosiery	1.30	1.30	1.30	1.30	1.30	1.30	1.30
6.5 Boys' outerwear	0.60	0.50	0.70	0.80	1.10	1.20	0.80
6.6 Girls' outerwear	0.90	1.10	1.00	1.20	1.10	1.10	1.00
6.7 Babies' outerwear	0.50	0.50	0.60	0.90	0.80	0.90	0.70
6.8 Boys', girls' and babies' underwear	0.30	0.30	0.40	0.40	0.50	0.50	0.40
6.9 Ties, belts, hats, gloves, etc	0.60	0.50	0.60	0.40	0.60	0.70	0.60
6.10 Haberdashery, textiles and clothes hire	0.40	0.40	0.40	0.30	0.20	0.40	0.40
6.11 Footwear	3.90	3.20	4.00	3.50	4.00	5.80	4.00

5.3 Detailed household expenditure by UK Countries and Government Office Regions (cont.)

1998-99 - 2000-01

based on weighted data and including children's expenditure

		North East	North West	Yorks and the Humber	East Midlands	West Midlands	East	London
Commodity or service		**Average weekly household expenditure (£)**						
7	**Household goods**	**26.40**	**28.10**	**29.50**	**31.20**	**31.00**	**35.00**	**31.60**
	Percentage standard error	*7*	*4*	*5*	*5*	*4*	*4*	*5*
7.1	Furniture	8.00	8.90	8.20	7.40	7.70	9.50	10.70
7.2	Floor coverings	2.60	2.90	3.60	3.30	3.70	3.60	2.60
7.3	Soft furnishings and bedding	1.90	1.70	1.80	2.70	2.20	2.30	1.60
7.4	Gas and electric appliances, inc repairs	3.50	3.50	4.50	4.60	4.30	5.60	3.80
7.5	Kitchen/garden equipment, household hardware	3.60	3.50	3.60	4.50	4.60	5.30	5.10
7.6	Kitchen and electrical consumables	0.80	0.90	0.90	1.00	1.00	1.10	1.00
7.7	Greetings cards, stationery and paper goods	1.70	1.60	1.60	1.70	1.80	1.90	2.00
7.8	Detergents and other cleaning materials	1.70	1.80	1.90	2.10	2.00	2.20	1.90
7.9	Toilet paper	0.60	0.60	0.60	0.70	0.70	0.70	0.70
7.10	Pets and pet food	2.10	2.60	2.80	3.10	3.20	2.80	2.20
8	**Household services**	**15.20**	**16.20**	**17.50**	**16.80**	**18.00**	**21.10**	**27.00**
	Percentage standard error	*8*	*4*	*4*	*3*	*4*	*4*	*5*
8.1	Insurance of contents of dwelling	1.70	2.00	1.90	1.80	1.70	2.10	2.50
8.2	Postage	0.40	0.50	0.50	0.50	0.50	0.60	0.70
8.3	Telephone	5.80	6.80	6.80	7.30	7.20	7.70	10.10
8.4	Domestic help and childcare	2.20	2.00	2.50	2.20	3.00	3.00	4.70
8.5	Repairs to footwear, watches, etc	0.30	0.20	0.10	0.20	0.10	0.70	0.20
8.6	Laundry, cleaning and dyeing	0.20	0.30	0.20	0.20	0.20	0.40	0.70
8.7	Subscriptions	0.70	1.00	0.90	1.10	0.90	0.90	1.20
8.8	Professional fees	0.90	1.10	1.40	1.20	1.40	3.10	2.70
8.9	Other services	2.90	2.40	3.30	2.30	3.00	2.70	4.10
9	**Personal goods and services**	**9.90**	**12.50**	**13.40**	**12.80**	**12.70**	**15.90**	**16.60**
	Percentage standard error	*5*	*4*	*5*	*4*	*4*	*4*	*4*
9.1	Leather and travel goods, jewellery, watches etc	1.10	1.80	2.40	1.80	1.70	2.30	2.60
9.2	Baby toiletries and equipment	0.70	0.80	0.70	0.80	0.70	0.80	0.80
9.3	Medicines, prescriptions, spectacles	1.70	2.40	2.70	2.80	2.60	3.90	2.90
9.4	Medical, dental, optical and nursing fees	0.60	1.50	1.10	1.10	1.30	1.70	2.30
9.5	Toiletries and soap	1.50	1.70	1.80	1.80	1.90	2.00	2.10
9.6	Cosmetics and hair products	2.40	2.10	2.20	2.30	2.60	2.60	2.90
9.7	Hairdressing, beauty treatment	1.90	2.30	2.50	2.20	2.00	2.50	3.00
10	**Motoring**	**36.80**	**51.40**	**52.80**	**54.50**	**56.10**	**63.80**	**48.40**
	Percentage standard error	*5*	*4*	*4*	*4*	*4*	*4*	*4*
10.1	Cars, vans and motorcycles purchase	14.30	23.00	24.00	24.80	24.10	29.00	21.30
10.2	Spares and accessories	1.30	2.00	2.00	1.60	2.00	1.90	1.40
10.3	Car and van repairs and servicing	2.90	3.60	4.40	3.90	4.30	5.00	5.00
10.4	Motor vehicle insurance and taxation	5.70	7.30	7.20	7.30	8.00	8.60	7.50
10.5	Petrol, diesel and other motor oils	11.60	13.80	13.30	14.90	15.90	16.80	11.00
10.6	Other motoring costs	1.10	1.70	1.80	2.00	1.80	2.30	2.20
11	**Fares and other travel costs**	**6.60**	**6.50**	**8.10**	**6.80**	**6.60**	**10.20**	**17.60**
	Percentage standard error	*8*	*6*	*14*	*10*	*10*	*9*	*5*
11.1	Rail and tube fares	1.00	0.80	0.90	0.60	0.60	3.70	4.50
11.2	Bus and coach fares	2.10	1.50	1.70	1.20	1.50	0.80	1.60
11.3	Taxis, air and other travel	2.70	3.60	3.90	4.50	3.10	4.70	11.10
11.4	Bicycles, boats, purchase and repair	0.80	0.50	1.60	0.50	1.30	1.00	0.40

ONS, Family Spending 2000-01, © Crown copyright 2002

5.3 Detailed household expenditure by UK Countries and Government Office Regions (cont.)

1998-99 - 2000-01

based on weighted data and including children's expenditure

Commodity or service	South East	South West	England	Wales	Scotland	Northern Ireland	United Kingdom
	Average weekly household expenditure (£)						
7 Household goods	**36.80**	**29.40**	**31.60**	**28.40**	**27.70**	**29.40**	**31.00**
Percentage standard error	*4*	*4*	*2*	*6*	*5*	*4*	*1*
7.1 Furniture	9.30	6.70	8.70	7.90	8.30	9.10	8.60
7.2 Floor coverings	3.50	3.10	3.20	2.90	3.00	3.80	3.20
7.3 Soft furnishings and bedding	2.40	2.50	2.10	2.00	1.30	1.80	2.00
7.4 Gas and electric appliances, inc repairs	5.30	4.60	4.50	3.30	4.00	4.20	4.40
7.5 Kitchen/garden equipment, household hardware	5.40	4.20	4.50	4.40	3.60	4.10	4.40
7.6 Kitchen and electrical consumables	1.20	1.10	1.00	0.90	0.90	0.80	1.00
7.7 Greetings cards, stationery and paper goods	2.10	1.80	1.80	1.50	1.60	1.30	1.80
7.8 Detergents and other cleaning materials	2.10	1.80	2.00	1.90	1.80	2.10	2.00
7.9 Toilet paper	0.70	0.70	0.70	0.70	0.70	0.80	0.70
7.10 Pets and pet food	4.70	2.80	3.00	2.80	2.40	1.40	2.90
8 Household services	**25.20**	**21.60**	**20.60**	**16.10**	**16.10**	**17.10**	**19.90**
Percentage standard error	*4*	*6*	*2*	*8*	*4*	*6*	*1*
8.1 Insurance of contents of dwelling	2.20	1.90	2.00	1.60	1.70	1.50	2.00
8.2 Postage	0.70	0.60	0.60	0.50	0.50	0.50	0.60
8.3 Telephone	8.40	7.20	7.70	6.70	6.80	7.30	7.60
8.4 Domestic help and childcare	3.70	2.60	3.00	1.60	1.90	3.00	2.90
8.5 Repairs to footwear, watches, etc	0.40	0.30	0.30	0.20	0.20	0.50	0.30
8.6 Laundry, cleaning and dyeing	0.40	0.40	0.40	0.20	0.30	0.20	0.40
8.7 Subscriptions	1.20	1.10	1.00	0.70	1.10	0.80	1.00
8.8 Professional fees	3.60	3.20	2.20	1.30	1.40	0.40	2.10
8.9 Other services	4.60	4.30	3.40	3.20	2.20	2.80	3.30
9 Personal goods and services	**17.10**	**14.60**	**14.40**	**11.60**	**11.40**	**12.00**	**14.00**
Percentage standard error	*3*	*6*	*2*	*5*	*4*	*4*	*1*
9.1 Leather and travel goods, jewellery, watches etc	2.40	3.00	2.20	1.60	1.70	1.60	2.10
9.2 Baby toiletries and equipment	0.80	0.70	0.80	1.10	0.60	0.80	0.80
9.3 Medicines, prescriptions, spectacles	3.60	2.80	2.90	2.10	2.10	1.80	2.80
9.4 Medical, dental, optical and nursing fees	2.50	1.70	1.70	1.00	0.90	0.70	1.50
9.5 Toiletries and soap	2.10	1.90	1.90	1.70	1.90	2.00	1.90
9.6 Cosmetics and hair products	2.50	2.20	2.40	2.20	2.20	2.60	2.40
9.7 Hairdressing, beauty treatment	3.20	2.40	2.50	2.00	2.00	2.40	2.50
10 Motoring	**62.00**	**56.60**	**54.60**	**44.30**	**46.20**	**44.50**	**53.10**
Percentage standard error	*3*	*4*	*1*	*5*	*4*	*6*	*1*
10.1 Cars, vans and motorcycles purchase	25.90	24.00	23.90	18.00	21.10	16.20	23.10
10.2 Spares and accessories	2.50	2.20	1.90	1.50	1.30	1.60	1.80
10.3 Car and van repairs and servicing	5.90	5.10	4.60	3.20	3.60	2.60	4.40
10.4 Motor vehicle insurance and taxation	8.50	7.80	7.70	6.30	6.00	8.40	7.50
10.5 Petrol, diesel and other motor oils	17.10	15.40	14.60	13.90	13.00	14.70	14.40
10.6 Other motoring costs	2.30	2.10	2.00	1.40	1.30	1.00	1.90
11 Fares and other travel costs	**10.90**	**5.90**	**9.40**	**5.30**	**7.90**	**5.90**	**9.00**
Percentage standard error	*7*	*10*	*3*	*10*	*10*	*7*	*3*
11.1 Rail and tube fares	3.50	0.80	2.10	0.60	1.20	0.30	1.90
11.2 Bus and coach fares	1.00	1.10	1.30	1.00	2.10	1.00	1.40
11.3 Taxis, air and other travel	4.90	3.50	5.00	3.00	4.00	4.10	4.80
11.4 Bicycles, boats, purchase and repair	1.60	0.60	0.90	0.70	0.50	0.50	0.90

5.3 Detailed household expenditure by UK Countries and Government Office Regions (cont.)

based on weighted data and including children's expenditure

		North East	North West	Yorks and the Humber	East Midlands	West Midlands	East	London
Commodity or service		**Average weekly household expenditure (£)**						
12	**Leisure goods**	**14.40**	**16.80**	**18.60**	**18.30**	**19.20**	**20.20**	**20.10**
	Percentage standard error	*7*	*5*	*6*	*7*	*6*	*4*	*5*
12.1	Books, maps, diaries	0.90	1.30	1.40	1.40	1.50	1.70	2.30
12.2	Newspapers	2.00	2.00	1.80	1.90	1.90	1.90	1.80
12.3	Magazines and periodicals	0.90	0.90	1.00	1.10	1.00	1.20	1.10
12.4	TVs, videos, computers and audio equipment	5.50	7.20	9.20	8.10	9.20	8.10	9.10
12.5	Sports and camping equipment	0.40	0.70	0.50	0.60	1.30	0.50	0.60
12.6	Toys and hobbies	2.40	1.80	1.70	2.10	1.80	2.60	1.60
12.7	Photography and camcorders	0.70	1.00	1.00	1.00	0.90	1.40	1.50
12.8	Horticultural goods, plants, flowers	1.60	1.90	2.00	2.10	1.70	2.70	2.00
13	**Leisure services**	**34.10**	**43.80**	**41.90**	**43.30**	**42.00**	**44.50**	**62.40**
	Percentage standard error	*6*	*4*	*4*	*5*	*4*	*4*	*5*
13.1	Cinema and theatre	0.60	1.00	0.90	0.80	0.80	1.20	1.60
13.2	Sports admissions and subscriptions	1.80	3.10	3.20	2.40	2.80	2.80	3.50
13.3	TV, video and satellite rental, television licences and Internet	4.10	4.30	3.90	3.80	4.20	3.80	4.10
13.4	Miscellaneous entertainments	1.10	1.10	1.30	1.80	1.30	1.30	1.40
13.5	Educational and training expenses	2.40	4.50	6.00	5.60	4.90	5.80	11.90
13.6	Holiday in UK	1.50	2.30	2.90	3.00	2.70	3.20	2.00
13.7	Holiday abroad	7.70	12.00	10.50	10.80	10.20	11.40	13.70
13.8	Other incidental holiday expenses	2.10	6.30	3.10	6.20	5.70	4.00	11.70
13.9	Gambling payments	5.50	3.70	4.00	3.40	3.80	3.30	3.50
13.10	Cash gifts, donations	7.20	5.40	6.20	5.40	5.80	7.70	8.90
14	**Miscellaneous**	**1.00**	**0.90**	**0.90**	**1.00**	**1.20**	**1.10**	**1.80**
	Percentage standard error	*15*	*10*	*16*	*14*	*18*	*11*	*16*
1-14	**All expenditure groups**	**297.20**	**340.40**	**347.50**	**347.90**	**353.20**	**386.60**	**435.70**
	Percentage standard error	*3*	*2*	*2*	*2*	*2*	*2*	*2*
15	**Other payments recorded**							
15.1	Life assurance, contributions to pension funds	17.80	18.60	20.10	19.10	20.80	22.20	24.80
15.2	Medical insurance premiums	0.50	1.10	0.90	1.00	1.10	1.60	1.80
15.3	Other insurance premiums	0.50	0.80	1.20	1.00	0.80	1.00	1.10
15.4	Income tax, payments less refunds	44.50	53.90	53.80	59.70	57.90	72.40	99.50
15.5	National insurance contributions	14.40	16.20	16.40	18.10	17.90	19.40	22.60
15.6	Purchase or alteration of dwellings, mortgages	17.90	14.70	17.00	19.10	20.10	28.50	26.20
15.7	Savings and investments	23.20	7.10	7.80	6.40	7.10	8.80	20.60
15.8	Repayment of loans to clear other debts	2.60	2.20	2.10	2.80	2.70	2.70	3.30

ONS, Family Spending 2000-01, © Crown copyright 2002

5.3 Detailed household expenditure by UK Countries and Government Office Regions (cont.)

1998-99 - 2000-01

based on weighted data and including children's expenditure

Commodity or service	South East	South West	England	Wales	Scotland	Northern Ireland	United Kingdom
	Average weekly household expenditure (£)						
12 Leisure goods	**20.90**	**20.30**	**19.10**	**16.10**	**17.90**	**13.80**	**18.70**
Percentage standard error	*4*	*6*	*2*	*6*	*6*	*5*	*2*
12.1 Books, maps, diaries	1.90	1.50	1.60	1.20	1.40	1.00	1.60
12.2 Newspapers	1.90	2.00	1.90	1.80	2.60	2.30	2.00
12.3 Magazines and periodicals	1.10	1.00	1.10	1.00	1.00	0.80	1.00
12.4 TVs, videos, computers and audio equipment	8.80	9.20	8.40	7.30	7.90	5.50	8.20
12.5 Sports and camping equipment	0.80	0.90	0.70	0.80	0.80	0.30	0.70
12.6 Toys and hobbies	2.30	2.00	2.00	1.80	1.80	1.60	2.00
12.7 Photography and camcorders	1.30	1.40	1.20	0.50	0.80	0.70	1.10
12.8 Horticultural goods, plants, flowers	2.80	2.30	2.20	1.70	1.60	1.50	2.10
13 Leisure services	**54.00**	**41.60**	**47.10**	**39.80**	**36.10**	**36.70**	**45.50**
Percentage standard error	*4*	*5*	*2*	*7*	*4*	*6*	*1*
13.1 Cinema and theatre	1.40	0.90	1.10	0.90	1.40	1.00	1.10
13.2 Sports admissions and subscriptions	3.60	2.40	3.00	2.20	2.80	1.90	2.90
13.3 TV, video and satellite rental, television licences and Internet	4.00	3.60	4.00	4.30	3.80	3.40	4.00
13.4 Miscellaneous entertainments	1.50	1.30	1.30	0.90	1.10	1.20	1.30
13.5 Educational and training expenses	8.00	6.10	6.60	3.20	3.20	3.40	6.10
13.6 Holiday in UK	3.10	2.70	2.60	1.90	1.80	1.00	2.50
13.7 Holiday abroad	13.10	11.00	11.60	10.20	10.00	7.20	11.30
13.8 Other incidental holiday expenses	6.90	4.60	6.20	6.20	3.00	6.70	5.90
13.9 Gambling payments	3.40	2.90	3.60	3.70	4.20	3.00	3.70
13.10 Cash gifts, donations	9.10	6.00	7.10	6.30	4.80	7.90	6.80
14 Miscellaneous	**1.30**	**0.90**	**1.20**	**1.00**	**0.80**	**1.70**	**1.10**
Percentage standard error	*9*	*12*	*5*	*14*	*11*	*9*	*4*
1-14 All expenditure groups	**417.80**	**354.10**	**373.80**	**315.40**	**330.70**	**323.50**	**365.80**
Percentage standard error	*1*	*2*	*1*	*2*	*2*	*2*	*1*
15 Other payments recorded							
15.1 Life assurance, contributions to pension funds	26.20	22.10	21.90	15.10	19.00	16.00	21.10
15.2 Medical insurance premiums	1.80	1.50	1.30	0.50	0.50	0.40	1.20
15.3 Other insurance premiums	1.20	1.40	1.00	0.70	0.60	0.50	1.00
16.4 Income tax, payments less refunds	95.60	57.20	70.20	39.90	53.90	37.80	66.40
15.5 National insurance contributions	20.80	16.10	18.50	13.60	16.70	13.20	18.00
15.6 Purchase or alteration of dwellings, mortgages	29.60	23.20	22.50	12.80	17.70	12.50	21.40
15.7 Savings and investments	19.10	9.40	12.40	3.80	5.60	1.70	11.10
15.8 Repayment of loans to clear other debts	3.50	2.30	2.80	2.50	1.90	0.40	2.60

5.4 Household expenditure by type of administrative area
based on weighted data and including children's expenditure

1998-99 - 2000-01

	Metropolitan districts		Non-Metropolitan Districts			All house-holds
	Greater London	Others & Central Clydeside	High population density[1]	Medium population density[2]	Low population density[3]	
Average number of grossed households (thousands)	3,070	5,320	5,970	4,750	5,890	25,010
Total number of households in sample (over 3 years)	1,983	3,984	5,147	3,737	5,513	20,364
Total number of persons in sample (over 3 years)	4,575	9,558	12,322	9,006	13,468	48,929
Total number of adults in sample (over 3 years)	3,347	7,040	9,124	6,642	10,017	36,170
Weighted average number of persons per household	2.3	2.3	2.3	2.4	2.4	2.3

Commodity or service	Average weekly household expenditure (£)					
1 Housing (Net)	83.00	50.20	58.90	57.70	57.10	59.40
Percentage standard error	2	1	1	2	1	1
2 Fuel and power	10.90	11.50	11.20	11.70	12.60	11.60
"	3	1	1	1	1	0
3 Food and non-alcoholic drinks	68.40	55.30	59.20	60.80	60.70	60.20
"	2	1	1	1	1	0
4 Alcoholic drink	16.40	15.60	14.40	14.80	13.50	14.80
"	4	2	2	3	2	1
5 Tobacco	5.40	7.10	6.10	5.60	5.40	6.00
"	5	3	3	4	3	1
6 Clothing and footwear	26.00	21.10	20.80	21.40	20.50	21.60
"	4	3	2	3	2	1
7 Household goods	31.70	26.30	29.10	33.60	34.70	31.00
"	5	3	2	4	2	1
8 Household services	26.90	16.00	18.60	19.50	21.50	19.90
"	5	3	2	3	3	1
9 Personal goods and services	16.60	11.50	13.90	14.40	14.50	14.00
"	4	3	2	3	3	1
10 Motoring	48.40	46.00	50.70	58.60	60.10	53.10
"	4	3	2	3	2	1
11 Fares and other travel costs	17.60	8.00	8.80	7.70	6.50	9.00
"	5	7	6	5	5	3
12 Leisure goods	20.00	16.80	19.30	18.20	19.60	18.70
"	5	4	3	3	3	2
13 Leisure services	62.50	40.40	44.00	46.00	42.50	45.50
"	5	3	3	3	3	1
14 Miscellaneous	1.80	1.00	1.10	1.10	1.10	1.10
"	16	11	7	7	6	4
1-14 All expenditure groups	435.60	326.90	356.10	371.00	370.40	365.80
Percentage standard error	2	1	1	1	1	1
Average weekly expenditure per person (£)						
All expenditure groups	186.80	140.10	153.60	157.70	155.70	156.00

1 Over 7.9 persons per hectare (over 3.2 persons per acre)
2 2.2 to 7.9 persons per hectare (0.9 to 3.2 persons per acre)
3 Under 2.2 persons per hectare (0.9 persons per acre)

ONS, Family Spending 2000-01, © Crown copyright 2002

5.5 Household expenditure by urban/rural areas (GB only) 1999-2000 - 2000-01
based on weighted data and including children's expenditure

	London built-up area	Other metropo-litan built-up areas	Other urban					Rural
			popu-lation over 250K	popu-lation 100K to 250K	popu-lation 25K to 100K	popu-lation 10K to 25K	popu-lation 3K to 10K	
Average number of grossed households (thousands)	3,540	3,560	2,910	2,600	3,870	2,040	1,810	2,530
Total number of households in sample (over 2 years)	1,596	1,767	1,510	1,368	2,031	1,107	977	1,367
Total number of persons in sample (over 2 years)	3,702	4,183	3,486	3,169	4,834	2,647	2,351	3,343
Total number of adults in sample (over 2 years)	2,734	3,080	2,631	2,382	3,610	1,933	1,756	2,533
Weighted average number of persons per household	2.3	2.3	2.3	2.3	2.3	2.3	2.4	2.4
Commodity or service	**Average weekly household expenditure (£)**							
1 Housing (Net)	87.30	49.90	55.10	54.60	55.70	56.80	57.50	62.10
Percentage standard error	3	2	2	2	2	3	3	3
2 Fuel and power	11.10	11.40	10.60	10.80	11.10	11.30	11.90	13.70
"	3	2	2	2	1	2	2	2
3 Food and non-alcoholic drinks	70.20	54.80	57.00	56.80	59.40	58.70	59.90	64.30
"	2	2	2	2	1	2	2	2
4 Alcoholic drink	16.80	15.40	15.40	14.10	15.40	14.50	14.00	14.70
"	4	3	4	4	4	4	4	4
5 Tobacco	5.50	7.10	6.70	6.40	6.10	5.00	5.70	5.00
"	6	5	5	5	5	7	6	6
6 Clothing and footwear	26.40	20.30	19.90	19.10	19.70	19.70	20.50	21.60
"	5	4	4	4	4	5	5	5
7 Household goods	34.60	25.80	27.70	28.10	30.20	28.30	34.10	42.50
"	6	5	4	5	5	5	7	5
8 Household services	28.00	15.60	17.40	18.00	19.00	19.40	18.90	23.40
"	6	3	4	4	5	6	5	5
9 Personal goods and services	17.40	11.20	13.30	14.00	13.90	13.90	14.70	15.50
"	5	4	4	5	4	5	5	5
10 Motoring	55.10	44.20	44.60	45.20	54.20	51.20	58.00	74.50
"	5	4	4	4	3	6	4	4
11 Fares and other travel costs	17.60	7.40	8.90	8.20	9.00	7.10	6.50	7.10
"	6	8	13	14	8	10	9	11
12 Leisure goods	20.40	15.10	18.00	18.60	20.20	21.20	20.10	21.90
"	5	6	5	7	6	7	7	5
13 Leisure services	65.10	40.30	42.70	39.60	45.20	43.50	44.40	47.90
"	6	5	5	6	4	5	6	5
14 Miscellaneous	1.70	1.00	1.00	0.70	1.00	0.80	1.00	0.90
"	20	18	13	12	10	14	14	16
1-14 All expenditure groups	457.30	319.60	338.20	334.10	360.20	351.40	367.20	415.20
Percentage standard error	2	2	2	2	2	2	2	2
Average weekly expenditure per person (£)								
All expenditure groups	196.80	138.70	149.00	147.70	154.70	151.50	154.60	172.20

ONS, Family Spending 2000-01, © Crown copyright 2002

Chapter *6*

Trends in household expenditure

All expenditure figures are shown at 2000-01 prices

- Spending on **leisure goods and services** continues to rise as a proportion of total expenditure. This group shows the largest increase since 1974, up from 11 per cent of the total in 1974 to 18 per cent in 2000-01.

- The proportion spent on motoring has also risen steadily, from 11 per cent of the total in 1974 to 14 per cent in 2000-01.

- The largest fall is in the proportion spent on **food and non-alcoholic drinks**, down from 24 per cent of spending in 1974 to 16 per cent in 2000-01.

- Over the period there have also been falls in the proportion spent on **tobacco**, from four per cent to two per cent of total expenditure, on **fuel and power**, from six per cent to three per cent, and on **clothing and footwear**, from nine per cent to six per cent.

- Total expenditure on all types of **services – leisure, household and personal** has doubled as a proportion from 10 per cent of all expenditure in 1974 to 20 per cent in 2000-01. The largest growth has been in **leisure services**, such as holidays and entertainment, from £17 a week in 1974 to £51 a week in 2000-01. **Household services**, such as telephone bills and domestic help, also grew substantially from £8.70 to £22 a week. **Personal services**, such as medical costs and hairdressing, increased in line with total spending, from £2.40 a week to £4.30.

- Household spending on **NHS services** averaged about 20 pence a week from the mid-1970s to the mid-1980s then rose to about 90 pence a week in the most recent three years. Spending on **private health services**, including dental and optical, rose from 50 pence a week in the mid-70s to £1.00 a week in the mid-1990s then fell to 75 pence a week in the most recent period.

- Expenditure on **postal services** rose from 50 pence a week in 1974 to about 80 pence a week in 1994-95 then dropped back to 50 pence a week in 2000-01. **Telephone account** expenditure more than doubled between 1974 and 2000-01, from £2.60 to £5.70 a week. Up to 1995-96 expenditure on **mobile phone accounts** averaged 20 pence a week or less, but rose to £1.60 a week in 1999-2000 and 2000-01,

- Among leisure services there was a large rise in spending on **participant sports and sports and social clubs**, from 70 pence a week in 1974 to £2.70 a week in 2000-01. Spending on **spectator sports** is lower but also increased over the period, from an average of 15 pence a week to over 60 pence a week.

- Since 1995 the largest increase in spending on both **leisure services** and **household services** was by younger households, with a head aged under 30. There was also a large increase for couples with children.

6 Trends in household expenditure

This chapter looks at long-term trends in average household expenditure since 1974 and medium term trends for the last five years for selected items. Inevitably, the definitions of some categories of expenditure have changed over the period. Definitions and changes to them since 1990 are outlined in **Appendices D and E** and in earlier reports for changes in years before 1990. **Table 6.1** shows results before 1995-96 on an unweighted basis and not including data from the children's diaries, which had not then been introduced. After 1995-96 the results are based on weighted data and include the spending from children's diaries. In 1995-96 itself results are shown on both bases to provide a link. For an explanation of the effect of weighting and children's data on expenditure see **Appendix F** – Differential grossing and children's data. All results in this chapter have been uprated to 2000-01 prices.

Tables 6.1, 6.2 and **Figure 6.1** show trends for broad categories of expenditure between 1974 and 2000-01. As a proportion of total expenditure spending on leisure goods and services combined shows the largest increase over the period. Expenditure has increased from 11 to 18 per cent of total expenditure, up from £30 a week in 1974 (in 2000-01 prices) to around £70 a week in 2000-01. However, it is the leisure services element that shows the largest rise, up from six per cent of total spending in 1974 to around

6.1 Percentage of total expenditure on selected categories, 1974 to 2000-01

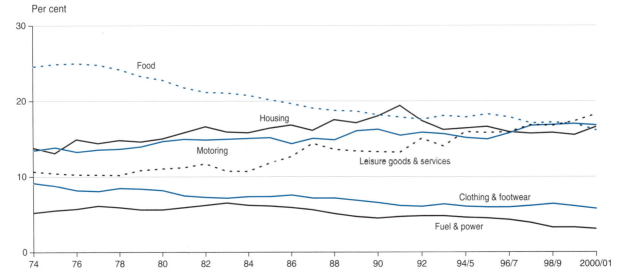

ONS, Family Spending 2000-01, © Crown copyright 2002

13 per cent in 2000-01. The leisure goods element increased in line with total spending and remained at a fairly constant five per cent (**Table 6.2**). Conversely expenditure on food has shown the largest proportionate decrease, down from 24 per cent in 1974 to 16 per cent in 2000-01. In monetary terms spending on food has declined from £69 a week (2000-01 prices) in 1974 to £62 a week in 2000-01. The proportion spent on housing rose from about 15 per cent in the mid-1970s to 17 per cent in the mid-1980s and has remained at about that level since then. Spending on motoring has risen fairly steadily from 11 per cent of total spending in the mid-1970s to 14 per cent in 2000-01. There have been falls in the proportion spent on tobacco (four per cent to two per cent), fuel and power (six per cent to three per cent) and clothing and footwear (nine per cent to six per cent).

Expenditure on services

Expenditure on services has increased from 10 per cent of total spending in 1974 to 20 per cent in 2000-01, as shown in **Figure 6.2**. The services consist of personal, household and leisure services. The largest part of the increase came from leisure services, but there was also substantial growth in household services. The proportion of spending on personal services remained fairly constant at around one per cent of total expenditure between 1974 and 2000-01. In monetary terms it has risen from £2.40 in 1974 to £4.30 in 2000-01. Personal services expenditure includes expenditure on medical, dental, optical and nursing fees and hairdressing and beauty treatment. Over the same period spending on household services has risen steadily from three per cent of total expenditure in 1974 to nearly six per cent in 2000-01. Leisure services expenditure showed by far the biggest increase over the period rising by seven percentage points. Spending in 1974 was around £17 a week, in 2000-01 it had risen to around £51 a week.

Figure 6.3 illustrates how spending on one part of personal services, medical, dental, optical and nursing fees, has changed since 1974. They are split into NHS and private, and three-year averages are shown to improve reliability. Spending on NHS services (dental fees, eye tests and hospital amenity beds) remained fairly steady between the mid-70s and the mid to late 80s at around 20 pence a week. It then rose steadily to 90 pence a week in the most recent three years. Spending on private medical,

6.2 **Services as a proportion of total expenditure**

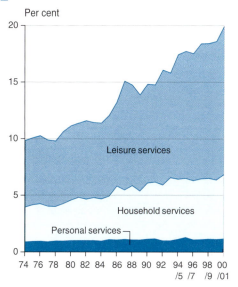

6.3 **Spending on medical, dental, optical and nursing fees, 1974 to 2000-01**

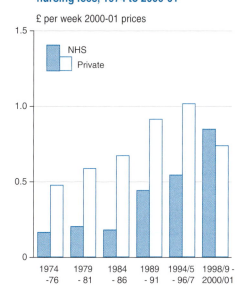

6.4 **Expenditure on postage, telephone accounts and mobile phone accounts, 1974 to 2000-01**

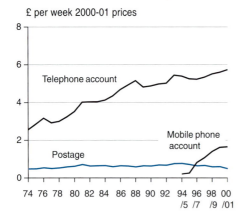

£ per week 2000-01 prices

dental, optical and nursing fees rose steadily from 50 pence a week in the mid-1970s to £1 a week in the mid-1990s, but fell to about 75 pence a week in the most recent period.

Figure 6.4 compares average weekly household expenditure on postage, telephone accounts and mobile phone accounts, part of household services. Spending on postage rose from 50 pence a week in 1974 to about 80 pence a week in 1994-95 then gradually dropped back to 50 pence a week in 2000-01. Telephone account expenditure more than doubled between 1974 and 2000-01, rising from £2.60 to £5.70 a week. From 1994-95 expenditure data has been collected on mobile phone accounts. For 1994-95 and 1995-96 spending on these accounts was relatively low at around 20 pence a week, it then increased to around £1.60 in 1999-00 and 2000-01.

6.5 **Expenditure on cinema, theatre and participant sports and subscriptions, 1974 to 2000-01**

£ per week 2000-01 prices

Figure 6.5 compares spending on a group of leisure services, admissions to cinema, theatre and concerts, spectator sports, and participant sports and subscriptions. In 1974 expenditure on cinema was just over 40 pence a week. By 1985 it had fallen to less than half that amount at 16 pence a week. Since then there has been a steady increase in spending, levelling out at just under 50 pence a week for the latest two years. Spending on theatre and concert tickets remained at around 30 pence a week between 1974 and 1977 before starting to rise. The trend continued upward reaching nearly 80 pence a week in 2000-01. Spending on spectator sports was the lowest of the four items in the mid-70s at about 15 pence a week. It rose to about 20 pence a week in the mid-80s and to over 60 pence a week in 2000-01, when it was higher than cinema admissions. Spending on participant sports and subscriptions to sports and social clubs showed much higher expenditure compared to the other items. Expenditure in 1974 was around 70 pence a week and remained below £1.00 a week up until 1984 when it was just over £1.00 a week. Over the next ten years spending on participant sports and subscriptions increased reaching around £2 a week in 1993. By 2000-01 spending on participant sports had risen to nearly £2.70 a week.

Recent trends by household characteristics

Age of head of household

Figure 6.6 Compares spending on leisure and household services by age of head of household between 1995-96 and 2000-01. All household expenditure on leisure services increased by rather under 40 per cent over the period. Households with a head aged under 30 showed the largest increase, up just over 40 per cent from around £27 in 1995-96 to around £38 in 2000-01. Households with a head aged 30 to 64 and with a head aged 65 or over both showed increases in spending of a third.

Although expenditure on household services was much less, the general trend was still upward. All household expenditure increased by about a quarter between 1995-96 and 2000-01 (£17 up to £22). The increase was greatest for households with a young head: under 30 the increase was just under 40 per cent (£15 to £21); at 30 to 64 it was about a quarter (£19 to £24); and at 65 and over it was under 15 per cent (£13 to £14).

Household composition

Figure 6.7 looks at spending on household and leisure services for retired households – for those mainly dependent on state pension and those with other sources of income. Pairs of years have been combined to improve reliability. The retired households with other sources of income spent three times as much on leisure services as those mainly dependent on state pension, reflecting their higher incomes. Their spending had also increased more over the last five years, by about 20 per cent compared with little change for those mainly dependent on state pensions.

Differences in spending on household services over the period were much less marked for both types of retired household. Those retired households with other sources of income spent about three-quarters as much again on household services as those mainly dependent on state pensions. The increase in spending over the five years was fairly similar, however, up by 20 to 25 per cent.

6.6 Services by age of head of household 1995-96 and 2000-01

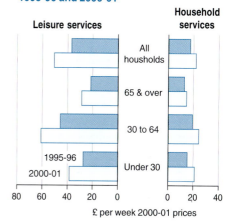

£ per week 2000-01 prices

6.7 Services by retired households, 1995-97 and 1999-2001

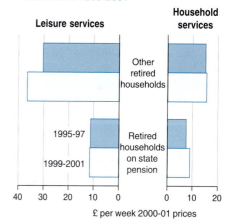

£ per week 2000-01 prices

6.8 Services by households with children, 1995-97 and 1999-2001

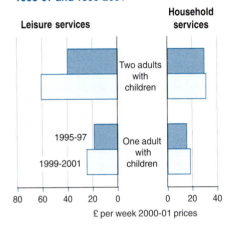

Figure 6.8 shows spending on household and leisure services for one and two adult households with children. Single parent households generally spent less than half of what couple households with children spent on leisure services. The general trend for the categories shown was upward. For single parent households spending on leisure services increased by about 40 per cent between 1995-96 and 2000-01 (£19 up to £27 a week). The increase was over 70 per cent for couple households with children (£38 up to £66 a week).

Gross income quintile

Expenditure on leisure services varied greatly between income groups. Households with the highest fifth of incomes spent nearly twice as much on leisure services as those in the fourth income group and nearly eight times as much as those in the lowest income group. The general trend for all groups over the five-year period was upward. The largest proportional increases were for households with the lowest fifth of incomes – up by a half, from £9 in 1995-96 to £14 in 2000-01 – and the highest income group – also up by a half, from £79 in 1995-96 to £116 in 2000-01.

6.9 Services by gross income quintile, 1995-96 and 2000-01

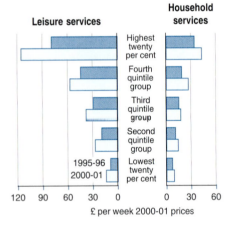

Households generally spent less on household services and trends in expenditure differed between the income quintiles. Those households with the top fifth of incomes spent between four and five times as much on household services as those with the lowest fifth of incomes. Over the five-year period spending increased by about a quarter in households as a whole, with no clear pattern in the increase for the different income groups. **(Figure 6.9).**

ONS, Family Spending 2000-01, © Crown copyright 2002

6.1 Household expenditure 1974 to 2000-01
2000-01 prices
based on unweighted, adult only data

Year	1974	1976	1978	1980	1982	1984	1986	1988	1990
Total number of households in sample	6,695	7,203	7,001	6,944	7,428	7,081	7,178	7,265	7,046
Total number of persons	18,974	19,793	19,019	18,844	20,022	18,557	18,330	18,280	17,437
Weighted average number of persons per household	2.8	2.7	2.7	2.7	2.7	2.6	2.6	2.5	2.5

Commodity or service	Average weekly household expenditure (£)								
1 Housing (Net)	38.80	38.90	40.00	41.60	46.10	45.40	51.40	57.40	60.40
2 Fuel and power	14.80	14.90	16.00	15.50	17.30	17.80	17.90	16.80	15.10
3 Food and non-alcoholic drinks	68.80	64.80	65.00	63.20	58.40	59.30	60.10	61.30	60.90
4 Alcoholic drink	13.50	13.10	13.20	13.40	12.70	13.70	14.10	14.70	13.60
5 Tobacco	10.10	9.70	9.20	8.30	8.00	8.20	7.80	7.10	6.50
6 Clothing and footwear	25.50	21.10	22.80	22.60	20.10	20.90	23.10	23.30	21.80
7 Household goods	23.00	18.60	20.80	21.30	20.40	21.60	23.50	24.10	27.20
8 Household services	8.70	8.60	8.20	9.90	10.10	10.60	14.60	15.70	16.70
9 Personal goods and services	9.40	8.40	8.80	9.80	9.10	9.90	11.10	13.00	12.90
10 Motoring	30.20	27.00	29.20	32.90	33.40	35.90	36.50	40.60	46.00
11 Fares and other travel costs	7.60	7.30	7.50	7.70	7.60	7.00	7.20	7.80	8.40
12 Leisure goods	13.20	10.90	11.60	12.10	13.20	14.40	14.70	15.50	15.30
13 Leisure services	16.50	15.60	15.60	18.20	19.20	19.10	22.60	29.10	29.30
14 Miscellaneous	1.30	1.40	2.30	1.30	1.10	1.20	1.30	1.30	1.90
1-14 All expenditure groups	281.30	260.20	270.20	277.90	276.50	285.10	306.00	327.60	335.80

Average weekly expenditure per person (£) All expenditure groups	100.50	96.40	99.50	102.40	102.90	109.40	119.80	130.20	135.70

	Average weekly household income (£)[3]								
Gross income (£)	342.00	332.70	340.50	352.80	348.20	353.00	379.80	429.40	431.00
Disposable income (£)	..	..	..	288.30	281.30	282.10	308.80	348.20	350.30

ONS, Family Spending 2000-01, © Crown copyright 2002

6.1
Household expenditure 1974 to 2000-01 (cont.)
2000-01 prices
based on unweighted, adult only data

Year	1992	1994 -95	1995[1] -96	1995[2] -96	1996 -97	1997 -98	1998 -99	1999 -2000	2000 -01
Grossed number of households (thousands)				24,130	24,310	24,560	24,660	25,330	25,030
Total number of households in sample	7,418	6,853	6,797	6,797	6,415	6,409	6,630	7,097	6,637
Total number of persons	18,174	16,617	16,586	16,586	15,732	15,430	16,218	16,786	15,925
Weighted average number of persons per household	2.5	2.4	2.4	2.4	2.5	2.4	2.4	2.3	2.4

Commodity or service	Average weekly household expenditure (£)								
1 Housing (Net)	58.60	54.70	55.10	55.60	54.60	55.50	59.80	58.70	63.90
2 Fuel and power	16.10	15.30	14.70	14.60	14.80	13.50	12.20	11.70	11.90
3 Food and non-alcoholic drinks	59.00	59.40	60.40	61.70	62.60	61.60	61.60	61.40	61.90
4 Alcoholic drink	13.70	14.50	13.00	14.00	14.60	15.30	14.60	15.80	15.00
5 Tobacco	6.70	6.60	6.70	6.70	6.90	6.80	6.10	6.20	6.10
6 Clothing and footwear	20.30	20.20	19.60	20.30	20.90	21.90	22.70	21.60	22.00
7 Household goods	27.10	26.70	26.80	27.20	29.70	29.10	31.00	31.60	32.60
8 Household services	16.60	17.80	17.30	17.30	18.00	19.10	19.80	19.50	22.00
9 Personal goods and services	12.60	12.70	13.20	13.40	13.20	13.70	13.90	14.30	14.70
10 Motoring	44.10	42.60	42.20	43.60	47.00	51.00	54.10	54.10	55.10
11 Fares and other travel costs	8.90	7.80	7.00	7.60	8.60	9.30	8.70	9.40	9.50
12 Leisure goods	16.50	16.40	15.70	16.50	17.60	18.70	18.60	19.10	19.70
13 Leisure services	34.10	36.70	36.60	37.40	39.00	42.60	43.90	45.30	50.60
14 Miscellaneous	2.20	2.70	2.70	1.40	1.10	1.20	1.30	1.50	0.70
1-14 All expenditure groups	336.40	334.00	330.90	337.30	348.50	359.20	368.40	370.20	385.70

Average weekly expenditure per person (£) All expenditure groups	137.30	141.60	135.60	141.00	139.40	149.70	153.50	160.90	163.90

	Average weekly household income (£)[3]								
Gross income (£)	427.60	447.00	434.80	444.80	450.30	463.10	478.00	494.20	502.50
Disposable income (£)	349.20	361.30	350.20	357.50	367.90	377.30	387.80	402.70	409.20

1 From 1974 to this version of 1995-96, figures shown are based on unweighted, adult only data.

2 From this version of 1995-96, figures are shown based on weighted data, including children's expenditure.

3 Does not include imputed income from owner-occupied and rent-free households.

6.2 Household expenditure
as a percentage of total expenditure 1974 to 2000-01
based on unweighted, adult only data

Year	1974	1976	1978	1980	1982	1984	1986	1988	1990
Total number of households in sample	6,695	7,203	7,001	6,944	7,428	7,081	7,178	7,265	7,046
Total number of persons	18,974	19,793	19,019	18,844	20,022	18,557	18,330	18,280	17,437
Weighted average number of persons per household	2.8	2.7	2.7	2.7	2.7	2.6	2.6	2.5	2.5
Commodity or service	**Percentage of total expenditure**								
1 **Housing (Net)**	14	15	15	15	17	16	17	18	18
2 **Fuel and power**	5	6	6	6	6	6	6	5	4
3 **Food and non-alcoholic drinks**	24	25	24	23	21	21	20	19	18
4 **Alcoholic drink**	5	5	5	5	5	5	5	4	4
5 **Tobacco**	4	4	3	3	3	3	3	2	2
6 **Clothing and footwear**	9	8	8	8	7	7	8	7	6
7 **Household goods**	8	7	8	8	7	8	8	7	8
8 **Household services**	3	3	3	4	4	4	5	5	5
9 **Personal goods and services**	3	3	3	4	3	3	4	4	4
10 **Motoring**	11	10	11	12	12	13	12	12	14
11 **Fares and other travel costs**	3	3	3	3	3	2	2	2	3
12 **Leisure goods**	5	4	4	4	5	5	5	5	5
13 **Leisure services**	6	6	6	7	7	7	7	9	9
14 **Miscellaneous**	0	1	1	0	0	0	0	0	1
1-14 **All expenditure groups**	100	100	100	100	100	100	100	100	100

ONS, Family Spending 2000-01, © Crown copyright 2002

6.2 Household expenditure
as a percentage of total expenditure 1974 to 2000-01 (cont.)
based on unweighted, adult only data

Year	1992	1994	1995[1] -96	1995[2] -96	1996 -97	1997 -98	1998 -99	1999 -2000	2000 -01
Grossed number of households (thousands)				24,130	24,310	24,560	24,660	25,330	25,030
Total number of households in sample	7,418	6,853	6,797	6,797	6,415	6,409	6,630	7,097	6,637
Total number of persons	18,174	16,617	16,586	16,586	15,732	15,430	16,218	16,786	15,925
Weighted average number of persons per household	2.5	2.4	2.4	2.4	2.5	2.4	2.4	2.3	2.4

Commodity or service	Percentage of total expenditure								
1 Housing (Net)	17	16	17	16	16	15	16	16	17
2 Fuel and power	5	5	4	4	4	4	3	3	3
3 Food and non-alcoholic drinks	18	18	18	18	18	17	17	17	16
4 Alcoholic drink	4	4	4	4	4	4	4	4	4
5 Tobacco	2	2	2	2	2	2	2	2	2
6 Clothing and footwear	6	6	6	6	6	6	6	6	6
7 Household goods	8	8	8	8	9	8	8	9	8
8 Household services	5	5	5	5	5	5	5	5	6
9 Personal goods and services	4	4	4	4	4	4	4	4	4
10 Motoring	13	13	13	13	13	14	15	15	14
11 Fares and other travel costs	3	2	2	2	2	3	2	3	2
12 Leisure goods	5	5	5	5	5	5	5	5	5
13 Leisure services	10	11	11	11	11	12	12	12	13
14 Miscellaneous	1	1	1	0	0	0	0	0	0
1-14 All expenditure groups	100	100	100	100	100	100	100	100	100

1 From 1974 to this version of 1995-96, figures shown are based on unweighted, adult only data.

6.3 Household expenditure by Standard Statistical Region and UK Countries, 1967 to 2000-01[1] (2000-01 prices)
based on unweighted, adult only data

	North	Yorks and Humber- side	North West	East Midlands	West Midlands	East Anglia	South East
	Average weekly household expenditure (£)						
1 Housing (Net)							
1967-1970	25.90	24.30	28.20	26.10	30.20	28.80	40.50
1977-1980	33.00	31.80	38.30	36.80	42.80	39.90	50.90
1987-1990	44.50	44.90	52.60	57.00	56.30	59.10	72.10
1998-99 - 2000-01	47.50	55.00	53.10	54.80	56.10	58.40	80.90
2 Fuel and power							
1967-1970	15.20	14.40	16.60	15.00	16.10	15.20	16.50
1977-1980	15.00	14.30	15.10	15.30	15.50	16.60	15.40
1987-1990	15.90	16.00	16.30	16.00	15.90	16.10	16.10
1998-99 - 2000-01	11.80	11.80	12.20	11.90	12.30	10.70	11.40
3 Food and non-alcoholic drinks							
1967-1970	63.80	63.10	65.30	64.80	68.30	63.10	69.50
1977-1980	62.50	62.30	62.60	62.80	64.60	60.10	67.50
1987-1990	55.40	56.20	58.30	59.10	58.40	60.20	66.90
1998-99 - 2000-01	53.70	57.70	57.70	60.40	60.20	60.60	68.00
4 Alcoholic drink							
1967-1970	12.20	10.40	12.90	10.70	12.60	8.00	10.10
1977-1980	14.80	13.80	14.00	13.50	14.30	11.00	12.90
1987-1990	14.50	14.30	16.20	13.80	13.10	11.80	14.90
1998-99 - 2000-01	16.40	16.00	16.00	14.70	15.00	12.60	15.90
5 Tobacco							
1967-1970	14.10	12.60	14.00	12.20	13.60	10.70	12.20
1977-1980	10.30	9.80	9.60	8.40	9.00	7.10	7.70
1987-1990	7.40	7.40	8.10	7.20	7.10	5.70	6.30
1998-99 - 2000-01	6.20	6.80	7.10	6.30	6.00	4.80	5.30
6 Clothing and footwear							
1967-1970	22.20	19.40	22.90	20.30	22.30	18.00	24.10
1977-1980	21.80	21.40	22.10	19.00	23.00	18.60	23.80
1987-1990	19.70	20.40	21.80	20.60	21.00	18.90	25.40
1998-99 - 2000-01	20.30	21.60	23.10	19.20	21.00	19.30	25.00
7 Household goods							
1967-1970	17.90	17.30	19.20	20.40	19.90	23.20	23.10
1977-1980	19.90	19.90	20.50	22.30	22.60	20.40	25.70
1987-1990	23.70	23.20	23.50	25.10	24.80	25.70	28.90
1998-99 - 2000-01	27.60	30.20	28.60	32.00	31.80	29.30	34.30

1 1967-1970 to 1987-1990 figures shown are based on unweighted, adult only data. From 1998-99 -2000-01 they are shown based on weighted data, including children's expenditure

ONS, Family Spending 2000-01, © Crown copyright 2002

6.3 Household expenditure by Standard Statistical Region and UK Countries, 1967 to 2000-01[1] (2000-01 prices) (cont.)
based on unweighted, adult only data

	London	South West	Wales	Scotland	Northern Ireland	United Kingdon
	Average weekly household expenditure (£)					
1 Housing (Net)						
1967-1970	44.80	33.50	27.00	24.90	21.40	31.20
1977-1980	52.00	39.70	32.70	28.00	26.30	40.00
1987-1990	72.40	60.00	44.90	42.10	38.30	57.10
1998-99 - 2000-01	80.20	59.00	46.50	50.80	32.30	60.80
2 Fuel and power						
1967-1970	15.70	16.90	15.90	16.90	16.30	16.10
1977-1980	14.40	16.60	17.00	16.50	26.00	15.80
1987-1990	15.60	16.30	17.20	16.60	22.70	16.30
1998-99 - 2000-01	11.30	11.50	12.30	12.70	16.10	11.90
3 Food and non-alcoholic drinks						
1967-1970	72.10	65.00	66.90	68.70	71.10	67.00
1977-1980	69.30	59.90	65.30	65.50	69.30	64.40
1987-1990	69.10	60.90	58.70	58.40	65.30	61.10
1998-99 - 2000-01	69.40	59.00	56.60	60.40	67.30	61.70
4 Alcoholic drink						
1967-1970	11.30	9.10	9.70	11.80	8.30	10.80
1977-1980	13.40	10.90	13.20	14.50	8.70	13.20
1987-1990	16.40	13.40	13.80	14.50	9.90	14.30
1998-99 - 2000-01	15.70	14.50	13.80	15.50	13.60	15.10
5 Tobacco						
1967-1970	13.70	10.80	13.30	15.10	14.40	13.00
1977-1980	8.20	7.30	9.00	11.40	9.90	8.90
1987-1990	6.70	5.90	7.80	9.40	8.20	7.10
1998-99 - 2000-01	5.20	4.80	6.60	8.30	9.40	6.10
6 Clothing and footwear						
1967-1970	26.70	19.60	23.10	24.50	32.60	22.70
1977-1980	24.10	18.20	23.40	24.70	30.00	22.40
1987-1990	26.60	20.40	22.30	23.80	27.10	22.50
1998-99 - 2000-01	25.00	18.20	21.10	23.00	27.80	22.10
7 Household goods						
1967-1970	24.10	21.10	17.80	19.60	16.30	20.40
1977-1980	25.40	19.70	19.70	21.60	15.40	22.10
1987-1990	26.10	27.80	24.00	21.00	25.40	25.60
1998-99 - 2000-01	35.40	30.00	29.10	28.40	30.20	31.80

1 1967-1970 to 1987-1990 figures shown are based on unweighted, adult only data. From 1998-99 -2000-01 they are shown based on weighted data, including children's expenditure

6.3 Household expenditure by Standard Statistical Region and UK Countries, 1967 to 2000-01[1] (2000-01 prices) (cont.)
based on unweighted, adult only data

	North	Yorks and Humber-side	North West	East Midlands	West Midlands	East Anglia	South East
	Average weekly household expenditure (£)						
8 Household services							
1967-1970	8.80	8.80	10.20	9.00	9.70	9.80	12.70
1977-1980	11.50	10.70	11.70	12.00	11.70	9.50	14.30
1987-1990	11.20	13.10	14.20	12.90	13.00	14.30	20.50
1998-99 - 2000-01	15.40	17.90	16.70	17.20	18.40	19.40	26.40
9 Personal goods and services							
1967-1970	5.90	5.90	6.50	6.50	6.80	6.80	8.10
1977-1980	6.70	6.70	7.00	7.30	7.20	6.80	8.60
1987-1990	9.60	10.90	12.00	12.10	11.30	12.10	15.20
1998-99 - 2000-01	10.30	13.70	12.90	13.10	13.00	14.70	17.20
10 Motoring							
1967-1970	22.30	21.70	24.10	25.70	26.80	29.00	30.60
1977-1980	26.50	25.80	28.60	30.80	30.70	30.70	34.80
1987-1990	37.10	38.30	41.60	45.90	44.80	42.90	45.90
1998-99 - 2000-01	40.30	54.10	52.30	55.90	57.40	55.80	56.00
11 Fares and other travel costs							
1967-1970	6.30	6.10	6.70	7.20	7.50	8.10	8.60
1977-1980	6.50	6.30	7.00	7.50	7.50	7.50	8.50
1987-1990	6.10	6.60	7.30	5.70	5.40	6.50	11.60
1998-99 - 2000-01	6.40	8.30	6.80	6.90	6.70	7.30	15.10
12 Leisure goods							
1967-1970	8.70	8.60	9.30	10.10	10.10	10.60	11.50
1977-1980	11.10	11.50	11.70	12.50	12.60	12.20	14.50
1987-1990	12.90	13.80	14.10	16.00	12.50	15.60	18.60
1998-99 - 2000-01	14.70	19.10	17.40	18.70	19.70	19.60	19.80
13 Leisure services							
1967-1970	9.00	9.10	10.60	9.30	10.00	10.00	13.10
1977-1980	12.70	11.80	12.90	13.20	12.80	10.40	15.80
1987-1990	20.70	22.90	27.90	23.90	22.20	30.50	37.80
1998-99 - 2000-01	36.80	43.00	44.40	44.40	43.00	39.30	59.00
14 Miscellaneous							
1967-1970	0.90	0.80	0.80	0.80	0.80	0.60	0.90
1977-1980	1.60	1.80	1.90	1.70	2.00	1.70	3.00
1987-1990	1.40	1.40	1.20	1.60	1.20	1.40	1.80
1998-99 - 2000-01	1.10	0.90	0.90	1.00	1.20	0.90	1.50
1-14 All expenditure groups							
1967-1970	233.00	222.40	247.30	238.20	254.80	242.00	281.40
1977-1980	254.10	247.90	263.10	263.30	276.20	252.60	303.30
1987-1990	280.00	289.30	315.10	316.90	307.10	328.40	382.50
1998-99 - 2000-01	307.30	354.80	346.20	353.00	360.70	351.30	434.90

1 1967-1970 to 1987-1990 figures shown are based on unweighted, adult only data. From 1998-99 -2000-01 they are shown based on weighted data, including children's expenditure

ONS, Family Spending 2000-01, © Crown copyright 2002

6.3 Household expenditure by Standard Statistical Region and UK Countries, 1967 to 2000-01[1] (2000-01 prices) (cont.)

based on unweighted, adult only data

		London	South West	Wales	Scotland	Northern Ireland	United Kingdon
		Average weekly household expenditure (£)					
8	**Household services**						
	1967-1970	13.60	10.90	8.10	9.50	9.50	10.40
	1977-1980	14.60	11.40	10.70	11.60	10.90	12.20
	1987-1990	23.60	15.60	12.60	14.00	13.20	15.60
	1998-99 - 2000-01	27.00	22.10	16.50	16.50	17.50	20.40
9	**Personal goods and services**						
	1967-1970	8.40	7.10	5.70	6.20	5.70	6.90
	1977-1980	8.30	7.10	6.80	6.60	6.30	7.40
	1987-1990	16.30	12.80	11.80	10.70	11.10	12.60
	1998-99 - 2000-01	17.20	15.00	11.90	11.70	12.30	14.30
10	**Motoring**						
	1967-1970	29.80	27.00	24.40	23.00	25.70	26.40
	1977-1980	34.40	28.70	29.80	28.40	29.30	30.50
	1987-1990	39.50	49.00	39.50	34.90	44.70	42.90
	1998-99 - 2000-01	55.40	57.90	45.30	47.40	45.60	54.40
11	**Fares and other travel costs**						
	1967-1970	8.30	7.60	6.90	6.50	7.20	7.40
	1977-1980	8.40	7.00	7.30	7.00	7.20	7.50
	1987-1990	15.50	6.20	6.20	7.90	6.50	8.00
	1998-99 - 2000-01	16.40	6.10	5.40	8.00	6.10	9.20
12	**Leisure goods**						
	1967-1970	11.80	10.30	8.70	9.20	7.80	10.00
	1977-1980	13.90	11.80	11.50	11.50	9.70	12.60
	1987-1990	18.10	16.90	14.10	13.90	12.50	15.60
	1998-99 - 2000-01	22.70	20.80	16.50	18.30	14.20	19.20
13	**Leisure services**						
	1967-1970	14.00	11.20	8.30	9.80	9.80	10.80
	1977-1980	16.10	12.60	11.80	12.70	12.20	13.50
	1987-1990	37.30	29.70	21.30	22.80	21.00	28.70
	1998-99 - 2000-01	61.70	42.60	40.80	37.00	37.60	46.60
14	**Miscellaneous**						
	1967-1970	0.90	0.80	0.90	0.90	1.10	0.80
	1977-1980	2.50	1.80	1.60	1.70	0.80	2.10
	1987-1990	1.90	1.30	1.80	1.40	1.80	1.50
	1998-99 - 2000-01	1.80	1.00	1.00	0.80	1.80	1.20
1-14	**All expenditure groups**						
	1967-1970	295.10	250.80	236.70	246.60	247.20	253.80
	1977-1980	305.10	252.90	259.80	261.50	261.90	270.10
	1987-1990	385.10	336.00	295.90	291.40	307.70	328.80
	1998-99 - 2000-01	439.70	387.00	345.70	325.80	337.80	351.30

1 1967-1970 to 1987-1990 figures shown are based on unweighted, adult only data. From 1998-99 -2000-01 they are shown based on weighted data, including children's expenditure

ONS, Family Spending 2000-01, © Crown copyright 2002

Chapter 7

Detailed expenditure, recent changes & place of purchase

Changes since 1995-96
All expenditures are shown at 2000-01 prices.

● Spending on **mortgage interest** fell between 1995-96 and 1999-2000, but rose in 2000-01.

● Expenditure on **fuel and power** fell by a fifth from £14.60 a week in 1995-96 to £11.70 a week in 1999-2000, but there was little change in 2000-01. The trend was exactly the same for each of gas and electricity as for fuel and power in total.

● Spending on **clothing and footwear** increased from to £20.30 a week in 1995-96 to £22.00 a week in 2000-01. The increase came mainly from women's and girl's outerwear. Spending on **women's outerwear** grew from £6.50 a week in 1995-96 to £7.60 a week in 2000-01. Spending on **men's outerwear** changed very little and was £4.40 in 2000-01.

● Spending on **mobile phones** grew rapidly between 1995-96 and 1999-2000, more than quadrupling from 40p a week to £2.00 a week. There was only a small further increase in 2000-01, to £2.10 a week.

● In 2000-01 spending on **fixed line telephone services and purchase** was nearly three times as high as on **mobiles**, £5.80 a week, and was still rising slowly.

● Spending on **fresh milk** fell by a quarter, from £2.80 in 1995-96 to £2.10 a week in 2000-01.

Frequency and place of purchase

● Eighty per cent of households bought **ready-prepared dishes**, including also pizzas, quiches or vegetarian pies, during a two week period.

● Although 78 per cent of spending on **food and non-alcoholic drink** was in large supermarket chains, 90 per cent of households made at least one purchase in a shop other than these in a two-week period.

● The food items most likely to be bought somewhere else than in a large supermarket chain were **fresh milk,** 50 per cent of spending, **sweets and chocolates,** 40 per cent, and **lamb**, also 40 per cent.

7.1 Expenditure on mortgage interest, rent etc.

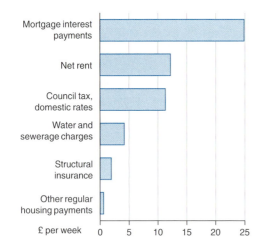

Detailed expenditure in 2000-01

Table 7.1 provides the most detailed breakdown of household expenditure, with a finer breakdown of housing than in previous years. Weekly expenditure is averaged over all households in the survey and is shown for 125 items, many of which are divided further into sub-categories. Details concerning another nine items that are not classified as expenditure items in the context of '*Family Spending*' are also shown, under the heading 'Other items recorded'.

The table also shows proportions of households recording expenditure on different items. Most small purchases are recorded in the fortnight's diary, so the proportions are just for a two-week period. Credit card purchases are recorded in the diary, but purchases with other types of deferred or spread payments are recorded in the questionnaire, with varying recording periods. Other expenditures, recorded only in the household interview, relate to payments in the last three months (e.g. central heating oil) or twelve months (e.g. household contents insurance) or, for regular bills, to the most recent payment (e.g. telephone bills). Proportions recording expenditure are not, therefore, all comparable.

Some of the standard errors shown in **Table 7.1** are a little higher than those shown elsewhere. They have been calculated by **a** better method, but one that is too resource-intensive to be used generally. **Appendix C** gives the details.

Rent, mortgage interest, water charges, property taxes and buildings insurance

Previous reports showed only the total of spending on rent, mortgage interest, water charges, property taxes and structural insurance. **Table 7.1** now gives a breakdown of these components. **Figure 7.1** shows that a large proportion of the total of £55 a week was made up by mortgage interest payments, which were £24.90 a week. The other two large items were net rent, at £12.20 a week, and property taxes at £11.30 a week. Water and sewerage charges were £4.20 a week and structural insurance was less than half that at £1.90 a week.

ONS, Family Spending 2000-01, © Crown copyright 2002

Net rent is rent after deduction of Housing Benefit, and property taxes are Council Tax in England, Scotland and Wales and rates in Northern Ireland. Like all figures in the table, the expenditures are averaged across all households. That means, for example, that rent averaged just over renters would be much higher than the figure shown.

Ready-prepared dishes and pizzas

Items 3.33 and 3.34 in **Table 7.1** show a breakdown of expenditure on ready-prepared dishes and pizzas, quiches and vegetarian pies. Eighty per cent of households were spending on ready-prepared dishes and pizzas during the two-week diary period, with an average expenditure of £2.80 a week. **Figure 7.2** shows proportions of expenditure spent on the different types of ready-prepared dishes and pizzas. Over a third of expenditure was spent on ready-prepared meat dishes at 34 per cent and just over a quarter was spent on pizzas, quiches and vegetarian pies. Proportions spent on vegetable dishes and vegetarian foods and other convenience foods were both the same at 12 to 14 per cent. Expenditure on fish dishes and sandwiches, filled rolls and baguettes were approximately half of this at 6 to 7 per cent.

Changes between 1995-96, 1999-2000 and 2000-01

There were significant changes in expenditure on a number of items in 2000-01 compared with the previous twelve months and with 1995-96. These are shown at 2000-01 prices.

Mortgages v rents

Figure 7.3 shows expenditure on mortgage interest payments compared with net rent over the period 1995-96 to 1999-2000 and 2000-01. Expenditure on mortgage interest payments fell between 1995-96 and 1999-2000, but increased substantially between then and 2000-01. One reason is that tax relief on mortgage interest ended in April 2000. Other reasons were that interest rates were higher in 2000-01 than in 1999-2000 and house prices were also higher. Averaged over all households, spending on rent (net of Housing Benefit) was about half of spending on mortgage interest. It rose throughout the period, from £9.60 a week in 1995-96 to £12.20 in 2000-01.

7.2 **Proportions of expenditure on ready-prepared dishes and pizzas**

Per cent

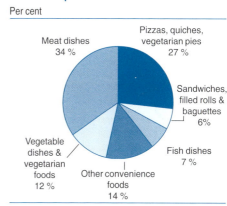

7.3 **Mortgages v rents**

£ per week, at 2000-01 prices

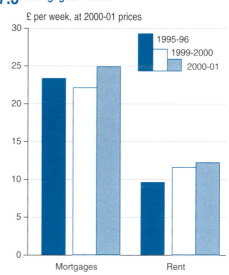

7.4 **Expenditure on fuel and power**

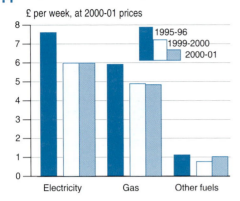

£ per week, at 2000-01 prices

Fuel and power

Figure 7.4 shows changes in expenditure on fuel and power since 1995-96. Average weekly household expenditure on fuel and power fell between 1995-96 and 1999-2000, from £14.60 to £11.70 a week, but there was little change between 1999-2000 and 2000-01. Expenditure on electricity fell by a fifth between 1995-96 and 1999-2000 from £7.60 to £6.00 a week, remaining the same in 2000-01. Gas expenditure fell by £1.00 between 1995-96 and 1999-2000 from £5.90 to £4.90 a week. This also remained constant for 2000-01.

7.5 **Expenditure on outerwear clothing**

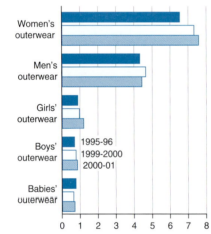

£ per week, at 2000-01 prices

Outerwear clothing

Over the period 1995-96 to 2000-01, expenditure on clothing and footwear rose from £20.30 to £22.00 a week. The detailed breakdown for outerwear in **Figure 7.5** shows that spending on both women's and girls' outerwear increased over the last five years, but there was little change in spending on men's or boys' outerwear. Women's outerwear had the highest expenditure, growing from £6.50 a week in 1995-96 to £7.60 a week in 2000-01. Spending on men's outerwear remained fairly constant in these years at about £4.50 a week. Expenditure on girls' outerwear rose from 90 pence a week in 1995-96, to £1.20 a week in 2000-01. Spending on boys' outerwear and on babies' outerwear remained fairly constant over the years at 60 to 80 pence a week for each.

Mobile and fixed line telephones

Growth in spending on mobile phones was rapid between 1995-96 and 1999-2000, when it quadrupled from 40p a week to £2.00 a week. It then slowed down with only a small increase between 1999-2000 and 2000-01. Purchase and running costs are combined for these comparisons, shown in **Figure 7.6**, which also shows the trends for fixed line telephones. There was a small but steady increase in spending on fixed line telephones. In 2000-01 spending on fixed line telephone services and purchase was still nearly three times as high as on mobiles, £5.80 a week compared with £2.10.

7.6 **Expenditure on telephones and mobile phones**

£ per week, at 2000-01 prices

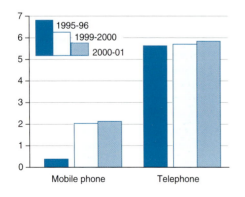

ONS, Family Spending 2000-01, © Crown copyright 2002

Analysis of expenditure by place of purchase

Food

Table 7.3 shows that 78 per cent of spending on food and non-alcoholic drink was in large supermarket chains and only 22 per cent in other outlets. Nevertheless 90 per cent of households made at least one purchase in a shop other than a large supermarket chain during the two week diary-keeping period. Supermarkets took high shares of spending for breakfast cereals, over 90 per cent, and for biscuits and cakes, over 80 per cent as shown in **Figure 7.7**. The highest shares for other outlets were for fresh milk, 50 per cent, sweets and chocolates, just over 40 per cent and for lamb, also just over 40 per cent. Expenditure on fresh fruit and vegetables had a lower share in other outlets at about 20 per cent.

Motor fuel and tobacco

Table 7.4 illustrates expenditure on selected items by place of purchase. **Figure 7.8** shows expenditure on petrol and diesel by place of purchase. Spending on both petrol and diesel were greater in other outlets in comparison with large supermarkets. Nearly half of all households purchased petrol from other outlets, whilst a quarter of all households bought petrol from large supermarket chains. Expenditure on petrol in other outlets was an average of £10.00 a week in 2000-01. Expenditure was less than half this amount in large supermarkets at £4.00 a week. Spending on diesel was £1.30 a week in other outlets and a third of this amount in large supermarkets at an average of 40 pence a week.

Figure 7.9 shows expenditure on tobacco in large supermarket chains and other outlets. Nearly a third of all households bought tobacco from other outlets whilst 16 per cent of all households purchased tobacco from large supermarket chains. Expenditure on cigarettes was £1.60 a week when bought in large supermarket chains and more than double this amount when purchased in other outlets at an average of £3.80 a week. Spending on tobacco and other tobacco products had similar patterns by place of purchase. Average weekly household expenditure on tobacco and other tobacco products was 20 pence a week when bought in large supermarket chains and more than double in other outlets at 50 pence a week.

7.7 Expenditure on selected food items by place of purchase

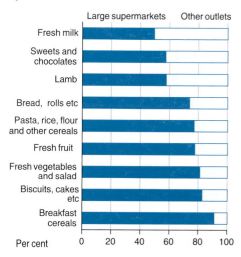

7.8 Petrol and diesel

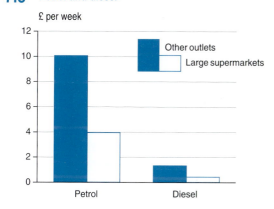

7.9 Tobacco

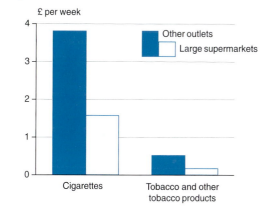

7.1 Components of household expenditure
based on weighted data and including children's expenditure

2000-01

	Average weekly expenditure all house-holds (£)	Total weekly expenditure (£ million)	Recording house-holds in sample	Percentage standard error (full method)
Total number of households			**6,637**	
Commodity or service				
1 Housing (Net)	**63.90**	**1,600**	**6,485**	*1.4*
1.1 Gross rent, mortgage interest payments, water charges, council tax, etc	64.70	1,621	6,595	*1.0*
1.1.1 Gross rent	21.90	548	4,117	*2.4*
1.2 *less* housing benefit, rebates and allowances received	9.70	243	2,704	*2.7*
1.3 Net rent, mortgage interest payments, water charges, council tax, etc	55.00	1,378	6,445	*1.3*
1.3.1 Mortgage interest payments	24.90	622	2,652	*2.2*
1.3.2 Net rent	12.20	305	1,413	*3.9*
1.3.3 Council tax, domestic rates	11.30	283	5,516	*0.9*
1.3.4 Water and sewerage charges	4.20	104	5,669	*1.0*
1.3.5 Structural insurance	1.90	48	4,003	*1.8*
1.3.6 Other regular housing payments	0.60	15	667	*10.2*
1.4 Repairs, maintenance and decorations	8.90	222	3,516	*5.2*
1.4.1 Central heating repairs	0.90	23	1,613	*7.8*
1.4.2 House maintenance etc (contracted out)	3.20	80	1,561	*5.5*
1.4.3 Paint, wallpaper, plaster, wood	1.50	36	791	*6.0*
1.4.4 Doors, electrical & other fittings	1.70	43	635	*15.3*
1.4.5 Tools, eg paint brushes, spanners	0.40	10	530	*8.9*
1.4.6 Other materials, hire of equipment	1.20	29	984	*15.7*
2 Fuel and power	**11.90**	**297**	**6,353**	*1.1*
2.1 Gas	4.80	121	4,712	*1.3*
2.2 Electricity	6.00	150	6,167	*1.7*
2.3 Other fuels	1.00	26	794	*6.1*
2.3.1 Coal and coke	0.30	8	357	*8.7*
2.3.2 Fuel oil for central heating	0.60	15	402	*7.4*
2.3.3 Paraffin, calor gas, candles, firewood	0.10	3	124	*16.5*
3 Food and non-alcoholic drinks	**61.90**	**1,550**	**6,631**	*0.8*
3.1 Bread, rolls etc	1.80	45	6,385	*1.0*
3.2 Pasta, rice, flour and other cereals	0.50	12	3,048	*3.4*
3.2.1 Pasta - dried or fresh	0.20	5	1,909	*3.8*
3.2.2 Flour, rice and other cereals	0.30	7	1,910	*4.9*
3.3 Biscuits, cakes etc	2.90	72	6,008	*1.3*
3.3.1 Biscuits, shortbread, wafers, chocolate biscuits	1.20	31	5,177	*1.4*
3.3.2 Cakes, buns, currant bread, fruit pies, pasties, scones	1.60	39	5,140	*1.7*
3.3.3 Pastry, cake mixes	0.00	1	496	*5.6*
3.4 Breakfast cereals	0.90	21	3,911	*1.6*
3.5 Beef and veal (uncooked)	1.50	37	3,535	*2.1*
3.6 Mutton and lamb (uncooked)	0.60	15	1,510	*3.5*
3.7 Pork (uncooked)	0.60	16	2,032	*2.5*
3.8 Bacon and ham (uncooked)	0.90	22	3,373	*1.9*
3.9 Poultry (uncooked)	2.00	50	4,080	*1.7*
3.10 Cold meats, ready to eat meats	1.40	36	4,781	*1.6*
3.11 Meat pies, sausages and other meats	1.30	32	4,602	*1.5*
3.11.1 Sausages (uncooked)	0.40	11	2,746	*2.3*
3.11.2 Offal and other uncooked meats	0.10	2	494	*7.4*
3.11.3 Tinned and bottled meat, meat products	0.10	4	1,393	*3.2*
3.11.4 Meat and poultry pies and pasties	0.60	15	2,999	*2.1*

ONS, Family Spending 2000-01, © Crown copyright 2002

7.1 Components of household expenditure (cont.)
based on weighted data and including children's expenditure

2000-01

Commodity or service	Average weekly expenditure all house-holds (£)	Total weekly expenditure (£ million)	Recording house-holds in sample	Percentage standard error (full method)
3 Food and non-alcoholic drinks (continued)				
3.12 Fish, shellfish and fish products	1.50	38	4,149	2.2
3.12.1 Fish (uncooked) and shellfish	0.80	20	2,223	2.9
3.12.2 Processed fish (smoked, dried, canned, bottled)	0.40	11	2,421	3.0
3.12.3 Fish (prepared) and fish products	0.30	7	1,573	3.3
3.13 Butter	0.30	7	2,223	2.6
3.14 Margarine	0.40	10	3,509	1.8
3.15 Cooking oils and fats	0.20	5	1,711	3.7
3.16 Fresh milk	2.10	52	6,150	1.3
3.17 Milk products including cream	1.40	35	5,004	1.6
3.17.1 Yoghurt & milk based desserts	1.10	28	4,545	1.7
3.17.2 Other milk and cream	0.30	7	2,092	3.8
3.18 Cheese	1.30	32	4,754	1.6
3.19 Eggs	0.40	10	3,891	1.6
3.20 Potatoes, potato products (excluding crisps)	1.20	31	5,372	1.2
3.20.1 Potatoes	0.80	20	4,728	1.4
3.20.2 Processed potatoes & products	0.40	11	2,893	2.0
3.21 Other vegetables	3.30	81	6,194	1.1
3.21.1 Fresh vegetables and salad	2.40	61	5,796	1.2
3.21.2 Processed & frozen vegetables	0.60	14	4,111	1.8
3.21.3 Pulses, dried and processed	0.30	7	3,447	2.1
3.22 Fruit, nuts	2.80	70	5,712	1.4
3.22.1 Fresh fruit	2.30	58	5,504	1.4
3.22.2 Processed fruit	0.20	4	1,730	3.3
3.22.3 Dried fruit and nuts	0.30	7	1,611	3.8
3.23 Sugar	0.20	5	2,475	2.6
3.24 Jam, jellies, preserves and other spreads	0.30	6	2,320	2.4
3.25 Sweets and chocolates	2.00	50	5,015	2.0
3.26 Ice cream and sorbets	0.50	12	2,392	2.5
3.27 Tea	0.50	12	2,816	2.2
3.28 Coffee	0.50	13	2,187	2.5
3.29 Drinking chocolate, other food drinks	0.20	4	890	5.3
3.30 Fruit juice, squashes, bottled water	1.40	34	4,706	1.6
3.30.1 Fruit juices, squashes	1.20	29	4,426	1.6
3.30.2 Bottled water (still & sparkling)	0.20	5	1,359	3.9
3.31 Fizzy drinks	1.00	26	4,058	2.0
3.32 Soup	0.30	7	2,432	2.6
3.33 Pizzas, quiches, vegetarian pies	0.80	19	3,048	2.0
3.34 Other convenience foods	2.20	55	4,808	1.8
3.34.1 Dishes ready prepared:	2.10	52	4,774	1.8
3.34.1.1 Meat dishes	1.00	25	2,773	2.4
3.34.1.2 Fish dishes	0.20	5	870	4.7
3.34.1.3 Vegetable dishes and vegetarian foods	0.30	8	2,023	3.6
3.34.1.4 Sandwiches, filled rolls and baguettes	0.20	4	803	4.9
3.34.1.5 Other convenience foods	0.30	8	1,954	2.9
3.34.1.6 Pasta cooked e.g tinned pasta	0.10	2	1,193	3.8
3.34.2 Baby and diet foods	0.10	3	228	9.1
3.35 Potato crisps and savoury snacks	1.00	25	4,318	1.5

7.1 Components of household expenditure (cont.)
based on weighted data and including children's expenditure

2000-01

	Average weekly expenditure all house-holds (£)	Total weekly expenditure (£ million)	Recording house-holds in sample	Percentage standard error (full method)
Commodity or service				
3 Food and non-alcoholic drinks (continued)				
3.36 Restaurant and café meals	10.40	260	4,634	2.3
3.37 Take-away meals eaten at home	3.60	90	3,065	2.3
3.38 Other take-away food and snack food	4.50	113	4,413	1.7
3.38.1 Hot and cold food	3.00	76	3,903	1.9
3.38.2 Confectionery	0.50	13	2,737	2.5
3.38.3 Ice cream	0.20	5	1,013	4.2
3.38.4 Soft drinks	0.80	19	2,887	2.3
3.39 State school meals and meals at work	2.00	50	2,393	2.6
3.39.1 Meals bought & eaten at the workplace	1.50	37	2,002	2.9
3.39.2 State school meals	0.50	13	754	4.7
3.40 Other foods	1.60	39	5,229	2.1
3.40.1 Pickles, sauces, flavourings, colourings	1.50	37	5,190	1.6
3.40.2 Other foods undefined	0.10	2	294	22.5
4 Alcoholic drink	**15.00**	**376**	**4,580**	*1.8*
4.1 Beer, cider	7.70	194	3,469	2.1
4.1.1 Beer and lager	7.40	186	3,362	2.2
4.1.2 Cider	0.30	8	536	9.3
4.2 Wines, fortified wines	3.60	91	2,712	2.8
4.2.1 Fortified wines	0.20	6	413	6.7
4.2.2 Non-fortified wines, still wines	3.20	80	2,508	2.9
4.2.3 Champagne & sparkling wine	0.20	5	185	13.4
4.3 Spirits, liqueurs	2.20	56	1,689	3.7
4.4 Other drinks	1.40	36	921	8.1
4.4.1 Alcoholic soft drinks	0.30	8	486	7.1
4.4.2 Other drinks undefined	1.10	28	490	10.4
5 Tobacco	**6.10**	**152**	**2,201**	*2.5*
5.1 Cigarettes	5.40	135	2,030	2.8
5.2 Tobacco & other tobacco products	0.70	17	565	6.4
5.2.1 Pipe and cigarette tobacco	0.50	13	451	6.6
5.2.2 Cigars and snuff	0.20	5	122	14.9

ONS, Family Spending 2000-01, © Crown copyright 2002

7.1 Components of household expenditure (cont.)
based on weighted data and including children's expenditure

2000-01

		Average weekly expenditure all house-holds (£)	Total weekly expenditure (£ million)	Recording house-holds in sample	Percentage standard error (full method)
Commodity or service					
6	**Clothing and footwear**	**22.00**	**550**	**4,679**	*2.0*
6.1	Men's outerwear	4.40	110	1,346	*4.0*
6.2	Men's underwear and hosiery	0.50	12	664	*5.6*
6.3	Women's outerwear	7.60	189	2,335	*2.8*
6.4	Women's underwear and hosiery	1.20	31	1,499	*4.3*
6.5	Boys' outerwear	0.80	21	493	*7.3*
6.6	Girls' outerwear	1.20	30	665	*5.7*
6.7	Babies' outerwear	0.70	17	555	*6.2*
6.8	Boys', girls' and babies' underwear	0.40	10	724	*5.0*
6.9	Ties, belts, hats, gloves, etc	0.60	14	924	*5.4*
6.9.1	Men's	0.20	5	312	*8.4*
6.9.2	Women's	0.20	6	393	*9.0*
6.9.3	Children's	0.10	3	328	*8.0*
6.10	Haberdashery, textiles & clothes hire	0.40	11	578	*10.1*
6.10.1	Haberdashery, wool	0.10	3	426	*10.0*
6.10.2	Textiles and clothes hire	0.30	8	200	*13.3*
6.11	Footwear	4.20	105	1,769	*4.0*
6.11.1	Men's	1.50	37	538	*7.7*
6.11.2	Women's	1.80	46	972	*4.3*
6.11.3	Children's	0.90	22	599	*5.7*
6.11.4	Undefined	0.00	0	3	*68.4*
7	**Household goods**	**32.60**	**817**	**6,421**	*2.6*
7.1	Furniture	9.30	232	1,446	*5.2*
7.2	Floor coverings	3.30	83	976	*6.4*
7.2.1	Soft floor coverings, carpets, mats	3.00	76	936	*6.5*
7.2.2	Hard floor coverings, vinyl, tiles etc	0.30	8	58	*23.8*
7.3	Soft furnishings and bedding	1.90	48	1,005	*6.7*
7.3.1	Bedspreads, blankets, duvets, pillows, sheets, excluding beds & mattresses	0.70	18	417	*8.7*
7.3.2	Curtains, cushions, towels etc	1.20	30	711	*8.2*
7.4	Gas and electric appliances, including repairs	4.60	114	1,287	*6.5*
7.4.1	Gas cookers	0.20	4	08	*51.8*
7.4.2	Other gas appliances eg fires, showers, water heaters	0.10	3	39	*57.9*
7.4.3	Electric cookers and combined electric/gas cookers	0.30	9	72	*27.7*
7.4.4	Washing machines, spin dryers	0.60	15	153	*18.4*
7.4.5	Refrigerators, freezers	0.50	13	109	*21.4*
7.4.6	Other major electrical appliances eg fires, dishwashers, microwave ovens, vacuum cleaners, showers	0.80	21	177	*11.1*
7.4.7	Electrical tools eg drills, paint strippers	0.40	10	77	*35.0*
7.4.8	Small electrical equipment eg hair dryers, shavers, irons	1.00	24	558	*6.0*
7.4.9	Repairs to gas and electric appliances, insurance and spare parts	0.60	15	305	*9.9*
7.5	Kitchen/garden equipment, household hardware	5.00	125	3,613	*6.7*
7.5.1	China, glassware (not mirrors), pottery, cutlery, silverware, clocks	0.70	18	699	*8.4*
7.5.2	Fancy, decorative goods, mirrors	1.80	45	1,474	*15.1*
7.5.3	Kitchen equipment, tableware and utensils	0.80	21	1,990	*4.4*
7.5.4	Other household hardware and appliances	0.80	19	1,300	*5.5*
7.5.5	Garden equipment - barbecues, lawn mowers, wheel barrows	0.30	8	152	*19.3*
7.5.6	Garden tools and accessories	0.20	5	248	*21.2*
7.5.7	Garden furniture	0.30	8	71	*30.4*
7.6	Kitchen & electrical consumables	1.00	26	3,968	*2.2*
7.6.1	Electrical consumables eg batteries, light bulbs	0.50	12	1,522	*3.7*
7.6.2	Kitchen disposables eg paper towels, foil, grease proof paper, drinking straws, bin liners, matches	0.60	14	3,381	*2.4*

7.1 Components of household expenditure (cont.)
based on weighted data and including children's expenditure

2000-01

	Average weekly expenditure all house-holds (£)	Total weekly expenditure (£ million)	Recording house-holds in sample	Percentage standard error (full method)
Commodity or service				
7 Household goods (continued)				
7.7 Greeting cards, stationery and paper goods	1.80	45	3,933	2.6
7.8 Detergents and other cleaning materials	2.00	50	5,054	1.6
7.8.1 Detergents, washing-up liquid, washing powder	1.00	25	3,765	1.9
7.8.2 Disinfectants, polishes, other cleaning materials	1.00	25	4,074	2.1
7.9 Toilet paper	0.70	18	3,581	1.6
7.10 Pets and pet food	3.00	75	2,598	5.2
7.10.1 Pet food	1.50	37	2,484	3.0
7.10.2 Pet care eg purchase, equipment, veterinary services	1.50	38	837	9.0
8 Household services	**22.00**	**550**	**6,504**	**2.3**
8.1 Insurance of contents of dwelling	2.00	51	4,923	2.0
8.2 Postage	0.50	13	2,038	3.9
8.3 Telephone	8.40	209	6,271	1.3
8.3.1 Telephone account	5.70	144	5,985	1.2
8.3.2 Payphones and phone cards	0.20	4	407	8.2
8.3.3 Mobile phone account	1.70	41	1,455	4.3
8.3.4 Mobile phone other payments - top up cards	0.80	20	743	4.8
8.4 Domestic help and child care	3.40	85	1,575	5.6
8.4.1 Domestic help, including service element in rent	1.60	39	1,291	5.7
8.4.2 Child care payments	1.20	31	234	10.0
8.4.3 Nursery, creche, playschools	0.60	15	158	16.6
8.5 Repairs to footwear, watches etc	0.30	7	154	24.8
8.5.1 Repairs to footwear	0.00	1	85	13.8
8.5.2 Repairs to other goods, eg furniture, jewellery, watches	0.20	6	71	29.5
8.6 Laundry, cleaning and dyeing	0.40	10	407	8.2
8.6.1 Laundry, launderettes	0.10	2	138	12.2
8.6.2 Dry cleaning, carpet cleaning and dyeing	0.30	8	281	9.7
8.7 Subscriptions	1.10	27	1,693	7.3
8.7.1 Subscriptions to trade unions and professional organisations	0.70	17	1,247	10.0
8.7.2 Subscriptions: leisure activities eg National Trust, Weight Watchers	0.30	7	481	11.1
8.7.3 Other subscriptions eg political parties, residents' associations, Scouts	0.10	3	222	16.8
8.8 Professional fees	2.20	55	477	9.6
8.8.1 Moving house	1.80	46	442	9.0
8.8.1.1 Buying and selling house	0.80	20	137	15.1
8.8.1.2 Selling house only	0.50	12	92	17.6
8.8.1.3 Buying house only	0.40	11	189	15.5
8.8.1.4 Unsuccessful transaction, second mortgage, remortgage	0.10	3	118	14.9
8.8.2 Legal fees excluding moving house	0.40	9	41	35.4
8.9 Other services	3.70	92	2,524	9.4
8.9.1 Bank charges	0.30	8	994	8.7
8.9.2 Stamp duties, fees & licences other than vehicle and TV licences eg marriage licence, passport fee, driving test fee, bank and Post Office counter charges	0.20	5	107	15.7
8.9.3 Second dwelling rent, council tax, water rates, mortgage payments, insurance	0.10	3	26	24.0
8.9.4 Moving & storage of furniture	0.30	7	249	12.5
8.9.5 Contract catering for weddings etc	0.70	17	29	36.9
8.9.6 Funeral expenses	0.10	2	13	42.5
8.9.7 Court fines, accountant, architect, bill paying services, other professional fees	0.50	13	53	37.9
8.9.8 Rental or hire of electrical or household equipment, skips, emptying septic tank, payment to friend for DIY, photocopying charges	0.50	12	616	10.5
8.9.9 Mortgage protection premiums	1.00	25	1,111	4.0

ONS, Family Spending 2000-01, © Crown copyright 2002

7.1

Components of household expenditure (cont.)
based on weighted data and including children's expenditure

2000-01

Commodity or service		Average weekly expenditure all house-holds (£)	Total weekly expenditure (£ million)	Recording house-holds in sample	Percentage standard error (full method)
9	**Personal goods and services**	**14.70**	**368**	**5,967**	*2.0*
9.1	Leather and travel goods, jewellery, watches etc	2.10	53	1,493	*6.2*
9.1.1	Leather & travel goods, umbrellas, walking sticks	0.70	17	698	*6.8*
9.1.2	Personal effects eg jewellery, watches, personal silverware	1.50	36	1,008	*8.8*
9.2	Baby toiletries and equipment	0.80	19	916	*6.6*
9.2.1	Baby toiletries and disposables	0.50	13	878	*4.0*
9.2.2	Baby equipment - prams, bedding	0.30	6	109	*17.6*
9.3	Medicines, prescriptions and spectacles	3.10	79	3,364	*5.6*
9.3.1	NHS prescription charges	0.30	6	368	*6.1*
9.3.2	Non NHS: medicines, lotions, surgical goods, dressings and appliances	1.30	33	3,041	*3.2*
9.3.3	Spectacles, lenses, prescription sunglasses	1.40	35	309	*11.7*
9.3.4	Accessories: eg contact lens cleaning fluid inc non-prescription sunglasses	0.10	3	200	*10.5*
9.4	Medical, dental, optical and nursing fees	1.60	41	554	*7.4*
9.4.1	NHS payments - dentists, medical & optical fees	0.90	23	347	*9.2*
9.4.2	Private medical, dental, nursing & optical fees	0.70	18	226	*12.9*
9.5	Toiletries and soap	1.90	47	4,588	*1.9*
9.5.1	Toiletries - cotton wool, toothpaste, shaving soap and brushes	1.20	30	3,933	*2.1*
9.5.2	Toilet soap	0.30	8	1,768	*3.7*
9.5.3	Other toilet requisites eg razors, toothbrushes	0.40	10	1,575	*4.0*
9.6	Cosmetics and hair products	2.50	62	3,563	*2.7*
9.6.1	Hair products - shampoo, colour rinses	0.70	18	2,325	*2.7*
9.6.2	Cosmetics and related accessories including after shave, sun lotion	1.80	44	2,509	*3.5*
9.7	Hairdressing, beauty treatment	2.70	67	1,989	*3.3*
10	**Motoring**	**55.10**	**1,379**	**4,948**	*1.8*
10.1	Cars, vans & motorcycle purchase	23.00	575	1,834	*3.5*
10.1.1	New cars and vans:	10.60	265	690	*6.0*
10.1.1.1	Outright purchases	5.30	131	192	*8.7*
10.1.1.2	Loans etc	5.30	134	548	*7.0*
10.1.2	Second-hand cars and vans:	11.80	295	1,235	*4.3*
10.1.2.1	Outright purchases	8.70	218	842	*5.0*
10.1.2.2	Loans etc	3.10	78	534	*5.7*
10.1.3	Motor cycles and scooters:	0.60	14	89	*14.6*
10.1.3.1	Outright purchases	0.40	9	50	*18.1*
10.1.3.2	Loans etc	0.20	5	49	*16.6*
10.2	Spares and accessories	1.70	43	570	*7.5*
10.2.1	Car accessories & fittings - durables eg radios, seat covers	0.30	7	158	*16.8*
10.2.2	Car spare parts	1.20	31	387	*8.6*
10.2.3	Motor cycle accessories & spare parts	0.20	4	36	*33.1*
10.2.4	Motor cycle service & repairs	0.10	2	35	*23.3*
10.3	Car and van repairs and servicing	4.50	113	2,011	*4.0*
10.4	Motor vehicle insurance and taxation	8.20	206	4,604	*1.4*
10.4.1	Vehicle taxation payments less refunds	2.50	62	4,448	*1.2*
10.4.2	Vehicle insurance	5.70	144	4,527	*1.6*
10.5	Petrol, diesel and other motor oils	15.80	396	4,261	*1.6*
10.5.1	Petrol	14.00	351	3,933	*1.6*
10.5.2	Diesel	1.80	44	584	*5.1*
10.5.3	Other motor oils	0.10	2	130	*12.1*

7.1 Components of household expenditure (cont.)
based on weighted data and including children's expenditure

2000-01

Commodity or service		Average weekly expenditure all house-holds (£)	Total weekly expenditure (£ million)	Recording house-holds in sample	Percentage standard error (full method)
10	**Motoring (continued)**				
10.6	Other motoring costs	1.80	46	2,597	4.2
10.6.1	Driving lessons	0.30	7	90	16.9
10.6.2	Garage rent, motoring fines, MOT tests, car wash, tools	0.60	14	498	7.8
10.6.3	AA, RAC etc subscriptions	0.30	8	922	6.9
10.6.4	Anti-freeze, battery water, cleaning materials	0.10	2	324	8.7
10.6.5	Parking fees, tolls and permits	0.60	14	1,635	4.8
11	**Fares and other travel costs**	**9.50**	**237**	**3,447**	**4.3**
11.1	Rail and tube fares	2.00	50	856	6.2
11.1.1	Season tickets	0.60	14	137	10.0
11.1.2	Other than season tickets	1.40	36	784	7.6
11.2	Bus and coach fares	1.40	35	2,017	3.5
11.2.1	Season tickets	0.30	7	235	8.8
11.2.2	Other than season tickets	1.10	28	1,924	3.5
11.3	Taxis, air and other travel	5.20	130	1,947	6.9
11.3.1	Domestic air travel	0.20	5	10	58.9
11.3.2	International air travel	1.10	28	43	25.0
11.3.3	Combined fares other than season tickets	0.20	5	144	11.6
11.3.4	Combined fares season tickets	0.70	17	134	11.7
11.3.5	Travel to state schools	0.00	1	65	18.0
11.3.6	Taxis and hired cars with drivers	1.40	34	1,335	3.9
11.3.7	Other personal travel - coach trips, furniture delivery, lift contributions	0.30	7	292	9.5
11.3.8	Hire of self-drive cars & vans	0.20	5	26	30.5
11.3.9	Car leasing payments	0.90	23	146	15.7
11.3.10	Water travel, ferries and season tickets	0.20	4	73	27.3
11.4	Bicycle, boats - purchases and repairs	0.80	21	232	11.2
11.4.1	Bicycle purchase	0.20	6	44	20.4
11.4.2	Bicycles, other costs	0.10	4	130	13.3
11.4.3	Boats etc, purchase and other costs	0.50	11	71	23.2
12	**Leisure goods**	**19.70**	**494**	**6,290**	**2.7**
12.1	Books, maps, diaries, address books, sheet music	1.70	41	1,757	4.5
12.2	Newspapers	2.00	50	5,063	1.8
12.3	Magazines and periodicals	1.00	26	3,334	3.1
12.4	TV, video, computers and audio equipment	8.80	221	2,591	5.2
12.4.1	Purchase of TV and digital TV decoder	1.10	28	200	19.3
12.4.2	Satellite dish purchase and installation	0.00	1	11	33.0
12.4.3	Audio equipment, CD players	0.80	21	182	12.9
12.4.4	CD's, audio cassettes, - hire and purchase	1.50	38	1,169	4.0
12.4.5	Accessories for audio equipment, cassette cases, racks	0.10	4	124	21.6
12.4.6	Video recorders	0.30	8	85	15.3
12.4.7	Purchase and rental of video cassettes, etc	0.90	24	1,174	4.5
12.4.8	Personal computers, printers, calculators	1.80	45	230	18.3
12.4.9	Computer games, cartridges and computer software	0.70	18	334	7.8
12.4.10	Musical instruments and hire of instruments	0.10	3	43	31.4
12.4.11	Repair of TV, computers, audio equipment inc insurance	0.60	16	309	14.7
12.4.12	Telephone purchase	0.10	2	55	20.4
12.4.13	Mobile phone purchase	0.50	12	176	10.0
12.4.14	Answering machines, faxes, modems	0.10	2	20	29.3
12.5	Sports and camping equipment	0.90	22	470	14.9
12.6	Toys and hobbies	2.10	52	1,637	4.5
12.7	Photography and camcorders, including developing	1.10	27	915	9.5
12.8	Horticultural goods, plants, flowers	2.20	55	2,369	4.4

ONS, Family Spending 2000-01, © Crown copyright 2002

7.1 Components of household expenditure (cont.)
based on weighted data and including children's expenditure

2000-01

Commodity or service	Average weekly expenditure all households (£)	Total weekly expenditure (£ million)	Recording households in sample	Percentage standard error (full method)
13 Leisure services	**50.60**	**1,267**	**6,545**	*2.7*
13.1 Cinema and theatre	1.20	30	936	*5.2*
13.1.1 Cinema admissions	0.50	11	629	*5.0*
13.1.2 Theatres, concerts, circuses, amateur shows	0.70	19	370	*7.8*
13.2 Sports admissions and subscriptions	3.30	82	2,209	*7.5*
13.2.1 Spectator sports - admission charges	0.60	16	228	*17.0*
13.2.2 Participant sports excluding subscriptions	1.30	33	1,516	*3.5*
13.2.3 Subscriptions to sports and social clubs	1.40	34	985	*15.3*
13.3 TV, video, satellite rental, TV licences and Internet	4.40	111	6,277	*1.6*
13.3.1 Television licences	2.00	49	6,201	*1.5*
13.3.2 Television slot meter payments	0.00	1	26	*23.6*
13.3.3 Rent for TV, VCR, satellite TV	0.50	13	626	*4.9*
13.3.4 Satellite TV subscription to channels	1.10	27	1,167	*3.2*
13.3.5 Cable TV subscription and connection	0.80	19	860	*4.5*
13.3.6 Internet subscription fees	0.10	2	91	*35.5*
13.4 Miscellaneous entertainments	1.40	34	1,586	*5.2*
13.4.1 Admission to dance & miscellaneous entertainment eg admissions to stately homes, museums, nightclubs etc	1.20	29	1,314	*5.5*
13.4.2 Social events & gatherings, including car boot sales, coffee mornings, toddler groups, youth clubs	0.20	5	391	*12.1*
13.5 Educational and training expenses	6.50	164	1,584	*7.2*
13.5.1 Education fees	5.00	126	565	*9.2*
13.5.2 Payments for school trips, other ad hoc school expenditure	0.20	5	211	*14.1*
13.5.3 Leisure classes - fees	1.30	33	1,106	*6.3*
13.6 Holiday in UK	2.50	63	927	*4.6*
13.6.1 Package holiday	0.70	17	214	*9.9*
13.6.2 Hotel holiday	1.10	26	393	*6.9*
13.6.3 Self-catering holiday	0.80	20	359	*6.8*
13.7 Holiday abroad	12.50	312	1,319	*3.9*
13.7.1 Package holiday	10.40	259	1,009	*4.5*
13.7.2 Hotel holiday	1.50	38	237	*12.5*
13.7.3 Self-catering holiday	0.60	15	137	*12.3*
13.8 Other incidental holiday expenses	6.80	169	342	*10.0*
13.8.1 Money spent abroad including duty free goods abroad	6.50	163	276	*10.3*
13.8.2 Duty free goods bought in the UK	0.00	1	11	*46.8*
13.8.3 Non-package holiday insurance/other travel insurance inc money paid to friend/relative	0.10	4	39	*23.3*
13.8.4 Commission on travellers cheques and foreign currency	0.10	2	178	*9.9*
13.9 Gambling payments	3.90	97	4,291	*3.1*
13.9.1 Football Pools	0.10	2	171	*12.9*
13.9.2 Bingo	0.40	9	332	*9.3*
13.9.3 Lotteries and scratch cards (including National Lottery)	2.70	66	3,981	*2.0*
13.9.3.1 National Lottery and scratch cards	2.60	64	3,918	*2.0*
13.9.3.2 Other lotteries and scratch cards	0.10	2	275	*11.5*
13.9.4 Bookmaker, betting shop, tote	0.80	20	1,096	*11.3*
13.10 Cash gifts, donations	8.10	203	3,083	*5.9*
13.10.1 Cash gifts to those outside household	3.00	75	1,310	*7.5*
13.10.2 Maintenance/separation allowance	1.90	49	201	*11.2*
13.10.3 Charitable donations and subscriptions (excluding money sent abroad)	1.80	46	2,092	*7.5*
13.10.4 Money sent abroad	1.00	26	348	*18.1*
13.10.5 Residential care fees for sick and elderly	0.30	7	8	*58.4*

7.1 Components of household expenditure (cont.)
based on weighted data and including children's expenditure

2000-01

		Average weekly expenditure all house- holds (£)	Total weekly expenditure (£ million)	Recording house- holds in sample	Percentage standard error (full method)
Commodity or service					
14	**Miscellaneous**	**0.70**	**18**	**1,529**	*5.9*
14.1	Pocket money and cash gifts to children under sixteen	0.10	3	208	*16.7*
14.2	Personal goods not otherwise specified	0.10	2	68	*15.4*
14.3	Household goods not otherwise specified	0.10	1	24	*39.3*
14.4	Interest on credit cards	0.40	10	518	*6.6*
14.5	Annual standing charge on credit or store card	0.10	2	1,267	*6.0*
14.6	Miscellaneous child expenditure	0.00	0	08	*41.7*
1-14	**All expenditure groups**	**385.70**	**9,654**	**6,637**	*0.9*
15	**Other items recorded**				
15.1	Life assurance, contributions to pension funds	21.20	530	4,192	*2.3*
	15.1.1 Life assurance premiums inc mortgage endowment policies	8.80	220	3,533	*2.6*
	15.1.2 Contributions to pension and superannuation funds deducted by employers (including contributions to widows and orphans funds)	7.60	190	1,968	*2.4*
	15.1.3 Personal pensions	4.80	120	1,039	*7.2*
15.2	Medical insurance premiums	1.30	32	718	*6.2*
15.3	Other insurance premiums including Friendly Societies	1.00	26	1,720	*5.1*
15.4	Income tax, payments less refunds	70.40	1,761	5,243	*2.4*
	15.4.1 Income tax paid by employees under PAYE	53.70	1,344	3,425	*2.6*
	15.4.2 Income tax paid direct eg by retired or unoccupied persons	2.10	51	270	*2.6*
	15.4.3 Income tax paid direct by self-employed	5.80	146	323	*14.6*
	15.4.4 Income tax deducted at source from income under covenant from investments or from annuities and pensions	8.10	202	3,656	*3.9*
	15.4.5 Income tax on bonus earnings	1.70	43	1,195	*8.4*
	15.4.6 Income tax refunds under PAYE	0.10	2	63	*24.2*
	15.4.7 Income tax refunds other than PAYE	0.90	23	515	*8.2*
15.5	National insurance contributions	18.40	460	3,457	*1.4*
	15.5.1 NI contributions paid by employees	18.20	455	3,394	*1.4*
	15.5.2 NI contributions paid by non-employees	0.20	5	101	*24.2*
15.6	Purchase or alteration of dwellings, mortgages	24.50	614	2,125	*6.1*
	15.6.1 Outright purchase of houses, flats etc, including deposits	1.50	37	53	*47.2*
	15.6.2 Capital repayment of mortgage	9.00	225	1,252	*4.5*
	15.6.3 Central heating installation	1.00	25	135	*21.8*
	15.6.4 Home improvements (contracted out)	11.40	285	1,027	*9.5*
	15.6.5 DIY improvements: double glazing, kitchen units, sheds	1.10	29	92	*30.0*
	15.6.6 Purchase of second dwelling	0.30	7	25	*22.8*
	15.6.7 Caravan purchase, including deposits	0.20	5	4	*91.4*
15.7	Savings and investments	10.40	259	1,402	*13.7*
	15.7.1 Savings, investments and food stamps	9.10	229	1,242	*15.4*
	15.7.2 Additional Voluntary Contributions	1.20	30	279	*8.7*
15.8	Repayment of loans to clear other debts	3.10	78	613	*5.4*
15.9	Windfall receipts from gambling etc	1.70	43	983	*10.3*

ONS, Family Spending 2000-01, © Crown copyright 2002

7.2

Expenditure on alcoholic drink by type of premises

2000-01

based on weighted data and including children's expenditure

	Average weekly expenditure all households (£)	Total weekly expenditure (£ million)	Recording households in sample	Percentage standard error
By type of premises				
4A Bought and consumed on licenced premises:				
4.1 Beer, cider	5.90	149	2,740	3
4.1.1 Beer and lager	5.80	145	2,698	3
4.1.2 Cider	0.20	4	260	13
4.2 Wines, fortified wines	1.00	25	1,108	5
4.2.1 Fortified wines	0.00	1	81	16
4.2.2 Non-fortified wines, still wines	0.90	23	1,048	5
4.2.3 Champagne & sparkling wine	0.00	1	21	31
4.3 Spirits, liqueurs	1.10	27	981	5
4.4 Other drinks	1.30	34	759	8
4.4.1 Alcoholic soft drinks	0.30	6	316	9
4.4.2 Other drinks undefined	1.10	27	480	10
4B Bought at off-licences (including large supermarket chains):				
4.1 Beer, cider	1.80	45	1,870	3
4.1.1 Beer and lager	1.60	41	1,717	3
4.1.2 Cider	0.20	4	336	8
4.2 Wines, fortified wines	2.60	66	2,245	4
4.2.1 Fortified wines	0.20	5	344	7
4.2.2 Non-fortified wines, still wines	2.30	57	2,041	4
4.2.3 Champagne & sparkling wine	0.20	4	167	12
4.3 Spirits, liqueurs	1.10	28	948	4
4.4 Other drinks	0.10	2	221	10
4.4.1 Alcoholic soft drinks	0.10	2	206	9
4.4.2 Other drinks undefined	0.00	0	18	32
4C Bought from large supermarket chains:				
4.1 Beer, cider	1.00	26	1,357	3
4.1.1 Beer and lager	1.00	24	1,226	4
4.1.2 Cider	0.10	2	241	9
4.2 Wines, fortified wines	1.80	45	1,863	3
4.2.1 Fortified wines	0.20	4	279	7
4.2.2 Non-fortified wines still wines	1.50	38	1,684	3
4.2.3 Champagne & sparkling wine	0.10	2	133	12
4.3 Spirits, liqueurs	0.80	21	712	4
4.4 Other drinks	0.10	1	149	11
4.4.1 Alcoholic soft drinks	0.00	1	142	11
4.4.2 Other drinks undefined	0.00	0	9	41
4D Bought from other off-licence outlets:				
4.1 Beer, cider	0.80	19	850	4
4.1.1 Beer and lager	0.70	17	782	5
4.1.2 Cider	0.10	2	129	5
4.2 Wines, fortified wines	0.90	21	782	13
4.2.1 Fortified wines	0.00	1	80	8
4.2.2 Non-fortified wines still wines	0.80	19	705	14
4.2.3 Champagne & sparkling wine	0.10	1	37	8
4.3 Spirits, liqueurs	0.30	8	319	27
4.4 Other drinks	0.00	1	80	7
4.4.1 Alcoholic soft drinks	0.00	1	71	18
4.4.2 Other drinks undefined	0.00	0	10	15

7.3 Expenditure on food and non-alcoholic drinks by place of purchase

based on weighted data and including children's expenditure

2000-01

		Large supermarket chains				Other outlets			
		Average weekly expenditure all house- holds (£)	Total weekly expenditure (£ million)	Recording house- holds in sample	% standard error	Average weekly expenditure all house- holds (£)	Total weekly expenditure (£ million)	Recording house- holds in sample	% standard error
3	**Food and non-alcoholic drinks**	**32.50**	**813**	**6,365**	*1*	**9.00**	**225**	**5,932**	*2*
3.1	Bread, rolls etc	1.30	33	5,843	*1*	0.50	12	3,055	*2*
3.2	Pasta, rice, flour and other cereals	0.40	9	2,737	*2*	0.10	3	519	*10*
3.2.1	Pasta - dried or fresh	0.20	5	1,745	*3*	0.00	1	231	*18*
3.2.2	Flour, rice and other cereals	0.20	4	1,661	*3*	0.10	2	336	*11*
3.3	Biscuits, cakes etc	2.40	59	5,586	*1*	0.50	12	2,552	*3*
3.3.1	Biscuits, shortbread, wafers, chocolate biscuits	1.10	26	4,660	*2*	0.20	5	1,508	*4*
3.3.2	Cakes, buns, currant bread, fruit pies, pasties	1.30	32	4,637	*2*	0.30	8	1,764	*4*
3.3.3	Pastry, cake mixes	0.00	1	444	*6*	0.00	0	58	*18*
3.4	Breakfast cereals	0.80	20	3,584	*2*	0.10	2	541	*6*
3.5	Beef and veal (uncooked)	1.00	25	2,839	*2*	0.50	12	1,101	*4*
3.6	Mutton and lamb (uncooked)	0.30	9	1,035	*4*	0.30	6	550	*6*
3.7	Pork (uncooked)	0.40	11	1,579	*3*	0.20	5	566	*6*
3.8	Bacon and ham (uncooked)	0.70	17	2,719	*2*	0.20	5	964	*4*
3.9	Poultry (uncooked)	1.70	42	3,595	*2*	0.30	8	850	*5*
3.10	Cold meats, ready to eat meats	1.20	30	4,219	*2*	0.20	6	1,268	*4*
3.11	Meat pies, sausages and other meats	1.00	24	3,965	*2*	0.30	8	1,607	*4*
3.11.1	Sausages (uncooked)	0.30	8	2,144	*2*	0.10	3	817	*5*
3.11.2	Offal and other uncooked meats	0.00	1	301	*9*	0.10	1	214	*12*
3.11.3	Tinned and bottled meat, meat products	0.10	3	1,217	*3*	0.00	0	220	*8*
3.11.4	Meat and poultry pies and pasties	0.50	12	2,480	*2*	0.10	3	839	*4*
3.12	Fish, shellfish and fish products	1.20	31	3,714	*2*	0.30	8	845	*6*
3.12.1	Fish (uncooked) and shellfish	0.60	15	1,828	*3*	0.20	6	532	*7*
3.12.2	Processed fish (smoked, dried, canned, bottled)	0.40	10	2,230	*3*	0.00	1	200	*9*
3.12.3	Fish (prepared) and fish products	0.30	6	1,414	*3*	0.00	1	193	*14*
3.13	Butter	0.20	6	1,921	*3*	0.00	1	416	*7*
3.14	Margarine	0.40	9	3,249	*2*	0.00	1	415	*6*
3.15	Cooking oils and fats	0.20	4	1,520	*3*	0.00	1	227	*12*
3.16	Fresh milk	1.00	26	5,029	*1*	1.10	27	3,436	*2*
3.17	Milk products including cream	1.30	31	4,678	*2*	0.20	4	1,044	*5*
3.17.1	Yoghurt & milk based desserts	1.00	26	4,245	*2*	0.10	2	806	*5*
3.17.2	Other milk and cream	0.20	5	1,868	*4*	0.10	2	351	*9*
3.18	Cheese	1.10	28	4,357	*2*	0.20	4	824	*5*
3.19	Eggs	0.30	7	2,917	*2*	0.10	3	1,276	*3*
3.20	Potatoes, potato products (excluding crisps)	1.00	25	4,656	*1*	0.20	6	1,760	*3*
3.20.1	Potatoes	0.60	15	3,845	*2*	0.20	5	1,537	*4*
3.20.2	Processed potatoes & products	0.40	10	2,645	*2*	0.00	1	421	*6*
3.21	Other vegetables	2.70	67	5,776	*1*	0.60	14	2,548	*3*
3.21.1	Fresh vegetables and salad	2.00	49	5,185	*1*	0.50	12	2,257	*3*
3.21.2	Processed & frozen vegetables	0.50	12	3,758	*2*	0.10	2	681	*6*
3.21.3	Pulses, dried and processed	0.20	6	3,089	*2*	0.00	1	544	*7*
3.22	Fruit, nuts	2.20	54	5,124	*2*	0.60	15	2,331	*3*
3.22.1	Fresh fruit	1.80	45	4,821	*2*	0.50	13	2,107	*3*
3.22.2	Processed fruit	0.20	4	1,526	*3*	0.00	1	273	*8*
3.22.3	Dried fruit and nuts	0.20	5	1,339	*4*	0.10	2	405	*7*

ONS, Family Spending 2000-01, © Crown copyright 2002

7.3 Expenditure on food and non-alcoholic drinks by place of purchase (cont.)
based on weighted data and including children's expenditure

2000-01

	Large supermarket chains				Other outlets			
	Average weekly expenditure all house-holds (£)	Total weekly expenditure (£ million)	Recording house-holds in sample	% standard error	Average weekly expenditure all house-holds (£)	Total weekly expenditure (£ million)	Recording house-holds in sample	% standard error
3 Food and non-alcoholic drinks (continued)								
3.23 Sugar	0.20	4	2,151	3	0.00	1	435	7
3.24 Jam, jellies, preserves and other spreads	0.20	5	2,024	2	0.00	1	400	6
3.25 Sweets and chocolates	1.10	29	3,897	2	0.90	21	3,224	3
3.26 Ice cream and sorbets	0.40	10	2,001	3	0.10	2	649	5
3.27 Tea	0.40	10	2,442	2	0.10	2	532	7
3.28 Coffee	0.50	12	1,957	2	0.10	2	302	8
3.29 Drinking chocolate, other food drinks	0.10	3	776	5	0.00	1	148	16
3.30 Fruit juice, squashes, bottled water	1.20	29	4,226	2	0.20	5	1,313	4
3.30.1 Fruit juices, squashes	1.00	25	3,955	2	0.20	4	1,132	4
3.30.2 Bottled water (still & sparkling)	0.20	4	1,169	4	0.00	1	272	10
3.31 Fizzy drinks	0.80	19	3,421	2	0.30	7	1,591	4
3.32 Soup	0.30	6	2,194	3	0.00	1	362	8
3.33 Pizzas, quiches, vegetarian pies	0.70	17	2,765	2	0.10	2	472	6
3.34 Other convenience foods	1.90	48	4,437	2	0.30	7	1,143	5
3.34.1 Dishes ready prepared:	1.80	46	4,411	2	0.20	6	1,078	5
3.34.1.1 Meat dishes	0.90	23	2,560	2	0.10	2	361	9
3.34.1.2 Fish dishes	0.20	4	798	4	0.00	1	83	20
3.34.1.3 Vegetarian foods	0.30	8	1,840	3	0.00	1	270	9
3.34.1.4 Sandwiches, filled rolls and baguettes	0.10	3	553	5	0.10	2	298	8
3.34.1.5 Other convenience foods	0.30	7	1,780	3	0.00	1	307	10
3.34.1.6 Pasta cooked	0.10	2	1,098	4	0.00	0	120	12
3.34.2 Baby and diet foods	0.10	2	177	10	0.00	1	100	14
3.35 Potato crisps and savoury snacks	0.90	21	3,844	2	0.20	4	1,374	4
3.40 Other foods	1.30	33	4,798	2	0.20	6	1,252	10
3.40.1 Pickles, sauces, flavourings, colourings	1.30	33	4,774	2	0.20	4	1,184	4
3.40.2 Other foods undefined	0.00	1	183	12	0.10	2	118	29

Note: Items 3.36 to 3.39 are not included because this place of purchase analysis is not applicable.

7.4 Expenditure on selected items by place of purchase
based on weighted data

2000-01

	Large Supermarket chains				Other outlets			
	Average weekly expenditure all house- holds (£)	Total weekly expenditure (£ million)	Recording house- holds in sample	% standard error	Average weekly expenditure all house- holds (£)	Total weekly expenditure (£ million)	Recording house- holds in sample	% standard error
10.5 Petrol, diesel & other motor oils	**4.40**	**110**	**1,668**	**3**	**11.50**	**286**	**3,463**	**2**
10.5.1 Petrol	3.90	99	1,522	3	10.10	251	3,175	2
10.5.2 Diesel	0.40	11	191	8	1.30	33	459	6
10.5.3 Other motor oils	0.00	0	19	37	0.10	2	111	12
7 Household goods								
7.6.1 Electrical consumable eg batteries, light bulbs	0.10	3	556	5	0.30	9	1,083	5
7.7 Greeting cards, stationery and paper goods	0.00	0	1,046	0	0.00	0	3,584	0
7.8 Detergents, other cleaning materials	1.60	39	4,348	2	0.50	11	1,715	4
7.9 Toilet paper	0.60	15	3,001	2	0.10	3	767	5
7.10.1 Pet food	0.90	22	1,954	3	0.60	15	1,236	5
9 Personal goods and services								
9.5.1 & 9.5.3 Toiletries and other toilet requisites - cotton wool, toothpaste, shaving soap, brushes, razors, tooth brushes	0.80	20	3,041	2	0.80	19	2,302	3
9.5.2 Toilet soap	0.20	4	1,150	4	0.10	3	732	6
9.6.2 Cosmetics and related accessories including after shave, sun lotion	0.30	8	1,075	5	1.40	36	1,796	4
5 Tobacco	**1.70**	**44**	**1,075**	**5**	**4.30**	**108**	**1,944**	**3**
5.1 Cigarettes	1.60	40	989	5	3.80	95	1,789	3
5.2 Tobacco & other tobacco products	0.20	4	191	12	0.50	13	476	6
5.2.1 Pipe and cigarette tobacco	0.10	2	144	11	0.40	10	378	7
5.2.2 Cigars and snuff	0.10	2	49	23	0.10	3	101	17
8.2 Postage	0.00	0	0	0	0.50	12	2,038	4
12.2 Newspapers	0.20	4	1,792	3	1.80	46	4,796	2
12.3 Magazines and periodicals	0.20	6	1,469	3	0.80	20	2,623	3

ONS, Family Spending 2000-01, © Crown copyright 2002

7.5 Expenditure on clothing and footwear by place of purchase

based on weighted data and including children's expenditure

		Large supermarket chains				Clothing chains				Other outlets			
		Average weekly expenditure all house-holds (£)	Total weekly expenditure (£ million)	Recording house-holds in sample	% standard error	Average weekly expenditure all house-holds (£)	Total weekly expenditure (£ million)	Recording house-holds in sample	% standard error	Average weekly expenditure all house-holds (£)	Total weekly expenditure (£ million)	Recording house-holds in sample	% standard error
6	Clothing and footwear	3.10	77	1,558	4	6.00	150	1,713	3	13.00	324	4,179	3
6.1	Men's outerwear	0.50	13	210	11	1.20	31	397	7	2.60	66	1,073	6
6.2	Men's underwear and hosiery	0.20	4	181	10	0.20	6	187	9	0.10	2	492	19
6.3	Women's outerwear	1.10	27	439	7	2.60	66	886	5	3.90	98	1,917	5
6.4	Women's underwear and hosiery	0.50	13	635	6	0.60	14	476	6	0.10	4	1,048	28
6.5	Boys' outerwear	0.10	2	77	14	0.10	4	74	17	0.60	15	417	8
6.6	Girls' outerwear	0.10	3	91	14	0.20	5	123	12	0.90	22	563	7
6.7	Babies' outerwear	0.10	3	123	12	0.20	4	105	12	0.40	11	437	9
6.8	Boys', girls' and babies' underwear	0.10	3	191	10	0.10	3	142	11	0.20	4	556	10
6.9	Ties, belts, hats, gloves, etc	0.10	2	138	13	0.10	4	152	11	0.30	8	750	7
6.9.1	Men's	0.00	1	61	19	0.10	2	80	13	0.10	2	224	15
6.9.2	Women's	0.00	1	50	20	0.00	1	52	21	0.20	4	325	11
6.9.3	Children's	0.00	0	33	25	0.00	0	29	22	0.10	2	276	10
6.10	Haberdashery, textiles & clothes hire	0.00	0	62	15	0.00	1	26	44	0.40	9	494	10
6.10.1	Haberdashery, wool	0.00	0	54	16	0.00	0	18	33	0.10	3	352	10
6.10.2	Textiles and clothes hire	0.00	0	8	44	0.00	1	10	51	0.30	7	179	13
6.11	Footwear	0.30	7	190	9	0.50	14	251	8	3.40	85	1,566	4
6.11.1	Men's	0.10	2	44	17	0.20	4	65	14	1.30	31	484	7
6.11.2	Women's	0.20	4	104	12	0.30	8	165	10	1.40	34	841	5
6.11.3	Children's	0.00	1	55	18	0.10	2	45	21	0.80	19	524	6
6.11.4	Undefined	0.00	0	1	100	0.00	0	0	0	0.00	0	2	71

ONS, Family Spending 2000-01, © Crown copyright 2002

Chapter 8

Household income

- Average gross income was £500 a week in 2000-01, around 15 per cent higher than five years earlier after allowing for inflation.

- One adult, retired households mainly dependent on state pensions had the lowest gross weekly income, an average of £110 a week. Households with four or more adults recorded the highest, £1,010 a week.

- In couple households with children, the more children the couple had the lower the proportion of income from **wages and salaries** and **self-employment** and the higher the proportion from **social security benefits.**

- **Wages and salaries** accounted for over 80 per cent of average gross weekly income for those buying their home with a mortgage and those renting furnished accommodation from the private sector.

- The highest weekly income was recorded in households where the head was in a non-manual job or was self-employed. Unemployed manual workers recorded the lowest weekly income.

- London, South East and East of England recorded an average gross weekly income higher than the UK national average. The lowest average incomes were in the North East, Wales and Northern Ireland, all more than 25 per cent below the UK average.

- Average household income varied with the population of the built-up area. It was highest in the London built-up area, at £650 a week. It was lowest in other metropolitan built-up areas, £390 a week, and increased steadily as the population of the built-up area decreased, reaching £550 a week in rural areas.

- Around 70 per cent of income for the London built-up area and urban areas with a population of between 25k and 100k, came from **wages and salaries** compared to 60 per cent in rural areas.

Household income

8.1 Gross household income, 1970 to 2000-01 at 2000-01 prices

£ per week, at 2000-01 prices

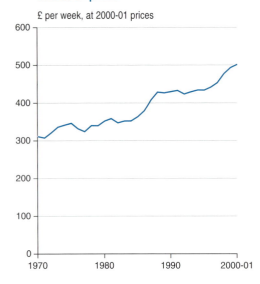

This chapter looks at the levels of gross household income, disposable income, and the proportions of gross income from different sources for a variety of household types in the United Kingdom.

Detailed information on income is also collected in the Family Resources Survey (FRS). The FRS has the advantage of a much larger sample than the FES, but detailed income is still required in the FES for analysis with expenditure. The box at the end of the chapter gives more information on the FRS and compares results from the two surveys. The FES provides a longer time series than the FRS and the 1998-99 edition of Family Spending showed changes over the last 20 or 30 years. This years report, as well as commenting on 2000-01 data, looks at income by urban/rural area and for household reference person. Income does not include any Housing Benefit (HB). HB is treated as a reduction in housing costs.

Table 8.9 shows the changes in income since 1970 at current and at constant prices, and **Figure 8.1** shows the trends at 2000-01 prices. Average gross income was £500 a week in 2000-01, around 15 per cent higher than five years earlier after allowing for inflation.

Figure 8.2 shows that in 2000-01, 67 per cent of this gross income was from wages and salaries. A further 9 per cent came from self-employment and 12 per cent came from social security benefits. The remainder was split between annuities and pensions, investments, and other sources.

Household composition

Table 8.1 shows how the size and the composition of the household affected its income and sources of income in 2000-01. One adult retired households mainly dependent on state pensions had the lowest gross income at an average £110 a week, less than 20 per cent of the average for all households. Households with four or more adults recorded the highest income at £1,010 a week, just over twice the overall average.

8.2 Source of income as a percentage of gross weekly household income for all households

Per cent

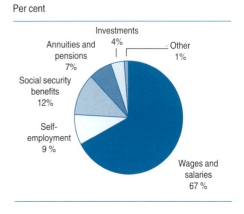

ONS, Family Spending 2000-01, © Crown copyright 2002

Couple households with one or two children showed the highest proportion of income from wages and salaries and self-employment at around 90 per cent. Social security benefits contributed between five and six per cent to their income. The more children the couple households had the lower the proportion of income from wages and salaries and self-employment and the higher the proportion from social security benefits.

Age of head of household (Table 8.2)

Households where the head was aged over 75 recorded the lowest gross income at £230 a week. Of this, just over 50 per cent came from social security benefits and 29 per cent from annuities and pensions. These households recorded seven per cent of income from wages and salaries and self-employment. Where the head of household was aged between 30 and 49 gross weekly income was £630 a week, 81 per cent coming from wages and salaries and six per cent from social security benefits. **Figure 8.3** shows that as the age of head of household increased the proportion of income from wages and salaries and self-employment combined decreased and income from social security benefits increased.

Income level

Table 8.3 illustrates the average gross weekly income by gross income quintile group for 2000-01. Households in the lowest quintile group had an average gross income of £110 a week, compared to £1,170 a week in the highest quintile group. There was a marked difference in the proportion of income from wages and salaries and self-employment combined for the lower income groups – around seven per cent for the lowest income group, 36 per cent for the second quintile group and 68 per cent for the middle income group. For the top two income groups over 80 per cent of their income came from wages and salaries and self-employment combined. The reverse was true for the proportion of income from social security benefits, from which those in the lowest income group gained 80 per cent of their income while those in the top income group gained only two per cent.

8.3 **Proportion of income from wages & salaries and self-employment from and social security benefit by age of head of household**

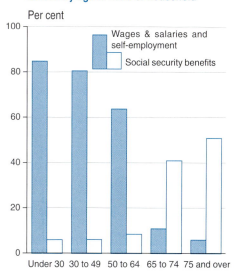

Per cent

Legend: Wages & salaries and self-employment / Social security benefits

X-axis: Under 30, 30 to 49, 50 to 64, 65 to 74, 75 and over

8.4 Gross weekly income by household tenure

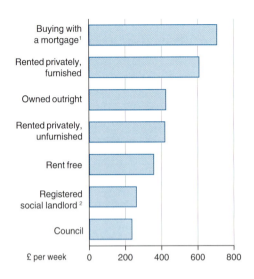

£ per week

1 See footnotes in Table 4.10
2 Formerly housing association

Tenure Type

Table 8.4 shows that wages and salaries accounted for over 80 per cent of the average gross income for those households buying their property with a mortgage and those renting furnished accommodation from the private sector. These household types also had the highest gross income, £710 and £610 a week respectively **(Figure 8.4).** For social renters, either from the council or a registered social landlord, wages and salaries accounted for around 50 per cent of gross income, most of the rest of their income coming from social security benefits. These households also recorded the lowest gross income, £230 and £260 respectively.

Economic status of head of household

Table 8.5 shows that households where the head was in a non-manual job or were self-employed had the highest salaries at £790 and £730 a week respectively. Of this around 90 per cent came from wages and salaries and self-employment. Unemployed manual workers had the lowest salaries at £200 a week. Around 50 per cent of this came from wages and salaries and 40 per cent from social security benefits.

(Note: When an employee has been away from work without pay for 13 weeks or less, his or her normal pay is used in estimating total income instead of unemployment benefits. Earnings of other household members besides the head are also included in the total).

Occupation of head of household [1] (employees and unemployed)

Households where the head was in a professional occupation recorded the highest salaries at £940 a week. The lowest income was recorded where the head of household was an unskilled manual worker at £320 a week. For all categories the majority of income came from wages and salaries – 79 per cent for unskilled manual workers up to 93 per cent for employers and managers. **(Table 8.6)**

---

1 Excludes households where the head is retired, unoccupied, self-employed, in the armed forces or with an inadequately described occupation.

Region

Table 8.7 shows regional variations in income and source of income averaged over three years to reduce sampling variability. The average gross weekly income for the UK was £480. The highest gross weekly income was recorded in London at £610 a week, followed by the South East at £580 a week and East of England at £510 a week. All other regions recorded less than the UK average; three of them – Northern Ireland, North East and Wales – recorded less than £400 a week.

Figure 8.5 shows that for all regions the majority of income – over 60 per cent – came from wages and salaries. The regions are ranked by the proportion of income coming from wages and salaries. It can be seen that the proportion from social security benefits is not always low when the proportion from wages and salaries is high. Nevertheless Northern Ireland recorded the most from social security benefits at 21 per cent closely followed by the North East and Wales at 19 and 18 per cent respectively. London and the South East recorded the lowest at eight and nine per cent respectively.

Urban /rural areas

Table 8.8 shows income and source of income by urban/rural area for the two-year period 1999-2000 to 2000-01. Data from the two years are combined to reduce sampling variability. Urban/rural indicators are only available for the GB sample. **Figure 8.6** shows that households in the London built-up area had the highest gross weekly income at an average of £650 a week, over 30 per cent above the GB average. London apart, there was a consistent relationship between the population of an area and average income, the smaller the population the larger the income. So the lowest was in other metropolitan areas, £390 a week, and highest in rural areas, £550 a week.

For all areas the main source of income was from wages and salaries. At the highest, seventy per cent of income for households in both the London built-up area and urban areas with a population of between 25k and 100k, came from wages and salaries compared to only 60 per cent in rural areas. Around 18 per cent of income for households in other metropolitan built-up areas had income from social security benefits compared to only seven per cent in the London built-up area.

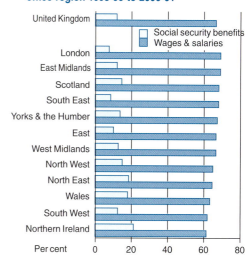

8.5 Proportion of income from wages and salaries and social security benefits by government office region 1998-99 to 2000-01

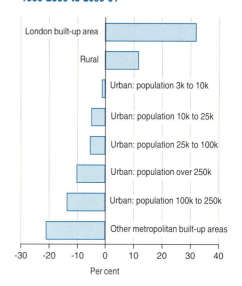

8.6 Average gross weekly income by urban/rural areas in relation to the GB average: 1999-2000 to 2000-01

8.7 **FES sources of income: all households 1999-2000 Great Britain**

Per cent

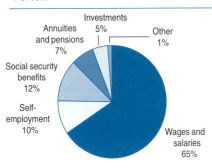

Family Resources Survey (FRS)

A major advantage of the Family Resources Survey is its large sample size. In the survey year 1999-2000 around 25,000 GB households were interviewed for the FRS compared to just over 6,500 GB households for the FES. The response rate was also higher than for the FES, 66 per cent compared to 63 per cent in 1999-2000.

Comparison of results from the FES and FRS

Family Expenditure Survey results have been compared with the FRS in the context of Households Below Average Income (HBAI) analysis. Appendix 9 of the 1979-1996/7 HBAI report details comparisons between the FES and the FRS. The main findings were that the FRS recorded lower equivalised disposable income, particularly for one adult and couples without children, and lower investment income, particularly for pensioners. This was due to a combination of both sampling variation and inherent differences between the two surveys. In particular it is thought that the FRS over represents some types of low-income households and under represents some types of high-income households.

The FES recorded the average gross household income at £480 a week in 1999-2000, compared to £470 a week recorded by the FRS for the same year. **Figures 8.7 and 8.8** compares the FRS and FES results on sources of gross income as a percentage of gross weekly household income, for all households in 1999-2000. In the FRS, 73 per cent of this income came from wages and salaries and self-employment compared to the 76 per cent recorded by the FES. The FES recorded a higher percentage of income from social security benefits than the FRS (12 per cent compared to 9 per cent). Conversely the FRS recorded a higher percentage of income from annuities and pensions than the FES (13 per cent compared to 7 per cent). The FES records investment income at five per cent compared to three per cent in the FRS. This supports the HBAI Appendix 9 finding that investment income was lower in the FRS.

8.8 **FRS sources of income: all households 1999-2000 Great Britain**

Per cent

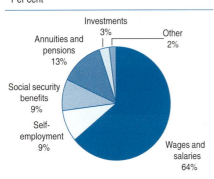

References

Department of Social Security, *Family Resources Survey Great Britain 1999-2000*. Corporate Document Services 2000.

Department of Social Security (1977), *Households below Average Income, 1979-1996-97*. ISBN 1 84123 059 6. Corporate Document Services 1998.

ONS, Family Spending 2000-01, © Crown copyright 2002

8.1 Income and source of income by household composition

2000-01

based on weighted data

| | Grossed number of house-holds | Number of house-holds in the sample | Weekly household income | | Source of income | | | | | |
			Dispo-sable	Gross	Wages and salaries	Self employ-ment	Invest-ments	Annuities and pensions[1]	Social security benefits[2]	Other sources
	(000s)	Number	£	£	Percentage of gross weekly household income					
All households	**25,030**	**6,637**	**409**	**503**	*67*	*9*	*4*	*7*	*12*	*1*
Composition of household										
One adult	7,470	1,900	215	261	*55*	*5*	*6*	*11*	*21*	*1*
Retired households mainly dependent on state pensions[3]	1,770	457	108	108	*0*	*0*	*2*	*5*	*93*	*0*
Other retired households	1,510	404	208	234	*0*	*0*	*17*	*43*	*38*	*1*
Non-retired households	4,190	1,039	263	334	*77*	*6*	*4*	*4*	*7*	*1*
One adult, one child	680	208	222	251	*56*	*9*	*1*	*1*	*27*	*6*
One adult, two or more children	690	241	237	255	*43*	*2*	*2*	*1*	*43*	*8*
One man and one woman	7,380	1,969	440	539	*62*	*6*	*6*	*13*	*12*	*0*
Retired households mainly dependent on state pensions[3]	610	178	169	170	*0*	*0*	*2*	*7*	*91*	*0*
Other retired households	1,840	548	350	390	*5*	*0*	*14*	*43*	*37*	*1*
Non-retired households	4,930	1,243	508	641	*77*	*8*	*4*	*7*	*4*	*1*
Two men or two women	550	135	441	553	*77*	*4*	*2*	*3*	*12*	*2*
One man one woman, one child	1,750	474	526	662	*81*	*10*	*2*	*1*	*5*	*1*
One man one woman, two children	2,250	650	571	723	*75*	*15*	*3*	*0*	*6*	*1*
One man one woman, three children	740	234	533	663	*70*	*16*	*1*	*1*	*10*	*1*
Two adults, four or more children	210	73	467	575	*66*	*11*	*4*	*0*	*18*	*1*
Three adults	1,650	348	592	728	*70*	*12*	*3*	*5*	*8*	*2*
Three adults, one or more children	800	208	638	782	*77*	*9*	*2*	*2*	*9*	*1*
Four or more adults	580	114	840	1,014	*76*	*12*	*3*	*2*	*4*	*3*
Four or more adults, one or more children	200	54	630	752	*67*	*15*	*2*	*0*	*13*	*2*

1 Other than social security benefits.

2 Excluding housing benefit and council tax benefit (rates rebates in Northern Ireland) - see appendix D.

3 Mainly dependent on state pension and not economically active - see appendix D.

8.2 Income and source of income by age of head of household

2000-01

based on weighted data

| | Grossed number of house-holds | Number of house-holds in the sample | Weekly household income | | Source of income | | | | | |
			Dispo-sable	Gross	Wages and salaries	Self employ-ment	Invest-ments	Annuities and pensions[1]	Social security enefits[2]	Other sources
Age of head of household	(000s)	Number	£	£	Percentage of gross weekly household income					
Under 30	2,670	687	383	474	*85*	*5*	*1*	*0*	*6*	*3*
30 and under 50	9,940	2,598	494	626	*81*	*10*	*2*	*0*	*6*	*1*
50 and under 65	6,220	1,646	450	551	*64*	*12*	*5*	*9*	*9*	*1*
65 and under 75	3,190	956	276	308	*11*	*3*	*10*	*33*	*41*	*1*
75 and over	3,010	750	210	226	*6*	*1*	*13*	*29*	*51*	*0*

1 Other than social security benefits.

2 Excluding housing benefit and council tax benefit (rates rebates in Northern Ireland) - see appendix D.

8.3 Income and source of income by gross income quintile group
based on weighted data

2000-01

Gross income quintile group	Grossed number of house- holds	Number of house- holds in the sample	Weekly household income		Source of income					
			Dispo- sable	Gross	Wages and salaries	Self employ- ment	Invest- ments	Annuities and pensions[1]	Social security benefits[2]	Other sources
	(000s)	Number	£	£	Percentage of gross weekly household income					
Lowest twenty per cent	5,000	1,373	103	105	6	1	3	8	80	2
Second quintile group	5,010	1,405	215	232	31	5	4	15	43	2
Third quintile group	5,010	1,333	338	398	62	6	4	11	15	1
Fourth quintile group	5,010	1,299	491	604	75	7	3	8	6	2
Highest twenty per cent	5,000	1,227	899	1,174	77	12	4	3	2	1

1 Other than social security benefits.

2 Excluding housing benefit and council tax benefit (rates rebates in Northern Ireland) - see appendix D.

8.4 Income and source of income by household tenure
based on weighted data

2000-01

Tenure of dwelling[3]	Grossed number of house- holds	Number of house- holds in the sample	Weekly household income		Source of income					
			Dispo- sable	Gross	Wages and salaries	Self employ- ment	Invest- ments	Annuities and pensions[1]	Social security benefits[2]	Other sources
	(000s)	Number	£	£	Percentage of gross weekly household income					
Owners										
Owned outright	6,870	1,873	360	422	35	10	11	22	21	1
Buying with a mortgage[3]	10,210	2,665	554	706	81	10	2	2	4	1
All	17,080	4,538	476	592	68	10	5	8	9	1
Social rented from										
Council	3,870	1,075	211	234	50	3	1	4	42	1
Registered social landlord [4]	1,470	395	229	259	55	4	1	4	35	1
All	5,340	1,470	216	241	51	3	1	4	40	1
Private rented										
Rent free	380	100	297	355	71	3	4	4	16	1
Rent paid, unfurnished	1,580	389	340	417	76	8	1	2	11	2
Rent paid, furnished	650	140	477	606	82	6	1	0	3	7
All	2,600	629	368	455	77	7	1	2	9	4

1 Other than social security benefits.

2 Excluding housing benefit and council tax benefit (rates rebates in Northern Ireland) - see appendix D.

3 See footnotes in Table 4.10.

4 Formerly housing association

ONS, Family Spending 2000-01, © Crown copyright 2002

8.5 Income and source of income by economic status of head of household
2000-01
based on weighted data

| | Grossed number of house-holds | Number of house-holds in the sample | Weekly household income | | Source of income | | | | | |
			Dispo-sable	Gross	Wages and salaries	Self employ-ment	Invest-ments	Annuities and pensions[1]	Social security benefits[2]	Other sources
Economic status of head of household	(000s)	Number	£	£	Percentage of gross weekly household income					
Economically active										
Manual	5,130	1,326	413	508	90	1	1	2	6	1
Non-manual	7,470	1,903	601	787	91	2	3	1	2	1
Self-employed	2,020	537	627	732	22	66	4	3	4	1
Unemployed	760	199	198	221	52	3	1	4	36	4
Manual	560	143	180	199	51	3	1	2	41	2
Non-manual	190	49	252	288	57	3	3	6	22	9
Economically inactive										
Other	3,390	950	233	260	24	1	9	22	40	4
Retired	6,170	1,700	228	250	6	1	11	33	48	1

1 Other than social security benefits.
2 Excluding housing benefit and council tax benefit (rates rebates in Northern Ireland) - see appendix D.

8.6 Income and source of income by occupation of head of household[1]
2000-01
based on weighted data

| | Grossed number of house-holds | Number of house-holds in the sample | Weekly household income | | Source of income | | | | | |
			Dispo-sable	Gross	Wages and salaries	Self employ-ment	Invest-ments	Annuities and pensions[2]	Social security benefits[3]	Other sources
Occupational groupings of head of household	(000s)	Number	£	£	Percentage of gross weekly household income					
Professional	1,050	251	719	938	88	4	4	1	2	1
Employers and managers	3,070	796	686	922	93	1	2	1	2	0
Intermediate non-manual	1,850	464	529	679	91	1	2	2	3	1
Junior non-manual	1,590	416	406	502	87	1	2	2	5	2
Manual	5,680	1,469	390	478	88	1	1	2	7	1
Skilled	2,920	749	446	555	91	1	1	2	5	1
Semi-skilled	2,170	560	348	417	85	1	1	2	9	2
Unskilled	600	160	275	323	79	0	2	2	16	1

1 Excludes households where the head is retired, unoccupied, self-employed, in the armed forces or with an inadequately described occupation.
2 Other than social security benefits.
3 Excluding housing benefit and council tax benefit (rates rebates in Northern Ireland) - see appendix D.

8.7 Income and source of income by UK Countries and Government Office Regions
based on weighted data

1998-99 - 2000-01

Government Office Regions	Average number of grossed house-holds	Total number of house-holds (over 3 years)	Weekly household income		Source of income					
			Dispo-sable	Gross	Wages and salaries	Self employ-ment	Invest-ments	Annuities and pensions[1]	Social security benefits[2]	Other sources
	(000s)	Number	£	£	Percentage of gross weekly household income					
United Kingdom	24,984	20,210	390	480	67	9	4	7	12	1
North East	1,166	886	318	379	65	5	3	8	19	1
North West	2,839	2,169	355	429	65	8	4	7	15	1
Yorkshire and the Humber	2,104	1,642	359	439	67	7	4	7	14	1
East Midlands	1,768	1,347	367	450	69	6	4	7	12	1
West Midlands	2,159	1,644	382	463	67	9	4	6	13	1
East	2,290	1,784	413	510	67	9	5	8	10	1
London	3,040	1,955	486	616	70	12	4	5	8	1
South East	3,468	2,582	463	586	68	10	6	7	9	1
South West	2,087	1,766	373	449	62	10	5	9	13	1
England	20,922	15,775	402	496	67	9	4	7	11	1
Wales	1,219	970	318	376	63	7	3	7	18	1
Scotland	2,206	1,756	343	418	68	6	3	7	15	2
Northern Ireland	639	1,709	316	371	62	9	2	6	21	1

1 Other than social security benefits.

2 Excluding housing benefit and council tax benefit (rates rebate in Northern Ireland) - see appendix D.

8.8 Income and source of income by GB urban/rural area
based on weighted data and children's income

1999-2000 – 2000-01

GB urban rural areas	Average number of grossed house-holds	Total number of house-holds (over 2 years)	Weekly household income		Source of income					
			Dispo-sable	Gross	Wages and salaries	Self employ-ment	Invest-ments	Annuities and pensions[1]	Social security benefits[2]	Other sources
	(000s)	Number	£	£	Percentage of gross weekly household income					
Urban										
London built-up area	3,540	1,596	514	651	70	13	4	4	7	1
Other metropolitan built up areas	3,560	1,767	326	391	67	4	3	7	18	1
Other urban:										
population over 250k	2,910	1,510	363	442	65	9	4	7	14	2
population 100k to 250k	2,600	1,368	358	430	66	7	4	7	14	1
population 25k to 100k	3,870	2,031	382	468	70	6	4	7	12	1
population 10k to 25k	2,040	1,107	386	469	62	11	5	7	13	1
population 3k to 10k	1,810	977	398	489	67	8	4	8	12	1
Rural	2,530	1,367	449	551	60	12	7	9	11	1

1 Other than social security benefits.

2 Excluding housing benefit and council tax benefit (rates rebate in Northern Ireland) - see appendix D.

ONS, Family Spending 2000-01, © Crown copyright 2002

8.9 Income and source of income
1970 to 2000-01
based on unweighted data unless footnoted otherwise

	Grossed number of households	Number f households in the sample	Weekly household income[1]				Source of income					
			Current prices		Constant prices		Wages and salaries	Self employ-ment	Invest-ments	Annuities and pensions[2]	Social security benefits[3]	Other sources
			Dispo-sable	Gross	Dispo-sable	Gross						
	(000s)	Number	£	£	£	£	Percentage of gross weekly household income					
1970		6,393	28	34	259	312	77	7	4	3	9	1
1980		6,944	115	140	288	353	75	6	3	3	13	1
1990		7,046	258	317	350	431	67	10	6	5	11	1
1995-96		6,797	307	381	350	435	64	9	5	7	14	2
1996-97		6,415	325	397	362	442	65	9	4	7	14	1
1997-98		6,409	343	421	370	454	67	8	4	7	13	1
1998-99[4]	24,664	6,630	371	457	388	478	68	8	4	7	12	1
1999-2000	25,335	7,097	391	480	403	494	66	10	5	7	12	1
2000-01	25,030	6,637	409	503	409	503	67	9	4	7	12	1

1 Does not include imputed income from owner-occupied and rent-free households.

2 Other than social security benefits.

3 Excluding housing benefit and council tax benefit (rates rebate in Northern Ireland)
and their predecessors in earlier years - see appendix D.

4 Based on grossed data from 1998-99

8.10 Income and source of income
by age of household reference person
based on weighted data

2000-01

Age of household reference person	Grossed number of households	Number of households in the sample	Weekly household income		Source of income					
			Dispo-sable	Gross	Wages and salaries	Self employ-ment	Invest-ments	Annuities and pensions[1]	Social security enefits[2]	Other sources
	(000s)	Number	£	£	Percentage of gross weekly household income					
Under 30	2,760	708	380	469	84	5	1	0	7	3
30 and under 50	10,070	2,635	497	630	80	10	2	1	6	1
50 and under 65	6,140	1,624	447	547	63	12	5	10	9	1
65 and under 75	3,120	937	272	303	9	3	11	34	42	1
75 and over	2,950	733	203	219	5	1	13	29	52	0

1 Other than social security benefits.

2 Excluding housing benefit and council tax benefit (rates rebates in Northern Ireland) - see appendix D.

8.11 Income and source of income by economic status of household reference person

based on weighted data

2000-01

| | Grossed number of house- holds | Number of house- holds in the sample | Weekly household income | | Source of income | | | | | |
			Dispo- sable	Gross	Wages and salaries	Self employ- ment	Invest- ments	Annuities and pensions[1]	Social security benefits[2]	Other sources
Economic status of household reference person	(000s)	Number	£	£	Percentage of gross weekly household income					
Economically active										
Manual	4,890	1,268	403	494	*89*	*1*	*1*	*2*	*6*	*1*
Non-manual	8,250	2,099	591	770	*90*	*2*	*3*	*2*	*3*	*1*
Self-employed	1,840	492	626	727	*18*	*68*	*4*	*4*	*4*	*1*
Unemployed	610	160	164	182	*44*	*3*	*2*	*6*	*41*	*4*
Manual	440	112	146	159	*41*	*3*	*1*	*3*	*49*	*2*
Non-manual	150	41	213	247	*53*	*4*	*3*	*9*	*23*	*8*
Economically inactive										
Other	3,240	916	229	257	*19*	*5*	*9*	*21*	*41*	*4*
Retired	6,130	1,685	226	246	*5*	*1*	*12*	*33*	*49*	*1*

1 Other than social security benefits.

2 Excluding housing benefit and council tax benefit (rates rebates in Northern Ireland) - see appendix D.

8.12 Income and source of income by occupation of household reference person[1]

based on weighted data

2000-01

| | Grossed number of house- holds | Number of house- holds in the sample | Weekly household income | | Source of income | | | | | |
			Dispo- sable	Gross	Wages and salaries	Self employ- ment	Invest- ments	Annuities and pensions[2]	Social security benefits[3]	Other sources
Occupational groupings of household reference person	(000s)	Number	£	£	Percentage of gross weekly household income					
Professional	1,070	257	710	923	*88*	*4*	*4*	*1*	*2*	*1*
Employers and managers	3,200	831	684	918	*92*	*1*	*3*	*1*	*2*	*0*
Intermediate non-manual	2,130	535	542	689	*89*	*2*	*2*	*3*	*3*	*1*
Junior non-manual	1,920	492	399	492	*87*	*2*	*1*	*2*	*6*	*2*
Manual	5,330	1,380	399	492	*87*	*2*	*1*	*2*	*6*	*2*
Skilled	2,620	670	382	466	*88*	*1*	*1*	*2*	*7*	*1*
Semi-skilled	2,140	554	438	546	*91*	*1*	*1*	*2*	*5*	*1*
Unskilled	570	156	344	411	*84*	*1*	*1*	*2*	*10*	*2*

1 Excludes households where the reference person is retired, unoccupied, self-employed, in the armed forces or with inadequately described occupation.

2 Other than social security benefits.

3 Excluding housing benefit and council tax benefit (rates rebates in Northern Ireland) - see appendix D.

Chapter 9

Household characteristics & ownership of consumer durables

- Between 1996-97 and 2000-01 ownership of **satellite receivers** has grown from under 20 per cent to 40 per cent, of **home computers** from 27 per cent to 44 per cent, **mobile phones** from 17 per cent to 47 per cent and **CD players** from 59 per cent to 77 per cent. The growth had slowed in the last year for mobile phones, however, **Internet access from the home** increased from 10 per cent in 1998-99 to 32 per cent in 2000-01.

- Possession of **central heating, washing machines,** and **telephones** has become almost universal, with over 90 per cent of households owning them.

- Even among households with the lowest tenth of incomes over four fifths had **central heating** and a **telephone** and three quarters owned a **washing machine**. Almost all households in the highest income group had these goods and 96 or 97 per cent of them also owned **CD players** and **video recorders**.

- The largest differences with income were in ownership of a **dishwasher**, 68 per cent in the highest income group but only 4 per cent in the lowest, **Internet access** from the home, 73 per cent for the highest group and 5 per cent for the one-from lowest, and a **home computer**, 81 per cent in the highest group and 14 per cent in the two lowest.

- A fifth of households in the lowest income group owned a **satellite receiver**, a higher proportion than those with **home computers**, **Internet access** or **dishwasher.**

- Households with children had higher levels of ownership of nearly all consumer durables than households without children. The highest priority items for households with children were **washing machines**, **freezers** and **video recorders**, all with 97 or 98 per cent of these households owning them. However, ownership of **telephones** was about the same for households with and without children.

- Ownership of at least one **car** increased rapidly with income, at low and medium incomes, but did not vary much between the highest four of the ten income groups, in all of which over 90 per cent had a car. In the highest income group over 70 per cent had two or more cars, including over 20 per cent who had three or more.

Household characteristics and ownership of consumer durables

This chapter describes the characteristics of households in 2000-2001 as estimated from the Family Expenditure Survey. The relationships between ownership of durable goods and income, household composition, type of tenure and region are also outlined in this chapter.

Characteristics of households – effect of the change in household definition

A change in the definition of the household has been mentioned in the Introduction and elsewhere. The purpose was to bring the survey into line with the harmonised definition used in other household surveys. The new and the old definitions are set out in full in Appendix E. In the large majority of cases the change makes no difference, but where a group of adults is sharing accommodation the new definition may allocate them to a single household when the old definition would have divided them into two or more households. The overall effect is likely to have been to increase average household size by 0.6 per cent, as explained below.

The table in **Figure 9.1** shows household composition as reported in the survey in the last three years. Average household size was 1.7 per cent higher in 2000-01 than in the year before, with one person households forming 29.9 per cent of the total compared with 31.4 per cent in 1999-2000. However the average size in 2000-01 was about the same as two years earlier. Looking at earlier reports, 1999-2000 looks like the anomalous year. The apparent increase in average household size between 1999-2000 and 2000-01 is likely to have been the result mainly of sampling variability and only to a small extent the change in household definition. The change in household definition can affect only sampled addresses which, on the old definition, were split into more than one household. The table in Appendix A shows that in 2000-01 149 extra households were found at addresses with more than one household, that is 1.5 per cent of eligible addresses. The comparable percentages for the two previous years were 2.0 and 2.1 per cent. On that evidence the change in household definition increased average household size by 0.5 to 0.6 per cent. A study carried out on the Labour Force Survey in 1981 also gave an estimate of a 0.6 per cent increase. This the best estimate for the FES as well.

Ownership of durable goods

Table 9.3 looks at ownership of durable goods within a household from 1970 to 2000-01. **Figure 9.2** illustrates the change in the proportions of households for those goods that have shown the

9.1 Household compositions 1998-99, 1999-2000 and 2000-01

	1998-99	1999-2000	2000-01
			Number
Average household size	2.37	2.31	2.35
			Per cent
One person	29.0	31.4	29.9
Two persons	35.1	33.4	34.3
Three or four persons	29.1	29.0	29.3
Five or more persons	6.7	6.1	6.4
One man			
Aged under 65	9.1	10.8	10.3
Aged 65 and over	3.6	3.5	3.3
One woman			
Aged under 60	5.5	6.1	5.8
Aged 60 and over	10.8	10.9	10.5
One adult with children	5.9	6.2	5.4
Two adults with children	20.1	19.5	20.2
Three or more adults with children	3.8	3.5	3.8
Two adults	32.3	30.5	31.6
Three or more adults	8.8	8.8	8.9
All households	100.0	100.0	100.0

ONS, Family Spending 2000-01, © Crown copyright 2002

largest increases since 1996-97. The Figure shows that in 1996-97, 59 per cent of all households owned a CD player. This item has shown a steady increase each year and in 2000-01, over three-quarters of households in the UK owned a CD player. Since it was first recorded in 1998-99, access to the Internet has increased from 10 per cent to 32 per cent of households in 2000-01. This is an average for the year and quarterly figures published in September 2001 show that 37 per cent had Internet access from the home in the January to March quarter of 2001. The increase in the proportion of households owning a home computer has been steady since 1996-97, increasing by between 2 and 6 percentage points each year. The largest increase was in the last year, where the proportion of households owning a home computer increased from 38 to 44 per cent.

Table 9.3 also shows that central heating, washing machines and telephones have become almost universal durable goods as over 90 per cent of households recorded ownership of each of these items. In 2000-01, households in the UK were more likely to have access to the Internet (one third of households) than a dishwasher (one quarter of households) and just over half of all households owned a tumble dryer. The survey does not ask about possession of a television as this has been almost universal for several years.

Table 9.4 shows ownership of durable goods by income and **Figure 9.3** compares the lowest and highest income deciles for each of the durable goods. The Figure illustrates that again, the most essential durable goods for both decile groups were central heating, telephones and washing machines. Over four fifths of the lowest income households had central heating and telephones, with three-quarters owning a washing machine. Almost all of the highest income households had these goods with very high proportions also owning CD players and video recorders, 96 and 97 per cent respectively.

There were some large disparities in ownership for some other items between the lowest and the highest income groups. By far the largest difference was seen for households owning dishwashers; the highest income households were 17 times more likely to own a dishwasher than the lowest income households. About 10 times as many households in the highest income group had access to the Internet than the lowest income group and almost 6 times as many of the highest income households had a home computer. Other large differences occurred for mobile phones and satellite receivers where about 3 times as many of the highest income households recorded

9.2 Households with selected durable goods, 1996-97 to 2000-01

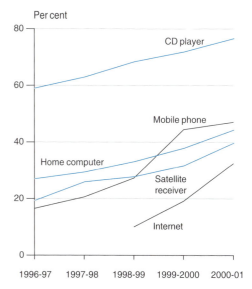

9.3 Ownership of durable goods for the lowest and highest gross income decile groups, 2000-01

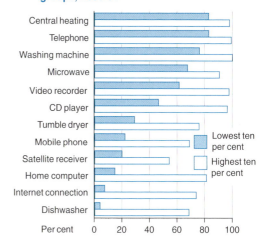

9.4 **Ownership of durable goods for households with and without children, 2000-01**

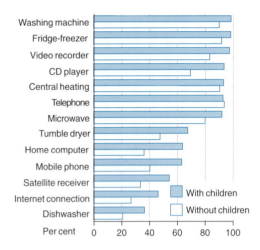

ownership than the lowest income households. The lowest priority durable good for the lowest income group was the dishwasher with only 4 per cent of households recording ownership. For the highest income group the satellite receiver had the lowest proportion but still had 54 per cent of households recording ownership. However, 20 per cent of the lowest income households owned a satellite receiver, a greater proportion than those with home computers, Internet access or dishwashers.

Figure 9.4 looks at the difference in the ownership of durable goods for households with and without children. Households with children had higher levels of ownership of almost every item, partly because they have higher incomes on average. The three highest priority goods for those with children were washing machines and freezers (fridge-freezer or deep freezer), both at 98 per cent, and video recorders, at 97 per cent. Ninety-four per cent of households without children recorded ownership of a telephone (the highest proportion recorded on an item for these households). This was the only item where households without children recorded a higher proportion of ownership than households with children but only by a small margin. The next two items with the highest proportion of ownership for households without children were central heating (90 per cent) and freezers (92 per cent). Those households with children were much more likely to have a home computer and access to the Internet. Out of all the durable goods both types of households were least likely to own dishwashers, satellite receivers and have access to the Internet.

9.5 **Households with cars by gross income decile groups, 2000-01**

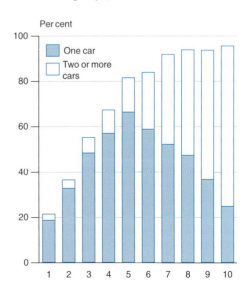

Table 9.5 looks at car ownership by income decile group, tenure and household composition. **Figure 9.5** illustrates car ownership by income decile group broken down into households with one car and households with two-or-more cars. In general, the number of households owning a car increased by income group. Nearly four-and-a-half times as many households in each of the top three income groups owned a car than in the lowest. The percentage increases in the proportions of car-owning households are greater between the first five income groups (between 12 and 19 percentage points) with considerably smaller increases between the highest four groups (a maximum increase of 2 percentage points).

Figure 9.5 also shows the proportion of households with one car or two-or-more cars in each income decile group. Again, the proportion with two-or-more cars increased with income. The 21 per cent with a car in the lowest income decile included only 3 per cent with more than one. Four times as many households owned a car in the fifth income group (81 per cent) including 15 per cent with more than one. In the eighth income group 94 per cent were car-owning households of which exactly half owned two-or-more cars. In the ninth and tenth groups, households were more likely to own two-or-more cars than just one. Seventy-one per cent of households in the highest income group owned two-or-more cars. The Table shows a large increase in households with three or more cars from the ninth decile, 12 per cent, to the tenth, at 21 per cent. **Table 9.5** also showed that almost all households in the process of buying (92 per cent) or consisting of one man, one woman and two children (93 per cent) were car-owning households.

Figure 9.6 and **Table 9.6** look at car ownership by Government Office Regions combined over the last three years (1998-99 – 2000-01). The Figure shows that the East had the highest proportion of car-owning households, at 79 per cent. This was closely followed by the South West with 78 per cent of households with a car and the South East with 77 per cent. Scotland and the North East had the lowest proportions of car-owning households, at 63 and 61 per cent respectively. London had the third lowest proportion of car-owning households at 64 per cent, 2 percentage points less than the proportion of households in Northern Ireland. The Figure also illustrates the proportions of households owning one or two-or-more cars in each region. Proportions of households owning one car were very similar for each region and only ranged between 42 and 46 per cent. Again the South West, East and South East were the three regions with the greatest proportion of households owning two or more cars, at 33, 34 and 35 per cent respectively. Households in the North East were the least likely to own two-or-more cars (18 per cent) with London the second least likely at 19 per cent.

Urban and rural households

Table 9.1 and **Figure 9.7** shows the proportions of households broken down by urban and rural areas for Great Britain only (also see Chapter 5, **Table 5.5**). Figures are based on data from the last two years (1999-2000 - 2000-01), in order to increase sample size and reliability. The Figure shows that 89 per cent of all households are situated in urban areas, with the remaining 11 per cent classed as rural households. The smallest of the urban areas, with 3 to 10 thousand households, include large villages and account for 8 per cent of households. Nearly a third of all households live in metropolitan built up areas. Nearly as many lived in the London built-up area as in the other metropolitan built-up areas combined.

9.6 Households with cars by region, 1998-99 - 2000-01

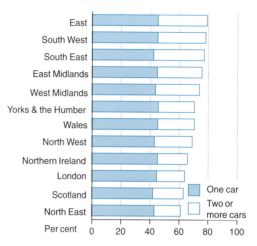

9.7 Household by urban/rural indicators, 1999-2000 - 2000-01

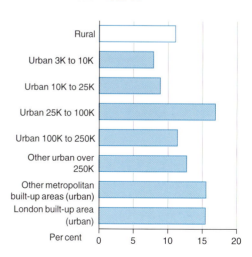

9.1 Characteristics of households
based on weighted data

2000-01

	% * of all house-holds	Grossed number of house-holds (000s)	House-holds in sample (number)		% * of all house-holds	Grossed number of house-holds (000s)	House-holds in sample (number)
Total number of households	100	25,030	6,637	**Composition of household (cont)**			
				Five adults	0	80	13
Size of household				Five adults, one or more children	0	20	6
One person	30	7,490	1,904				
Two persons	34	8,600	2,312	All other households without children	0	30	6
Three persons	16	3,900	990	All other households with children	0	40	10
Four persons	14	3,440	947				
Five persons	5	1,150	345	**Number of economically active**			
Six persons	1	290	92	**persons in household**			
Seven persons	0	90	26	No person	32	8,130	2,275
Eight persons	0	50	13	One person	29	7,200	1,910
Nine or more persons	0	30	8	More than one person	39	9,690	2,452
				Two persons	31	7,640	1,988
Composition of household				Three persons	6	1,540	349
One adult	30	7,470	1,900	Four persons	2	430	99
Retired households mainly				Five persons	0	70	14
dependent on state pensions[1]	7	1,770	457	Six or more persons	0	10	2
Other retired households	6	1,510	404				
Non-retired households	17	4,190	1,039				
One man	14	3,390	800	**Households with married women**	50	12,450	3,383
Aged under 65	10	2,570	559	Households with married women			
Aged 65 and over	3	830	241	economically active	28	7,100	1,875
One woman	16	4,080	1,100	With no dependent children	14	3,590	887
Aged under 60	6	1,440	428	With dependent children	14	3,510	988
Aged 60 and over	11	2,640	672	One child	6	1,440	377
				Two children	6	1,540	447
One adult, one child	3	680	208	Three children	2	440	135
One man, one child	0	110	26	Four or more children	0	90	29
One woman, one child	2	560	182				
One adult, two or more children	3	690	241	Households with married women			
One man, two or more children	0	50	12	not economically active	21	5,350	1,508
One woman, two or more children	3	630	229	With no dependent children	16	4,000	1,108
				With dependent children	5	1,350	400
One man, one woman	29	7,380	1,969	One child	2	410	114
Retired households mainly				Two children	2	570	165
dependent on state pensions[1]	2	610	178	Three children	1	270	86
Other retired households	7	1,840	548	Four or more children	0	100	35
Non-retired households	20	4,930	1,243				
Two men or two women	2	550	135				
				Economic status of head of household			
Two adults with children	20	5,050	1,460	Economically active	62	15,460	3,987
One man one woman, one child	7	1,750	474	Employee at work	50	12,610	3,232
Two men or two women, one child	0	60	20	Full-time	45	11,150	2,835
One man one woman, two children	9	2,250	650	Part-time	6	1,460	397
Two men or two women, two children	0	20	6				
One man one woman, three children	3	740	234	Government-supported training	0	70	19
Two men or two women, three children	0	10	3	Unemployed	3	760	199
Two adults, four children	1	170	57	Self-employed	8	2,020	537
Two adults, five children	0	30	11				
Two adults, six or more children	0	20	5	Economically inactive	38	9,570	2,650
Three adults	7	1,650	348	**Occupational groupings of**			
				head of household			
Three adults with children	3	800	208	Employee	54	13,440	3,450
Three adults, one child	2	510	128	Professional	4	1,050	251
Three adults, two children	1	180	50	Employers and managers	12	3,070	796
Three adults, three children	0	60	17	Intermediate non manual	7	1,850	464
Three adults, four or more children	0	50	13	Junior non manual	6	1,590	416
Four adults	2	480	95	Manual	23	5,680	1,469
				Skilled	12	2,920	749
Four adults, one child	0	90	23	Semi-skilled	9	2,170	560
Four adults, two or more children	0	50	15	Unskilled	2	600	160

* Based on grossed number of households

ONS, Family Spending 2000-01, © Crown copyright 2002

9.1 Characteristics of households (cont.)
based on weighted data

2000-01

	% * of all house- holds	Grossed number of house- holds (000s)	House- holds in sample (number)
Occupational groupings of			
head of household (continued)			
Member of armed forces	0	98	25
Others[2]	0	101	29
Self-employed	8	2,020	537
Professional	1	284	69
Employers and managers	2	404	106
Intermediate and junior non manual	1	230	61
Manual	4	1,097	298
Retired	25	6,173	1,700
Other	14	3,394	950
Age of head of household			
15 and under 20 years	0	112	33
20 and under 25 years	3	801	204
25 and under 30 years	7	1,760	450
30 and under 35 years	11	2,634	655
35 and under 40 years	11	2,729	713
40 and under 45 years	10	2,409	620
45 and under 50 years	9	2,165	610
50 and under 55 years	10	2,496	659
55 and under 60 years	8	1,921	512
60 and under 65 years	7	1,802	475
65 and under 70 years	6	1,582	481
70 and under 75 years	6	1,605	475
75 and under 80 years	6	1,425	391
80 and under 85 years	3	865	206
85 and under 90 years	2	549	116
90 years or more	1	175	37
Government Office Regions and Countries			
1998-99 - 2000-01			
United Kingdom	100	25,009	20,364
North East	5	1,162	886
North West	11	2,841	2,181
Yorkshire and the Humber	8	2,100	1,657
East Midlands	7	1,763	1,356
West Midlands	9	2,159	1,658
East	9	2,293	1,799
London	12	3,063	1,980
South East	14	3,477	2,613
South West	8	2,086	1,770
England	84	20,943	15,900
Wales	5	1,221	976
Scotland	9	2,205	1,779
Northern Ireland	3	640	1,709

	% * of all house- holds	Grossed number of house- holds (000s)	House- holds in sample (number)
Type of administrative area 1998-99 - 2000-01			
Greater London	12	3,067	1,983
Metropolitan Districts and Central			
Clydeside Conurbation	21	5,323	3,984
Non-Metropolitan Districts	66	16,619	14,397
High population density	24	5,973	5,147
Medium population density	19	4,752	3,737
Low population density	24	5,894	5,513
GB urban/rural areas 1999-2000 - 2000-01			
Urban			
London built-up area	15	3,501	1,564
Other metropolitan built up areas	16	3,577	1,754
Other urban:			
population over 250k	13	2,903	1,493
population 100k to 250k	11	2,604	1,356
population 25k to 100k	17	3,877	2,008
population 10k to 25k	9	2,000	1,074
population 3k to 10k	8	1,825	972
Rural	11	2,532	1,355
Tenure of dwelling[3]			
Owners			
Owned outright	27	6,872	1,873
Buying with a mortgage	41	10,211	2,665
All	68	17,083	4,538
Social rented from			
Council	15	3,873	1,075
Registered social landlord	6	1,471	395
All	21	5,344	1,470
Private rented			
Rent free	2	378	100
Rent paid, unfurnished	6	1,576	389
Rent paid, furnished	3	649	140
All	10	2,602	629
Households with durable goods			
Car/van	72	18,027	4,799
One	44	11,066	2,978
Two	22	5,533	1,480
Three or more	6	1,428	341
Central heating, full or partial	91	22,822	6,080
Fridge-freezer or deep freezer	94	23,434	6,223
Washing machine	92	23,152	6,185
Tumble dryer	53	13,374	3,573
Dishwasher	25	6,343	1,719
Microwave oven	84	20,901	5,600
Telephone	93	23,377	6,195
Mobile phone	47	11,776	3,080
Video recorder	87	21,880	5,847
Satellite receiver[4]	40	9,919	2,606
Compact disc player	77	19,149	5,035
Home computer	44	11,070	2,862
Internet connection	32	8,133	2,074

* Based on grossed number of households

1 Mainly dependent on state pension and not economically active - see appendix D.

2 Consists of 19 households where the head was on Government-supported training and 10 households where the head was a school leaver or had never worked.

3 See footnotes in Table 4.10.

4 Includes digital and cable receivers

9.2 Characteristics of persons
based on weighted data

2000-01

	Males				Females				All persons			
	Percentage* of		Grossed number of persons (000s)	Persons in the sample (number)	Percentage* of		Grossed number of persons (000s)	Persons in the sample (number)	%* of all persons	Grossed number of persons (000s)	Persons in the sample (number)
	all males	all persons			all females	all persons					
All persons	100	49	28,960	7,610	100	51	29,950	8,315	100	58,910	15,925
Adults	77	38	22,190	5,554	78	39	23,240	6,298	77	45,420	11,852
Persons aged under 60	59	29	16,970	4,084	56	28	16,720	4,557	57	33,690	8,641
Persons aged 60 or under 65	5	2	1,460	376	5	3	1,540	423	5	2,990	799
Persons aged 65 or under 70	4	2	1,200	366	4	2	1,250	378	4	2,450	744
Persons aged 70 or over	9	4	2,560	728	12	6	3,730	940	11	6,290	1,668
Children	23	12	6,780	2,056	22	11	6,710	2,017	23	13,490	4,073
Children under 2 years of age	2	1	700	208	2	1	710	210	2	1,410	418
Children aged 2 or under 5	4	2	1,110	332	4	2	1,050	318	4	2,160	650
Children aged 5 or under 16	15	7	4,210	1,304	14	7	4,260	1,311	14	8,470	2,615
Children aged 16 or under 18	3	1	760	212	2	1	700	178	2	1,450	390
Economic activity											
Persons active (aged 16 or over)	55	27	16,050	3,895	44	22	13,210	3,516	50	29,250	7,411
Persons not active	45	22	12,920	3,715	56	28	16,750	4,799	50	29,660	8,514
Men 65 or over and women 60 or over	12	6	3,530	1,026	20	10	5,990	1,600	16	9,520	2,626
Others (Including children under 16)	32	16	9,390	2,689	36	18	10,750	3,199	34	20,140	5,888

* Based on grossed number of households

9.3 Percentage of households with durable goods
1970 to 2000-01

	Car/ van	Central heating[1]	Washing machine	Tumble dryer	Dish-washer	Micro-wave	Tele-phone	Mobile phone	Video recorder	Satellite receiver[2]	Cd player	Home computer	Internet connec-tion
1970	52	30	65	--	--	--	35	--	--	--	--	--	--
1975	57	47	72	--	--	--	52	--	--	--	--	--	--
1980	60	59	79	--	--	--	72	--	--	--	--	--	--
1985	63	69	83	--	--	--	81	--	30	--	--	13	--
1990	67	79	86	--	--	--	87	--	61	--	--	17	--
1994-95	69	84	89	50	18	67	91	--	76	--	46	--	--
1995-96	70	85	91	50	20	70	92	--	79	--	51	--	--
1996-97	69	87	91	51	20	75	93	16	82	19	59	27	--
1997-98	70	89	91	51	22	77	94	20	84	26	63	29	--
1998-99	72	89	92	51	24	80	95	26	86	27	68	32	9
1998-99*	72	89	92	51	23	79	95	27	85	28	68	33	10
1999-2000*	71	90	91	52	23	80	95	44	86	32	72	38	19
2000-01*	72	91	92	53	25	84	93	47	87	40	77	44	32

1 Full or partial.

2 Includes digital and cable receivers

-- Data not available.

* Based on weighted data and including children's expenditure

ONS, Family Spending 2000-01, © Crown copyright 2002

9.4 Percentage[1] of households with durable goods by income group and household composition
2000-01

based on weighted data

	Central heating[2]	Washing machine	Tumble dryer	Micro-wave	Dish-washer	CD player
All households	91	92	53	84	25	77
Gross income decile group						
Lowest ten per cent	83	76	29	67	4	46
Second decile group	88	84	37	74	6	46
Third decile group	86	91	45	81	12	58
Fourth decile group	91	92	48	83	14	73
Fifth decile group	91	96	52	86	16	83
Sixth decile group	89	96	58	88	25	87
Seventh decile group	95	98	63	88	29	91
Eighth decile group	95	97	62	90	35	92
Ninth decile group	97	97	65	88	44	93
Highest ten per cent	98	100	76	90	68	96
Household composition						
One adult, retired households[3]	85	74	26	62	2	23
One adult, non-retired households	88	83	37	75	10	75
One adult, one child	87	95	47	89	12	91
One adult, two or more children	91	99	64	89	16	85
One man and one woman, retired households[3]	84	91	39	72	7	33
One man and one woman, non-retired households	93	99	60	90	33	90
One man and one woman, one child	94	98	68	93	36	94
One man and one woman, two or more children	94	99	71	93	44	95
All other households without children	92	94	59	86	26	85
All other households with children	91	95	47	86	36	88

	Home computer	Internet connection	Tele-phone	Mobile phone	Satellite receiver[4]	Video recorder
All households	44	32	93	47	40	87
Gross income decile group						
Lowest ten per cent	14	7	83	22	20	61
Second decile group	14	5	87	24	20	71
Third decile group	21	12	91	28	27	81
Fourth decile group	27	17	93	41	39	88
Fifth decile group	39	26	94	47	43	94
Sixth decile group	47	32	94	57	44	92
Seventh decile group	59	43	98	60	47	97
Eighth decile group	65	49	97	60	49	96
Ninth decile group	75	60	99	64	54	96
Highest ten per cent	81	73	99	69	54	97
Household composition						
One adult, retired households[3]	4	2	95	5	10	48
One adult, non-retired households	34	25	85	41	30	80
One adult, one child	42	21	86	62	42	95
One adult, two or more children	42	24	79	55	48	94
One man and one woman, retired households[3]	9	3	96	10	17	82
One man and one woman, non-retired households	53	41	96	56	45	95
One man and one woman, one child	63	49	95	65	55	98
One man and one woman, two or more children	71	53	96	64	57	98
All other households without children	57	47	96	58	51	91
All other households with children	59	37	90	60	49	91

1 See table 9.5 for number of recording households.

2 Full or partial.

3 Mainly dependent on state pension and not economically active - see appendix D.

4 Includes digital and cable receivers

9.5 Percentage of households with cars by income group, tenure and household composition

based on weighted data

2000-01

	One car/van	Two cars/vans	Three or more cars/vans	All with cars/vans	Grossed number of house-holds (000s)	House-holds in the sample (number)
All households	44	22	6	72	25,030	6,637
Gross income decile group						
Lowest ten per cent	19	2	0	21	2,500	664
Second decile group	33	4	0	36	2,500	709
Third decile group	48	6	1	55	2,500	710
Fourth decile group	57	10	1	67	2,500	695
Fifth decile group	66	13	2	81	2,500	668
Sixth decile group	59	22	4	84	2,500	664
Seventh decile group	52	31	9	92	2,500	667
Eighth decile group	47	39	8	94	2,500	631
Ninth decile group	37	45	12	94	2,500	619
Highest ten per cent	25	50	21	96	2,510	610
Tenure of dwelling[1]						
Owners						
Owned outright	50	19	4	74	6,870	1,873
Buying with a mortgage	47	36	10	92	10,210	2,665
All	48	29	7	85	17,080	4,538
Social rented from						
Council	32	4	1	38	3,870	1,075
Registered social landlord [2]	33	6	1	40	1,470	395
All	33	4	1	38	5,340	1,470
Private rented						
Rent free	44	16	4	64	380	100
Rent paid, unfurnished	43	15	3	62	1,580	389
Rent paid, furnished	37	6	5	49	650	140
All	42	13	4	59	2,600	629
Household composition						
One adult, retired mainly dependent on state pensions[3]	14	1	0	15	1,770	457
One adult, other retired	41	1	0	42	1,510	404
One adult, non-retired	55	4	1	60	4,190	1,039
One adult, one child	45	4	0	50	680	208
One adult, two or more children	46	5	0	51	690	241
One man and one woman, retired dependent on state pensions[3]	53	3	0	56	610	178
One man and one woman, other retired	65	17	1	82	1,840	548
One man and one woman, non-retired	46	37	5	88	4,930	1,243
One man and one woman, one child	49	36	7	92	1,750	474
One man and one woman, two children	43	45	5	93	2,250	650
One man and one woman, three children	45	39	5	88	740	234
Two adults, four or more children	42	33	4	79	210	73
Three adults	33	32	22	87	1,650	348
Three adults, one or more children	32	38	21	90	800	208
All other households without children	30	21	22	74	1,130	249
All other households with children	38	22	15	75	290	83

1 See footnotes in Table 4.10.

2 Formerly housing association

3 Mainly dependent on state pension and not economically active - see appendix D.

ONS, Family Spending 2000-01, © Crown copyright 2002

9.6 Percentage of households with durable goods by UK countries and Government Office Regions

1998-99 - 2000-01

based on weighted data

	North East	North West	Yorks and the Humber	East Midlands	West Midlands	East	London
Average number of grossed households (thousands)	1,160	2,840	2,100	1,760	2,160	2,290	3,060
Total number of households in sample (over 3 years)	886	2,181	1,657	1,356	1,658	1,799	1,980
Percentage of households							
by Government Office Region and country							
Car/van	61	69	71	76	74	79	64
One	43	43	46	45	44	45	45
Two	15	21	21	25	23	26	16
Three or more	3	5	4	6	7	8	3
Central heating full or partial	97	85	84	92	86	95	91
Fridge-freezer or deep freezer	92	93	92	93	93	95	91
Refrigerator[1]	45	48	59	62	51	55	43
Washing machine	95	92	95	94	91	92	88
Tumble dryer	49	51	55	55	55	53	44
Dishwasher	16	20	21	23	22	27	26
Microwave	88	83	85	83	81	79	72
Telephone	92	94	95	94	94	97	95
Mobile phone	35	39	40	42	42	41	43
Video recorder	86	87	87	87	87	86	84
Satellite receiver[2]	36	35	32	32	34	33	34
CD player	70	73	73	74	71	73	73
Home computer	32	36	36	39	39	42	45
Internet connection	15	20	18	20	20	23	27

	South East	South West	England	Wales	Scotland	Northern Ireland	United Kingdom
Average number of grossed households (thousands)	3,480	2,090	20,940	1,220	2,200	640	25,010
Total number of households in sample (over 3 years)	2,613	1,770	15,900	976	1,779	1,709	20,364
Percentage of households							
by Government Office Region and country							
Car/van	77	78	73	70	63	66	71
One	42	45	44	45	42	45	44
Two	27	26	23	22	17	18	22
Three or more	8	7	6	4	4	2	5
Central heating full or partial	91	88	90	90	91	94	90
Fridge-freezer or deep freezer	93	92	93	93	89	87	92
Refrigerator[1]	56	58	53	60	47	45	52
Washing machine	91	91	91	93	95	93	92
Tumble dryer	54	51	52	53	56	42	52
Dishwasher	31	27	25	17	20	26	24
Microwave	80	81	80	86	82	81	81
Telephone	96	94	95	94	93	93	94
Mobile phone	44	37	41	38	35	24	40
Video recorder	87	85	86	88	84	84	86
Satellite receiver[2]	31	28	33	40	31	31	33
CD player	75	73	73	67	72	59	72
Home computer	44	39	40	31	32	22	38
Internet connection	25	22	22	15	15	12	21

1 Data for 1998-99 and 1999-2000

2 Includes digital and cable receivers

9.7 Percentage of households by size, composition and age in each income decile group
based on weighted data

2000-01

	Lowest ten per cent	Second decile group	Third decile group	Fourth decile group	Fifth decile group	Sixth decile group
Lower boundary of group (£ per week)		107	163	231	310	397
Grossed number of households (thousands)	**2,500**	**2,500**	**2,500**	**2,500**	**2,500**	**2,500**
Number of households in the sample	**664**	**709**	**710**	**695**	**668**	**664**
Size of household						
One person	80	56	41	34	29	23
Two persons	14	26	42	41	39	37
Three persons	3	11	6	12	14	18
Four persons	1	6	7	6	11	16
Five persons	1	1	3	4	4	6
Six or more persons	1	0	1	2	2	1
All sizes	100	100	100	100	100	100
Household composition						
One adult, retired mainly dependent on state pensions[1]	44	19	6	1	0	0
One adult, other retired	2	23	16	8	5	3
One adult, non-retired	33	14	19	25	24	20
One adult, one child	10	4	3	3	3	2
One adult, two or more children	2	11	3	4	3	3
One man and one woman, retired mainly dependent on state pensions[1]	0	12	10	2	0	0
One man and one woman, other retired	0	2	15	18	14	9
One man and one woman, non-retired	4	8	11	16	19	23
One man and one woman, one child	1	2	3	5	5	9
One man and one woman, two children	1	3	5	4	9	12
One man and one woman, three children	0	0	2	3	3	4
Two adults, four or more children	1	0	0	1	1	1
Three adults	0	1	2	5	6	7
Three adults, one or more children	0	0	1	1	2	3
All other households without children	1	1	3	4	3	4
All other households with children	1	0	1	1	1	1
All compositions	100	100	100	100	100	100
Age of head of household						
15 and under 20 years	2	1	0	0	1	0
20 and under 25 years	5	4	3	4	4	3
25 and under 30 years	6	5	4	5	8	10
30 and under 35 years	5	6	5	10	11	15
35 and under 40 years	5	6	6	7	12	15
40 and under 45 years	5	5	5	9	8	9
45 and under 50 years	6	4	4	6	7	8
50 and under 55 years	8	4	6	9	8	10
55 and under 60 years	6	5	6	8	9	7
60 and under 65 years	9	7	9	10	9	7
65 and under 70 years	6	11	11	9	8	7
70 and under 75 years	8	12	17	9	6	4
75 and under 80 years	12	14	10	7	5	3
80 and under 85 years	10	8	7	4	2	2
85 and under 90 years	7	7	3	2	1	1
90 years or more	2	1	2	1	1	0
All ages	100	100	100	100	100	100

1 Mainly dependent on state pension and not economically active - see appendix D.

9.7 Percentage of households by size, composition and age in each income decile group (cont.)

2000-01

based on weighted data

	Seventh decile group	Eighth decile group	Ninth decile group	Highest ten per cent	All house-holds
Lower boundary of group (£ per week)	489	597	739	993	
Grossed number of households (thousands)	**2,500**	**2,500**	**2,500**	**2,510**	**25,030**
Number of households in the sample	**667**	**631**	**619**	**610**	**6,637**
Size of household					
One person	14	9	9	4	30
Two persons	39	39	35	33	34
Three persons	21	24	24	22	16
Four persons	18	17	24	30	14
Five persons	5	8	6	9	5
Six or more persons	3	3	3	3	2
All sizes	100	100	100	100	100
Household composition					
One adult, retired mainly dependent on state pensions[1]	0	0	0	0	7
One adult, other retired	1	1	1	1	6
One adult, non-retired	14	7	8	3	17
One adult, one child	1	1	1	0	3
One adult, two or more children	2	1	0	0	3
One man and one woman, retired mainly dependent on state pensions[1]	0	0	0	0	2
One man and one woman, other retired	7	4	3	2	7
One man and one woman, non-retired	28	30	30	28	20
One man and one woman, one child	13	10	12	9	7
One man and one woman, two children	13	12	13	17	9
One man and one woman, three children	3	6	4	4	3
Two adults, four or more children	1	1	1	1	1
Three adults	7	13	12	12	7
Three adults, one or more children	4	5	6	8	3
All other households without children	4	6	7	12	5
All other households with children	2	2	1	2	1
All compositions	100	100	100	100	100
Age of head of household					
15 and under 20 years	0	0	0	0	0
20 and under 25 years	3	2	2	1	3
25 and under 30 years	8	8	7	8	7
30 and under 35 years	15	15	13	10	11
35 and under 40 years	15	15	16	13	11
40 and under 45 years	10	16	14	16	10
45 and under 50 years	10	9	13	18	9
50 and under 55 years	10	12	15	19	10
55 and under 60 years	10	10	9	7	8
60 and under 65 years	7	5	5	4	7
65 and under 70 years	5	3	3	1	6
70 and under 75 years	4	2	2	1	6
75 and under 80 years	2	2	1	1	6
80 and under 85 years	1	1	1	0	3
85 and under 90 years	0	0	0	0	2
90 years or more	0	0	0	0	1
All ages	100	100	100	100	100

1 Mainly dependent on state pension and not economically active - see appendix D.

9.8 Percentage of households by occupation, economic activity, and tenure in each income decile group
based on weighted data

2000-01

	Lowest ten per cent	Second decile group	Third decile group	Fourth decile group	Fifth decile group	Sixth decile group
Lower boundary of group (£ per week)		107	163	231	310	397
Grossed number of households (thousands)	2,500	2,500	2,500	2,500	2,500	2,500
Number of households in the sample	664	709	710	695	668	664
Occupational grouping of head of household						
Employee	20	15	22	45	57	68
Professional	0	0	0	1	2	2
Employers and managers	2	0	1	3	7	9
Intermediate non-manual	1	1	2	3	9	11
Junior non-manual	2	3	5	12	9	9
Manual	14	11	14	25	29	36
Skilled	4	2	3	9	16	18
Semi-skilled	7	6	8	11	10	15
Unskilled	3	3	3	5	3	3
Member of the armed forces	0	0	0	0	0	1
Others[1]	1	1	0	1	0	0
Self-employed	2	3	5	7	9	9
Professional	0	0	1	0	0	1
Employers and managers	0	1	1	1	1	2
Intermediate non-manual	0	0	0	1	1	1
Manual	1	2	3	5	7	6
Retired	47	56	50	31	23	15
Other	32	27	22	17	12	8
All occupational groups	100	100	100	100	100	100
Number of economically active persons in household						
No person	78	80	66	39	24	15
One person	20	18	27	46	50	40
Two persons	2	2	6	15	23	42
Three persons	0	1	1	0	3	4
Four or more persons	0	0	0	0	0	0
All economically active persons	100	100	100	100	100	100
Tenure of dwelling[2]						
Owners						
Owned outright	25	35	43	36	34	26
Buying with a mortgage	6	6	12	27	38	47
All	31	41	56	63	72	73
Social rented from						
Council	41	35	23	18	12	10
Registered social landlord[3]	11	13	11	8	6	4
All	52	48	34	26	18	14
Private rented						
Rent free	3	2	1	3	1	3
Rent paid, unfurnished	10	7	7	5	6	7
Rent paid, furnished	4	2	2	3	3	2
All	17	11	11	10	10	12
All tenures	100	100	100	100	100	100

1Consists of 19 households where the head was on Government-supported training and 10 households where the head was a school leaver or had never worked.

2 See footnotes in Table 4.10.

3 Formerly housing association

ONS, Family Spending 2000-01, © Crown copyright 2002

9.8 Percentage of households by occupation, economic activity, and tenure in each income decile group (cont.)

2000-01

based on weighted data

	Seventh decile group	Eighth decile group	Ninth decile group	Highest ten per cent	All house-holds
Lower boundary of group (£ per week)	489	597	739	993	
Grossed number of households (thousands)	**2,500**	**2,500**	**2,500**	**2,510**	**25,030**
Number of households in the sample	**667**	**631**	**619**	**610**	**6,637**
Occupational grouping of head of household					
Employee	71	77	82	81	54
Professional	3	7	11	15	4
Employers and managers	15	16	27	42	12
Intermediate non-manual	10	13	13	11	7
Junior non-manual	8	6	7	4	6
Manual	34	34	24	8	23
Skilled	20	22	18	5	12
Semi-skilled	12	10	6	2	9
Unskilled	3	2	0	1	2
Member of the armed forces	1	1	1	1	0
Others[1]	0	0	0	0	0
Self-employed	12	9	10	15	8
Professional	1	1	1	6	1
Employers and managers	2	1	2	4	2
Intermediate non-manual	1	1	1	2	1
Manual	8	5	5	3	4
Retired	10	7	4	2	25
Other	6	6	4	2	14
All occupational groups	100	100	100	100	100
Number of economically active persons in household					
No person	9	7	4	3	32
One person	33	21	20	14	29
Two persons	50	57	54	55	31
Three persons	6	12	17	18	6
Four or more persons	2	3	6	10	2
All economically active persons	100	100	100	100	100
Tenure of dwelling[2]					
Owners					
Owned outright	22	20	19	15	27
Buying with a mortgage	63	63	69	75	41
All	86	83	87	91	68
Social rented from					
Council	6	5	4	1	15
Registered social landlord [3]	2	2	1	1	6
All	8	7	6	1	21
Private rented					
Rent free	1	1	1	1	2
Rent paid, unfurnished	4	8	4	3	6
Rent paid, furnished	1	2	2	4	3
All	6	10	7	8	10
All tenures	100	100	100	100	100

1 Consists of 19 households where the head was on Government-supported training and 10 households where the head was a school leaver or had never worked.

2 See footnotes in Table 4.10.

3 Formerly housing association

Appendices

Appendix A

Description and response rate of the survey

The survey

The Family Expenditure Survey (FES) is a voluntary sample survey of private households. The basic unit of the survey is the household. In the 2000-01 survey the FES adopted the harmonised definition used in other government household surveys: a group of people living at the same address with common housekeeping, that is sharing household expenses such as food and bills, **or** sharing a living room (see Appendix D). The previous definition differed from the harmonised definition by requiring both common housekeeping **and** a shared living room. This resulted in the FES having slightly more one person households and fewer large households than the other surveys. An analysis of the effect of the change is in Chapter 9.

Each individual aged 16 or over in the household visited is asked to keep diary records of daily expenditure for two weeks. Information about regular expenditure, such as rent and mortgage payments, is obtained from a household interview along with retrospective information on certain large, infrequent expenditures such as those on vehicles. Since 1998-99 the results have also included information from simplified diaries kept by children aged between 7 and 15. The effects were shown in Appendix F of Family Spending for 1998-99 and again for 1999-2000. The analysis is not repeated this year as inclusion of the data is now a standard feature of the survey.

Detailed questions are asked about the income of each adult member of the household. In addition, personal information such as age, sex and marital status is recorded for each household member. Paper versions of the computerised household and income questionnaires can be obtained from the address given in the Introduction.

The survey has been conducted each year since 1957. The survey is continuous, interviews being spread evenly over the year to ensure that seasonal effects are covered. From time to time changes are made to the information sought. Some changes reflect new forms of expenditure or new sources of income, especially benefits. Others are the result of new requirements by the survey's users. An important example is the re-definition of housing costs for owner occupiers in 1992 (see Appendix E).

The sample design

The FES sample for Great Britain is a multi-stage stratified random sample with clustering. It is drawn from the Small Users file of the Postcode Address File - the Post Office's list of addresses. All Scottish offshore islands and the Isles of Scilly are excluded from the sample because of excessive interview travel costs. Postal sectors (ward size) are the primary sample unit. 672 postal sectors are randomly selected during the year after being arranged in strata defined by standard regions (sub-divided into metropolitan and non-metropolitan areas) and two 1991 Census variables - socio-economic group and ownership of cars. These were new stratifiers introduced for the 1996-97 survey. The Northern Ireland sample is drawn as a random sample of addresses from the Valuation and Lands Agency list.

Response to the survey

Great Britain

Some 10,400 households are selected each year for the FES in Great Britain, but it is never possible to get full response. A small number cannot be contacted at all, and in other households one or more members decline to co-operate. In all, over 6,100 households in Great Britain co-operated fully in the survey in 2000-01, that is they answered the household questionnaire and all adults in the household answered the income questionnaire and kept the expenditure diary. The response rate for the 2000-01 FES was 59 per cent in Great Britain. This compares with 63 per cent in 1999-2000, which saw the first year-on-year increase since 1992, and is the same as the 59 per cent achieved in 1998-99.

Details of response are shown in the following table.

Response in 2000-01 - Great Britain

		No of households or addresses	Percentage of effective sample
i.	Sampled addresses	11,424	-
ii.	Ineligible addresses: businesses, institutions, empty, demolished/derelict	1,167	-
iii.	Extra households (multi-household addresses)	149	-
iv.	Total eligible (i.e. i less ii, plus iii)	10,406	100.0
v.	Co-operating households	6,115	58.8
vi.	Refusals	3,904	37.5
vii.	Households at which no contact could be obtained	387	3.7

Northern Ireland

In the Northern Ireland survey, the eligible sample was 990 households. The number of co-operating households who provided usable data was 522, giving a response rate of 56 per cent. Northern Ireland is over-sampled in order to provide a large enough sample for some separate analysis. The re-weighting procedure compensates for the over-sampling.

The fieldwork

The fieldwork is carried out by the Social Survey Division of the Office for National Statistics (ONS) in Great Britain and by the Northern Ireland Statistics and Research Agency of the Department of Finance and Personnel in Northern Ireland using almost identical questionnaires. Households at the selected addresses are visited and asked to co-operate in the survey. In order to maximise response, interviewers make at least four separate calls, and sometimes many more, at different times of day on households which are difficult to contact. Interviews are conducted by Computer Assisted Personal Interviewing (CAPI) using portable computers. During the interview information is collected about the household, about certain regular payments such as rent, gas, electricity and telephone accounts, about expenditure on certain large items (for example vehicle purchases over the previous 12 months), and about income. Each individual aged 16 or over in the household keeps a detailed record of expenditure every day for two weeks. Children aged between 7 and 15 are also asked to keep a simplified diary of daily expenditure (though not in the Northern Ireland enhanced sample). In 2000-01 a total of 1952 children aged between 7 and 15 in responding households in Great Britain were asked to complete expenditure diaries; only 29 or about 1½ per cent did not do so. This number includes both refusals and children who had no expenditure during the two weeks. Information provided by all members of the household is kept strictly confidential.

If all persons aged 16 and over in the household co-operate each is subsequently paid £10 for the trouble involved. Children who keep a diary are given a £5 payment. A refusal by an under 16 to keep a diary does not invalidate the household from inclusion in the survey. In the last two months of the 1998-99 survey, as an experiment, a small book of postage stamps was enclosed with the introductory letter sent to every address. It seemed to help with response and the measure has become a permanent feature of the survey. It is difficult to quantify the exact effect on response but the cognitive work that was carried out as part of the Expenditure and Food Survey development indicated that it was having a positive effect.

The new strategy for reissues adopted in 1999-2000 was continued in 2000-01. Addresses where there had been no contact or a refusal, but were judged suitable for reissue, were accumulated to form complete batches consisting only of reissues. The interviewers dealing with them were specially selected and given extra briefing. The information from households converted from non-responding to responding was included with the data for the quarter of the year when the interview was carried out. The increase in response rate, however, was attributed to the original month of issue. Over 2,100 addresses were reissued, that is about a half of addresses where there had been no response initially. About 240 of them were converted into fully responding households, which added 2.4 percentage points to the response rate.

The change in household definition will have made achieving response harder at some addresses. Under FES rules, a refusal by just one person invalidates the response of the whole household. If the group of people in a household would have been divided into two households on the previous definition, a non-response by one person in the group would still yield one responding household on the previous definition, but none on the new definition. The analysis in Chapter 9 shows that the new definition probably increased average household size by 0.6 per cent. A simple model of response in households affected by the change suggests that it may have reduced response by about 0.1 to 0.2 percentage points.

Reliability

Great care is taken in collecting information from households and comprehensive checks are applied during processing, so that errors in recording and processing are minimised. The main factors that affect the reliability of the survey results are sampling variability, non-response bias and some incorrect reporting of certain items of expenditure and income. Measures of sampling variability are given alongside some results in this report and are discussed in detail in Appendix C.

The households which decline to respond to the survey tend to differ in some respects from those which co-operate. It is therefore possible that their patterns of expenditure and income also differ. A comparison has been made of the households responding in the 1991 FES with those not responding, based on information from the 1991 Census of Population (*A comparison of the Census characteristics of respondents and non-respondents to the 1991 FES* by K Foster, ONS Survey Methodology Bulletin No. 38, Jan 1996). Results from the study indicate that response was lower than average in Greater London, higher in non-metropolitan areas and that non-response tended to increase with increasing age of the head of the household, up to age 65. Households which contained three or more adults, or where the head was born outside the United Kingdom or was classified to an ethnic minority group were also more likely than others to be non-responding. Non-response was also above average where the head of the household had no post-school qualifications, was self-employed, or was in a manual social class group. The data are now re-weighted to compensate for the main non-response biases identified from the 1991 Census comparison, as described in Appendix F.

Checks are included in the CAPI program which are applied to the responses given during the interview. Other procedures are also in place to ensure that users are provided with high quality data. For example, quality control is carried out to ensure that any outliers are genuine, and checks are made on any unusual changes in average spending compared with the previous year.

When aspects of the survey change, rigorous tests are used to ensure the proposed changes are sensible and work both in the field and on the processing system. For example, in 1996-97 an improved set of questions was introduced on income from self-employment. This was developed by focus groups and then tested by piloting before being introduced into the main survey.

It has been suggested that averages of household income recorded in the FES are too low, principally because certain forms of income, including investments, occupational pensions or self-employment, may be under-estimated. The evidence for this is limited and now very dated. Currently FES levels are generally within a few per cent of levels indicated by other sources such as the Family Resources Survey (the Department for Work and Pensions), the New Earnings Survey and Labour Force Survey (ONS) and national income statistics.

The information obtained by the survey does not permit the construction of household accounts in the form of an income-expenditure balance sheet. The definitions of weekly household expenditure and income used are such that it is not to be expected that expenditure and income will balance, either for an individual household or even when averaged over a group of households. Hence, the difference between expenditure and income is not a measure of savings or dis-savings.

Experience of household surveys in the United Kingdom and in other countries indicates that reported expenditure on a few items, notably tobacco and alcohol, is below the levels which might be expected by comparison with other sources of information. In 2000-01 the estimated average expenditure on tobacco was 63 per cent of the figure based on HM Customs and Excise data, and for alcohol was 56 per cent. Chapter 14 of the *FES Handbook* (Kemsley, Redpath and Holmes) published in 1980 examines the possible causes of the understatement of alcohol and tobacco expenditure in the FES results, as well as other problems of understatement. The conclusion then was that it was mainly due to non-response by very heavy drinkers and smokers. Under-reporting by responding households will also be a factor

National Lottery spending is significantly under-recorded in the FES, the FES estimate in 2000-01 being about 68 per cent of recorded sales.

Although FES response is based on complete households responding, there are areas in the survey for which missing values can be imputed. These missing values are imputed on a case by case basis using other information collected in the interview. The procedure is used, for example, for council tax payments and for interest received on savings.

Appendix B

Uses of the survey

FES Expenditure Data

Retail Prices Index - The main reason, historically, for instituting a regular survey on expenditure by households has been to provide information on spending patterns for the Retail Prices Index (RPI). The RPI plays a vital role in the uprating of state pensions and welfare benefits and in general economic policy and analysis. The RPI measures the change in the cost of a selection of goods and services representative of the expenditure of the vast majority of households. The pattern of expenditure gradually changes from one year to the next, and the composition of the basket needs to be kept up-to-date. Accordingly, regular information is required on spending patterns and much of this is supplied by the FES. The expenditure weights for the general RPI need to relate to people within given income limits, for which the FES is the only source of information.

Consumers' expenditure and GDP - FES data on spending are an important source used in compiling national estimates of consumers' expenditure which are published regularly in United Kingdom National Accounts (ONS Blue Book). Consumers' expenditure estimates feed into the National Accounts and estimates of GDP. They will provide the weights for the Harmonised Index of Consumer prices (HICP) which is calculated by each member of the European Union, and for Purchasing Power Parities (PPPs) for international price comparisons. FES data are also used in the estimation of taxes on expenditure, in particular VAT.

Regional accounts - FES expenditure information is one of the sources used by ONS to derive regional estimates of consumers' expenditure. It is also used in compiling some of the other estimates for the regional accounts.

Pay Review Bodies governing the salaries of HM Armed Forces and the medical and dental professions receive estimates of the minimum valuation of the benefit of a company car. This is based on FES data on the cost of buying and running private cars.

The Statistical Office of the European Communities (Eurostat) collates information from household budget surveys conducted by the member states. The FES is the UK's contribution to this. The UK is one of only a few countries with such a regular, continuous and detailed survey.

Other Government uses - The Department of Trade and Industry and the Department for Transport, Local Government and the Regions both use FES expenditure data in their own fields, e.g. - relating to energy, housing, cars and transport. Several other government publications include FES expenditure data, such as *Social Trends, Regional Trends* and the *Social Focus* series.

Non-Government uses - There are also numerous users outside Central Government, including academic researchers and business and market researchers.

FES Income Data

Redistribution of income - FES information on income and expenditure is used to study how Government taxes and benefits affect household income. The Government's interdepartmental tax benefit model is based on the FES and enables the economic effects of policy measures to be analysed across households. This model is used by HM Treasury, Inland Revenue and HM Customs and Excise to estimate the impact on different households of possible changes in taxes and benefits.

Non-Government users - As with the expenditure data, FES income data are also studied extensively outside Government. In particular, academic researchers in the economic and social science areas of many universities use the FES. For example the Institute for Fiscal Studies uses FES data in research it carries out both for Government and on its own account to inform public debate.

Other FES Data

The Office for National Statistics uses the information on access to the Internet in a quarterly News Release on Internet access. The Department for Transport, Local Government and the Regions uses FES data to monitor and forecast levels of car ownership and use, and in studies on the effects of motoring taxes.

Note: Great care is taken to ensure complete confidentiality of information and to protect the identity of FES households. Anonymised data only are supplied to users.

Appendix C

Standard errors and estimates of precision

Because the FES is a survey of a sample of households and not of the whole population, the results are liable to differ to some degree from those that would have been obtained if every single household had been covered. Some of the differences will be systematic, in that lower proportions of certain types of household respond than of others. That aspect is discussed in Appendices A and F. This Appendix discusses the effect of sampling variability, the differences in expenditure and income between the households in the sample and in the whole population that arise from random chance. The degree of possible error will depend on how widely particular categories of expenditure (or income) vary between households. This "sampling error" is smallest for the average expenditure of large groups of households on items purchased frequently and when the level of spending does not vary greatly between households. Conversely it is largest for small groups of households, and for items purchased infrequently or for which expenditure varies considerably between households. A numerical measure of the likely magnitude of such differences (between the sample estimate and the value of the entire population) is provided by the quantity known as the standard error.

Two methods are used in this report to calculate the standard error.

Simple method This is an approximation, used generally in this report, regarding the co-operating households as if they were a sample obtained by single-stage random selection of all private households in the United Kingdom.

Full method This is more elaborate, and takes into account the fact that the sample is drawn in two stages, first a sample of areas (primary sampling units) then a sample of addresses within each of these areas. The main features of the sample design are described in Appendix A to this Report. This year the full method also takes account of the effect of weighting. The two stage sample increases sampling variability slightly, but the weighting reduces it for some items.

Standard errors using the full method are shown in percentage terms in **table 7.1** (standard error as a percentage of the average to which it refers). As the calculation of full method standard errors is complex, this is the only table where they are shown. Comparisons of simple method and full method percentage standard errors are given in **tables C1** and **C2** which also show the design factor (DEFT), which is the ratio of the full to the simple method standard errors.

Table C1

Percentage standard errors of expenditure of households and number of recording households   2000-01

| Commodity or service | Weighted average weekly household expenditure (£) | Percentage standard error | | Percentage standard error | Households recording expenditure | |
		Simple method	Design factor (DEFT)	Full method	Recording households in sample	Percentage of all households
All expenditure groups	**385.70**	*1.0*	**1.0**	*0.9*	**6,637**	*100*
Housing (net)	63.90	*1.3*	1.1	*1.4*	6,485	*98*
Fuel and power	11.90	*1.0*	1.1	*1.1*	6,353	*96*
Food and non-alcoholic drinks	61.90	*0.8*	1.0	*0.8*	6,631	*100*
Alcoholic drink	15.00	*1.9*	1.0	*1.8*	4,580	*69*
Tobacco	6.10	*2.5*	1.0	*2.5*	2,201	*33*
Clothing and footwear	22.00	*2.0*	1.0	*2.0*	4,679	*70*
Household goods	32.60	*2.6*	1.0	*2.6*	6,421	*97*
Household services	22.00	*2.4*	1.0	*2.3*	6,504	*98*
Personal goods and services	14.70	*2.0*	1.0	*2.0*	5,967	*90*
Motoring expenditure	55.10	*1.9*	1.0	*1.8*	4,948	*75*
Fares and other travel costs	9.50	*4.7*	0.9	*4.3*	3,447	*52*
Leisure goods	19.70	*2.9*	0.9	*2.7*	6,290	*95*
Leisure services	50.60	*2.5*	1.1	*2.7*	6,545	*99*
Miscellaneous	0.70	*5.8*	1.0	*5.9*	1,529	*23*

Table C2

Percentage standard errors of income of households and number of recording households   2000-01

| Source of income | Weighted average weekly household income (£) | Percentage standard error | | Percentage standard error | Households recording income | |
		Simple method	Design factor (DEFT)	Full method	Recording households in sample	Percentage of all households
Gross household income	**503**	*1.2*	**0.9**	*1.0*	**6,637**	*100*
Wages and salaries	337	*1.6*	0.9	*1.4*	3,892	*59*
Self-employment	44	*7.9*	0.9	*6.9*	710	*11*
Investments	20	*5.1*	0.9	*4.6*	3,907	*59*
Annuities and pensions (other than social security benefits)	35	*3.3*	0.9	*3.1*	1,800	*27*
Social security benefits	60	*1.3*	0.8	*1.1*	4,727	*71*
Other sources	6	*6.4*	1.1	*6.9*	1,217	*18*

ONS, Family Spending 2000-01, © Crown copyright 2002

Using the standard errors – confidence intervals

A good way of using standard errors is to calculate 95% confidence intervals from them. Simplifying a little, these can be taken to mean that there is only a 5% chance that the true population value lies outside that confidence interval. The 95% confidence interval is calculated as 1.96 times the standard error on either side of the mean. For example the average expenditure on fuel and power is £11.90 and the corresponding percentage standard error (full method) is 1.1%. The amount either side of the mean for 95% confidence is then:

1.96 x (1.1 ÷100) x £11.90 = £0.30 (rounded to nearest 10p)

Lower limit is 11.90 – 0.30 = £11.60

Upper limit is 11.90 + 0.30 = £12.20

Similar calculations can be carried out for other estimates of expenditure and income. The 95% confidence intervals for main expenditure categories are given in **Table C3**.

Table C3
95 per cent confidence intervals for average household expenditure 2000-01

Commodity or service	Weighted average weekly household expenditure (£)	95% confidence interval	
		Lower limit	Upper limit
All expenditure groups	**385.70**	**378.70**	**392.70**
Housing (net)	63.90	62.20	65.60
Fuel and power	11.90	11.60	12.10
Food and non-alcoholic drinks	61.90	61.00	62.90
Alcoholic drink	15.00	14.50	15.60
Tobacco	6.10	5.80	6.40
Clothing and footwear	22.00	21.10	22.90
Household goods	32.60	31.00	34.30
Household services	22.00	20.90	23.00
Personal goods and services	14.70	14.10	15.30
Motoring expenditure	55.10	53.20	57.00
Fares and other travel costs	9.50	8.70	10.30
Leisure goods	19.70	18.70	20.80
Leisure services	50.60	47.90	53.30
Miscellaneous	0.70	0.60	0.80

When using standard errors and confidence intervals to assess the precision of survey estimates, it is best to use standard errors which take into account the survey design (referred to here as full method standard errors) whenever possible. For those estimates where only simple method standard errors are given, the full method standard error can be approximated by multiplying the simple method standard error by a suitable design factor. Design factors are shown in **Tables C1** and **C2**; they are the complex standard errors divided by the corresponding simple random sample standard errors. A design factor should be chosen from the most appropriate expenditure group or income.

Details of the calculation of standard errors

The user does not need the formulae for calculating the standard errors but they are given here for completeness.

Simple method

This formula takes no account of the multi-stage design of the actual sample. The method of calculation is as follows: Let n be the total number of responding households in the survey, x_r the expenditure on a particular item of the r-th household, and $\bar{x}$ the average expenditure per household on that item (averaged over the n households). Then the standard error s is given by:

$$\frac{\sum_{r=1}^{n} (x_r - \bar{x})^2}{n-1}$$

Full method

The sample in Great Britain is a multi-stage stratified random sample with clustering, described further in Appendix A. First a sample of areas is drawn, the Primary Sampling Units (PSUs). Then within each PSU a random sample of households is drawn. In Northern Ireland, however, the sample is drawn in a single stage and there is no clustering. The results are also weighted to match the population separately by sex, by age (mostly 10 year ranges), and by region, as described in Appendix F.

The method for calculating complex standard errors has changed somewhat. Instead of the successive differences used before, consecutive PSUs in the ordered list are now grouped up into pairs, or triples at the end of a regional stratum. The formula used for the variance of a total is:

$$\hat{v}\mathrm{ar}(\hat{X}) = \sum_s \frac{k_s}{k_s - 1} \sum_i (x_{si} - \bar{x}_s)^2$$

where the s denote the pairs (rather than the whole regional stratum), k_s is the number of PSUs in s (either 2 or 3), the x_{si} are the weighted PSU totals and the $\bar{x}$ is the mean of these totals over the pair. Further details of this method of estimating sampling errors are described in *A sampling Errors Manual* (B Butcher and D Elliot, ONS 1987).

The effect of the re-weighting is calculated using the jackknife linearisation estimator. It uses the formula given above on a linear combination of residuals from a regression of the survey variables on the number of people in each household in each of the region and age by sex categories used in the weighting. Details are available from the editor.

The formulae have been expressed in terms of expenditures on a particular item, but of course they can also be applied to expenditures on groups of items, commodity groups and incomes from particular sources.

Appendix D

Definitions

Major changes in definitions since 1991 are described in Appendix E. Changes made between 1980 and 1990 are summarised in Appendix E of Family Spending 1994-95. For earlier changes see Annex 5 of Family Expenditure Survey 1980.

Household

The Family Expenditure Survey adopted the harmonised definition of the household for the 2000-01 survey. This is the definition used for the Census and most other surveys since 1981:

> One person or a group of people who have the accommodation as their only or main residence

and (for a group)

> Share the living accommodation, that is a living room or sitting room
>
> **or**   share meals together or have common housekeeping

Up to the 1999-2000 survey the FES kept to the definition used for Censuses and surveys before 1981, which has in the last line:

> **and**   share meals together or have common housekeeping

The effect of the harmonised definition is to increase the number of multi-adult households among groups of unrelated adults in shared accommodation. Chapter 9 of this report contains an analysis of the effect of the change.

Inclusions and exclusions remain the same. Resident domestic servants are included. The members of a household are not necessarily related by blood or marriage. As the survey covers only private households, people living in hostels, hotels, boarding houses or institutions are excluded. Households are not excluded if some or all members are not British subjects, but no attempt is made to obtain information from households containing members of the diplomatic service of another country or members of the United States armed forces. Nor are attempts made to obtain information from Roman Catholic priests living in accommodation provided by the parish church.

Retired households

Retired households are those where the head of the household is retired. The head of the household is defined as retired if 65 years of age or more and male or 60 years of age or more and female, and economically inactive. Hence if, for example, a male head of household is over 65 years of age, but working part-time or waiting to take up a part-time job, this household would not be classified as a retired household. For analysis purposes two categories are used in this report:

a.   "A retired household mainly dependent upon state pensions" is one in which at least three quarters of the total income of the household is derived from national insurance retirement and similar pensions, including housing and other benefits paid in supplement to or instead of such pensions. The term "national insurance retirement and similar pensions" includes national insurance disablement and war disability pensions, and income support in conjunction with these disability payments.

b.   "Other retired households" are retired households which do not fulfil the income conditions of "retired household mainly dependent upon state pensions" because more than a quarter of the household's income derives from occupational retirement pensions and/or income from investments, annuities etc.

Head of household

The head of the household must be a member of that household. By statistical convention the head is the person, or the husband of the person who:

a.   owns the household accommodation, or

b.   is legally responsible for the rent of the accommodation, or

c.   has the household accommodation as an emolument or perquisite, or

d.   has the household accommodation by virtue of some relationship to the owner who is not a member of the household.

When two members of different sex have equal claim, the male is taken as head of household. When two members of the same sex have equal claim, the elder is taken as head of household.

Household reference person

The concept of head of household will be discontinued on all government-sponsored household surveys after the 2000-01 round and replaced with the household reference person. To provide an overlap the household reference person has been identified in the 2000-01 FES and the chapters with tables by the characteristics of the head of household also include some tables by the characteristics of the household reference person, for comparison.

The household reference person is the householder, as defined in (a) to (d) above. If there are joint householders it will be the one with the higher income. A key difference is that the household reference person must always be a householder, whereas the head of household was always the husband, who might not even be a householder himself.

Members of household

In most cases the members of co-operating households are easily identified as the people who satisfy the conditions in the definition of a household, above, and are present during the record-keeping period. However difficulties of definition arise where people are temporarily away from the household or else spend their time between two residences. The following rules apply in deciding whether or not such persons are members of the household:

a.   married persons living and working away from home for any period are included as members provided they consider the sampled address to be their main residence; in general, other people (e.g. relatives, friends, boarders) who are either temporarily absent or who spend their time between the sampled address and another address, are included as members if they consider the sampled address to be their main residence. However, there are exceptions which override the subjective main residence rule:

i.   Children under 16 away at school are included as members;

ii.   Older persons receiving education away from home, including children aged 16 and 17, are excluded unless they are at home for all or most of the record-keeping period.

iii.   Visitors staying temporarily with the household and others who have been in the household for only a short time are treated as members provided they will be staying with the household for at least one month from the start of record-keeping.

Household composition

A consequence of these definitions is that household compositions quoted in this report include some households where certain members are temporarily absent. For example, "one adult and children" households will contain a few households where one parent is temporarily away from home.

Adult

In the report, persons who have reached the age of 18 or who are married are classed as adults.

Children

In the report, persons who are under 18 years of age and unmarried are classed as children.

However, in the definition of clothing, clothing for persons aged 16 years and over is classified as clothing for men and women; clothing for those aged five but under 16 as clothing for boys and girls; and clothing for those under five as babies clothing.

Spenders

Members of households who are aged 16 or more, excluding those who for special reasons are not capable of keeping diary record-books, are described as spenders.

Economically active

These are persons aged 16 or over who fall into the following categories:

a.   *Employees at work* - those who at the time of interview were working full-time or part-time as employees or were away from work on holiday. Part-time work is defined as normally working 30 hours a week or less (excluding meal breaks) including regularly worked overtime.

b.   *Employees temporarily away from work* - those who at the time of interview had a job but were absent because of illness or accident, temporary lay-off, strike etc.

c.   *Government supported training schemes* - those participating in government programmes and schemes who in the course of their participation receive training, such as Employment Training, including those who are also employees in employment.

d.   *Self-employed* - those who at the time of interview said they were self-employed.

e.   *Unemployed* - those who at time of interview were out of employment, and had sought work within the last four weeks and were available to start work within two weeks, or were waiting to start a job already obtained.

f.   *Unpaid family workers* - those working unpaid for their own or a relative's business. In this report, unpaid family workers are included under economically inactive in analyses by economic status (tables 3.1, 8.5 and 9.1) because insufficient information is available to assign them to an economic status group.

Economically inactive

a.   *Retired* - persons who have reached national insurance retirement age (60 and over for women, 65 and over for men) and are not economically active.

b.   *Unoccupied* - persons under national insurance retirement age who are not working, nor actively seeking work. This category includes certain self-employed persons such as mail order agents and baby-sitters who are not classified as economically active.

In this report, unpaid family workers are classified as economically inactive in analyses by economic status, although they are economically active by definition. This is because insufficient information is available to assign them to an economic status group.

Occupation

The occupational classification used in the survey is the socio-economic groups defined in the *Standard Occupational Classification (1990)* prepared by the Office for National Statistics. Separate results are shown for the following groups: professional workers; employers and managerial workers; intermediate non-manual workers; junior non-manual workers; skilled manual workers; semi-skilled manual workers; unskilled manual workers; Armed Forces. As far as possible, occupation is classified according to an individual's current or most recent job; if an individual has more than one job, the most remunerative is used as the basis for the classification.

Social Class

Social class is based on occupation and is a classification system that has grown out of the original Registrar-General's social class classification. These are defined in the *Classification of Occupations (1990)* prepared by the Office for National Statistics. The 5 categories are:

I.	Professional, etc. occupations
II.	Managerial and technical occupations
III.	Skilled occupations
	(N) non-manual
	(M) manual
IV.	Partly skilled occupations
V.	Unskilled occupations

For the FES, social class of a household refers to the social class based on the occupation of the head of household. It is coded where the head is currently in paid work, or is economically inactive and has worked in the last 12 months, or is unemployed and has ever worked.

Regions

These are the Government Office Regions as formed in 1994. See Appendix D (page 191) for more details.

Types of administrative area

These are Greater London, former Metropolitan Counties in England with the Central Clydeside Conurbation in Scotland, and non-metropolitan districts with high and low population densities, i.e. 3.2 persons or more, and less than 3.2 persons, per acre respectively (7.9 persons per hectare). The types of administrative area are defined by the Office for National Statistics on the basis of the definitions of local authority areas and the Central Clydeside Conurbation used by the Registrars General for England and Wales, Scotland, and Northern Ireland. Local authorities in England and Wales and in Scotland are those existing after the reorganisation of local government in 1974 and 1975. For Northern Ireland local authority areas as they existed after the reorganisation of local government in 1973 are used, classified by the population density factors applied generally in the United Kingdom. All Northern Ireland districts are treated as non-Metropolitan.

Urban and rural areas

This classification is based on the population of the continuous built-up areas, irrespective of administrative boundaries derived by the Department for Transport, Local Government and the Regions (DTLR) based on the 1991 Census. Note that the metropolitan built-up areas are not the same as the metropolitan administrative districts. They exclude any rural areas within the metropolitan districts and include any built up areas adjoining them.

Expenditure

Any definition of expenditure is to some extent arbitrary, and the inclusion of certain types of payment is a matter of convenience or convention depending on the purpose for which the information is to be used. In the tables in this report, total expenditure represents current expenditure on goods and services. Total expenditure, defined in this way, excludes those recorded payments which are really savings or investments (e.g. purchases of national savings certificates, life assurance premiums, contributions to pension funds). Similarly, income tax payments, national insurance contributions, mortgage capital repayments and other payments for major additions to dwellings are excluded. Expenditure data are collected in the diary record-book and in the household schedule. Informants are asked to record in the diary any payments made during the 14 days of record-keeping, whether or not the goods or services paid for have been received. Certain types of expenditure which are usually regular though infrequent, such as insurance, licences and season tickets, and the periods to which they relate, are recorded in the household schedule as well as regular payments such as utility bills.

The cash purchase of motor vehicles is also entered in the household schedule. In addition, expenditure on some items purchased infrequently (thereby being subject to high sampling errors) has been recorded in the household schedule using a retrospective recall period of either three or 12 months. These items include carpets, furniture, holidays and some housing costs. In order to avoid duplication, all payments shown in the diary record-book which relate to items listed in the household or income schedules are omitted in the analysis of the data irrespective of whether there is a corresponding entry on the latter schedules. Amounts paid in respect of periods longer than a week are converted to weekly values.

Expenditure tables in this report show the main commodity groups of spending and these are broken down into items which are numbered hierarchically. Table 7.1 shows a further breakdown in the items themselves into components which can be separately identified. The items are numbered as in the main expenditure tables and against each item or component are shown the average weekly household expenditure and percentage standard error.

Qualifications which apply to this concept of expenditure are described in the following paragraphs:

a.   *Goods supplied from a household's own shop or farm*
       Spenders are asked to record and give the value of goods obtained from their own shop or farm, even if the goods are withdrawn from stock for personal use without payment. The value is included as expenditure.

b.   *Hire purchase and credit sales agreements, and transactions financed by loans repaid by instalments*
       Expenditure on transactions under hire purchase or credit sales agreements, or financed by loans repaid by instalments, consists of all instalments which are still

being paid at the date of interview, together with down payments on commodities acquired within the preceding three months. These two components (divided by the periods covered) provide the weekly averages which are included in the expenditure on the separate items given in the tables in this report.

c. *Club payments and budget account payments, instalments through mail order firms and similar forms of credit transaction*

When goods are purchased by forms of credit other than hire purchase and credit sales agreement, the expenditure on them may be estimated either from the amount of the instalment which is paid or from the value of the goods which are acquired. Since the particular commodities to which the instalment relates may not be known, details of goods ordered through clubs, etc. during the month prior to the date of interview are recorded in the household schedule. The weekly equivalent of the value of the goods is included in the expenditure on the separate items given in the tables in this report. This procedure has the advantage of enabling club transactions to be related to specific articles. Although payments into clubs, etc. are shown in the diary record-book, these entries are excluded from expenditure estimates.

d. *Credit card transactions*

From 1988 purchases made by credit card or charge card have been recorded in the survey on an *acquisition* basis rather than the formerly used payment basis. Thus, if a spender acquired an item (by use of credit/charge card) during the two week survey period, the value of the item would be included as part of expenditure in that period whether or not any payment was made in this period to the credit card account. Payments made to the card account are ignored. However any payment of credit/ charge card *interest* is included in expenditure if made in the two week period.

e. *Income Tax*

Amounts of income tax deducted under the PAYE scheme or paid directly by those who are employers or self-employed are recorded (together with information about tax refunds). For employers and the self-employed the amounts comprise the actual payments made in the previous twelve months and may not correspond to the tax due on the income arising in that period, e.g. if no tax has been paid but is due or if tax payments cover more than one financial year. However, the amounts of tax deducted at source from some of the items which appear in the Income Schedule are not directly available. Estimates of the tax paid on bank and building society interest and amounts deducted from dividends on stocks and shares are therefore made by applying the appropriate rates of tax. In the case of income tax paid at source on pensions and annuities, similar adjustments are made. These estimates mainly affect the relatively few households with high incomes from interest and dividends, and households including someone receiving a pension from previous employment.

f.   *Rented dwellings*

Housing expenditure is taken as the sum of expenditure on rent, rates, council tax, water rates etc. For local authority tenants the expenditure is gross rent less any rebate (including rebate received in the form of housing benefit), and for other tenants gross rent less any rent allowance received under statutory schemes including the Housing Benefit Scheme. Rebate on Council Tax or rates (Northern Ireland) is deducted from expenditure on Council Tax or rates. Receipts from sub-letting part of the dwelling are not deducted from housing costs but appear (net of the expenses of the sub-letting) as investment income: see page 188.

g.   *Rent-free dwellings*

Rent-free dwellings are those owned by someone outside the household and where either no rent is charged or the rent is paid by someone outside the household. Households whose rent is paid directly to the landlord by the DSS do not live rent-free. Payments Council Tax, water rates etc., are regarded as the cost of housing. Rebate on rates(Northern Ireland)/Council Tax/water rates(Scotland) (including rebate received in the form of housing benefit), is deducted from expenditure on rates/Council Tax/water rates. Receipts from sub-letting part of the dwelling are not deducted from housing costs but appear (net of the expenses of the sub-letting) as investment income.

h.   *Owner-occupied dwellings*

Payments for Council Tax, rates (Northern Ireland), water rates, ground rent, mortgage interest payments, insurance of structure etc., are regarded as the cost of housing. Rebate on rates(Northern Ireland)/Council Tax/water rates(Scotland) (including rebate received in the form of housing benefit for the rented element of shared ownership dwellings) is deducted from expenditure on Council Tax/rates. Receipts from letting part of the dwelling are not deducted from housing costs but appear (net of the expenses of the letting) as investment income. Mortgage capital repayments and amounts paid for the outright purchase of the dwelling or for major structural alterations are not included as housing expenditure, but are entered under "Other payments recorded".

i.   *Second-hand goods and part-exchange transactions*

The survey expenditure data are based on information about actual payments and therefore include payments for second-hand goods and part-exchange transactions. Net payments only are included for part-exchange transactions, i.e. the costs of the goods obtained less the amounts allowed for the goods which are traded in. Receipts for goods sold or traded in are not included in income.

j.   *Business expenses*

The survey covers only private households and is concerned with payments made by members of households as private individuals. Spenders are asked to state whether expenditure which has been recorded on the schedules includes amounts which will be refunded as expenses from a business or organisation or which will be entered as business expenses for income tax purposes, e.g. rent, telephone charges, travelling expenses, meals out. Any such amounts are deducted from the recorded expenditure.

Income

The standard concept of income in the survey is, as far as possible, that of gross weekly cash income current at the time of interview, i.e. before the deduction of income tax actually paid, national insurance contributions and other deductions at source. However, for a few tables a concept of disposable income is used, defined as gross weekly cash income less the statutory deductions and payments of income tax (taking refunds into account) and national insurance contributions. Some other analyses of FES data use "equivalisation" of incomes - i.e. adjustment of household income to allow for the different size and composition of each household. Equivalisation is not used in this volume. Analyses by specific household compositions, show a full picture. The cash levels of certain items of income (and expenditure) recorded in the survey by households receiving supplementary benefit were affected by the Housing Benefit Scheme introduced in stages from November 1982. From 1984 housing expenditure is given on a strictly net basis and all rent/council tax rebates and allowances and housing benefit are excluded from gross income.

Although information about most types of income is obtained on a current basis, some data, principally income from investment and from self-employment, are estimated over a twelve-month period.

The following are excluded from the assessment of income:

a.   money received by one member of the household from another (e.g. housekeeping money, dress allowance, children's pocket money) other than wages paid to resident domestic servants;

b.   withdrawals of savings, receipts from maturing insurance policies, proceeds from sale of financial and other assets (e.g. houses, cars, furniture, etc.), winnings from betting, lump-sum gratuities and windfalls such as legacies;

c.   the value of educational grants and scholarships not paid in cash;

d.   the value of income in kind, including the value of goods received free and the abatement in cost of goods received at reduced prices, and of bills paid by someone who is not a member of the household;

e.   loans and money received in repayment of loans.

Details are obtained of the income of each member of the household. The income of the household is taken to be the sum of the incomes of all its members. The information does not relate to a common or a fixed time period. Items recorded for periods greater than a week are converted to a weekly value.

Particular points relating to some components of income are as follows:

a.   *Wages and salaries of employees*

The normal gross wages or salaries of employees are taken to be their earnings. These are calculated by adding to the normal "take home" pay amounts deducted at source, such as income tax payments, national insurance contributions and other deductions, e.g. payments into firm social clubs, superannuation schemes, works transport, benevolent funds etc. Employees are asked to give the earnings actually received including bonuses and commission the last time payment was made and, if different, the amount usually received. It is the amount usually received which is regarded as the normal take-home pay. Additions are made so as to include in normal earnings the value of occasional payments, such as bonuses or commissions received quarterly or annually. One of the principal objects in obtaining data on income is to enable expenditure to be classified in ranges of normal income. Average household expenditure is likely to be based on the long-term expectations of the various members of the household as to their incomes rather than be altered by short-term changes affecting individuals. Hence if an employee has been away from work without pay for 13 weeks or less he is regarded as continuing to receive his normal earnings instead of social security benefits, such as unemployment or sickness benefit, that he may be receiving. Otherwise, his normal earnings are disregarded and his current short-term social security benefits taken instead. Wages and salaries include any earnings from subsidiary employment as an employee and the earnings of HM Forces.

b.   *Income from self-employment*

Income from self-employment covers any personal income from employment other than as an employee; for example, as a sole trader, professional or other person working on his own account or in partnership, including subsidiary work on his own account by a person whose main job is as an employee. It is measured from estimates of income or trading profits, after deduction of business expenses but before deduction of tax, over the most recent twelve-month period for which figures can be given. Should either a loss have been made or no profit, income would be taken as the amounts drawn from the business for own use or as any other income received from the job or business. Persons working as mail order agents or baby-sitters, with no other employment, have been classified as unoccupied rather than as self-employed, and the earnings involved have been classified as earnings from "other sources" rather than self-employment income.

c.   *Income from investment*

Income from investments or from property, other than that in which the household is residing, is the amount received during the twelve months immediately prior to the date of the initial interview. It includes receipts from sub-letting part of the dwelling (net of the expenses of the sub-letting). If income tax has been deducted at source the gross amount is estimated by applying a conversion factor during processing.

d.   *Social security benefits*

Income from social security benefits does not include the short-term payments such as unemployment or sickness benefit received by an employee who has been away from work for 13 weeks or less, and who is therefore regarded as continuing to receive his normal earnings as described on page 190.

Quantiles

The quantiles of a distribution, e.g. of household expenditure or income, divide it into a number of equal parts; each of which contains the same number of households.

For example, the median of a distribution divides it into two equal parts, so that half the households in a distribution of household income will have income more than the median, and the other half will have income less than the median. Similarly, quartiles, quintiles and deciles divide the distribution into four, five and ten equal parts respectively.

Most of the analysis in Family Spending is done in terms of quintile groups and decile groups.

In the calculation of quantiles for this report, zero values are counted as part of the distribution.

Income headings

Headings used for identifying 2000-01 income information

	Source of income	
References in tables	Components separately identified	Explanatory notes
a. Wages and salaries	Normal "take-home" pay from main employment "Take-home" pay from subsidiary employment Employees' income tax deduction Employees' National Insurance contribution Superannuation contributions deducted from pay Other deductions	(i) In the calculation of house hold income in this report, where an employee has been away from work without pay for 13 weeks or less his normal wage or salary has been used in estimating his total income instead of social security benefits, such as unemployment or sickness benefits that he may have received. Otherwise such benefits are used in estimating total income (see notes at reference e) (ii) Normal income from wages and salaries is estimated by adding to the normal "take-home" pay deductions made at source last time paid, together with the weekly value of occasional additions to wages and salaries (see page 187). (iii) The components of wages and salaries for which figures are separately available amount in total to the normal earnings of employees, regardless of the operation of the 13 week rule in note (i) above. Thus the sum of the components listed here does not in general equal the wages and salaries figure in tables of this report.
b. Self-employment	Income from business or profession, including subsidiary self-employment	The earnings or profits of a trade or profession, after deduction of business expenses but before deduction of tax
c. Investments	Interest on building society shares and deposits Interest on bank deposits and savings accounts including National Savings Bank Interest on ISAs Interest on TESSAs Interest on Gilt-edged stock and War Loans Interest and dividends from stocks, shares, bonds, trusts, PEPs, debentures and other securities Rent or income from property, after deducting expenses but inclusive of income tax (including receipts from letting or sub-letting part of own residence, net of the expenses of the letting or sub-letting). Other unearned Income	

d. Annuities and pensions, other than social security	Annuities and income from trust or covenant Pensions from previous employers Personal pensions	
e. Social security benefits	Child benefit Guardian's allowance Invalid care allowance Retirement pension (National Insurance) or old person's pension Widow's pension or widowed mother's allowance (NI) War disablement pension or war widow's pension Severe disablement allowance Disabled person's tax credit Care component of disability living allowance Mobility component of disability living allowance Attendance allowance Job seekers allowance, contributions based Job seekers allowance, income based Income support Family credit/working families tax credit Incapacity benefit Statutory sick pay (from employer) Industrial injury disablement benefit Maternity allowance Statutory maternity pay Any other benefit including lump sums and grants Social security benefits excluded from income calculation by 13 week rule	I. The calculation of household income in this report takes account of the 13 week rule described at reference a, note (i) ii. The components of social security benefits for which figures are separately available amount in total to the benefits received in the week before interview. That is to say, they include amounts that are discounted from the total by the operation of the 13 week rule in note i. Thus the sum of the components listed here differs from the total of social security benefits used in the income tables of this report. iii Housing Benefit is treated as a reduction in housing costs and not as income
f. Other sources	Married person's allowance from husband/wife temporarily away from home Alimony or separation allowances; allowances for foster children, allowances from members of the Armed Forces or Merchant Navy, or any other money from friends or relatives, other than husband outside the household Benefits from trade unions, friendly societies etc., other than pensions Value of meal vouchers Earnings from intermittent or casual work over twelve months, not included in a or b above Student loans and money scholarships received by persons aged 16 and over and aged under 16. Other income of children under 16	e.g. from spare-time jobs or income from trusts or investments

STANDARD STATISTICAL REGION	COUNTY*	GOVERNMENT OFFICE REGION
NORTH	Cleveland* Durham Northumberland Tyne and Wear	NORTH EAST
	Cumbria	
NORTH WEST	Cheshire Greater Manchester Lancashire Merseyside	NORTH WEST
YORKSHIRE AND HUMBERSIDE	Humberside* North Yorkshire* South Yorkshire West Yorkshire	YORKSHIRE AND THE HUMBER
EAST MIDLANDS	Derbyshire Leicestershire Lincolnshire Northamptonshire Nottinghamshire	EAST MIDLANDS
WEST MIDLANDS	Hereford and Worcester Shropshire Staffordshire Warwickshire West Midlands	WEST MIDLANDS
EAST ANGLIA	Cambridgeshire Norfolk Suffolk	EAST OF ENGLAND
	Bedfordshire Essex Hertfordshire	
	Greater London	LONDON
SOUTH EAST	Berkshire Buckinghamshire East Sussex Hampshire Isle of Wight Kent Oxfordshire Surrey West Sussex	SOUTH EAST
SOUTH WEST	Avon* Cornwall Devon Dorset Gloucestershire Somerset Wiltshire	SOUTH WEST

* Counties prior to local government reorganisation

Appendix E

Changes in definitions, 1991 to 2000-01

1991
No significant changes.

1992
Housing – Imputed rent for owner occupiers and households in rent-free accommodation was discontinued. For owner occupiers this had been the rent they would have had pay themselves to live in the property they own, and for households in rent-free accommodation it was the rent they would normally have had to pay. Up to 1990 these amounts were counted both as income and as a housing cost. Mortgage interest payments were counted as a housing cost for the first time in 1991.

1993
Council Tax - Council Tax was introduced to replace the Community Charge in Great Britain from April 1993.

1994-95
New expenditure items - The definition of expenditure was extended to include two items previously shown under "other payments recorded". These were:

> gambling payments;
> mortgage protection premiums.

Expenditure classifications - A new classification system for expenditures was introduced in April 1994. The system is hierarchical and allows more detail to be preserved than the previous system. New categories of expenditure were introduced and are shown in detail in table 7.1. The 14 main groups of expenditure were retained, but there were some changes in the content of these groups.

Gambling Payments - data on gambling expenditure and winnings are collected in the expenditure diary. Previously these were excluded from the definition of household expenditure used in the FES. The data are shown as memoranda items under the heading "Other payments recorded" on both gross and net bases. The net basis corresponds approximately to the treatment of gambling in the National Accounts. The introduction of the National Lottery stimulated a reconsideration of this treatment. From April 1994, (gross) gambling payments have been included as expenditure in "Leisure Services". Gambling winnings continued to be noted as a memorandum item under "Other items recorded". They are treated as windfall income. They do not form a part of normal household income, nor are they subtracted from gross gambling payments. This treatment is in line with the PRODCOM classification of the Statistical Office of the European Communities (SOEC) for expenditure in household budget surveys.

ONS, Family Spending 2000-01, © Crown copyright 2002

1995-96

Geographical overage - The FES geographical coverage was extended to mainland Scotland north of the Caledonian Canal.

Under 16s diaries - Two week expenditure diaries for 7-15 year olds were introduced following three feasibility pilot studies which found that children of that age group were able to cope with the task of keeping a two week expenditure record. Children are asked to record everything they buy with their own money but to exclude items bought with other people's money. Purchases are coded according to the same coding categories as adult diaries except for meals and snacks away from home which are coded as school meals, hot meals and snacks, and cold meals and snacks. Children who keep a diary are given a £5 incentive payment. A refusal to keep an under 16's diary does not invalidate the household from inclusion in the survey.

Pocket money given to children is still recorded separately in adult diaries; and money paid by adults for school meals and school travel is recorded in the Household Questionnaire. Double counting is eliminated at the processing stage.

Tables in Family Spending reports did not include the information from the children's diaries until the 1998-99 report. Appendix F in the 1998-99 and 1999-2000 reports show what difference the inclusion made.

1996-97

Self-employment - The way in which information about income from self-employment is collected was substantially revised in 1996-97 following various tests and pilot studies. The quality of such data was increased but this may have lead to a discontinuity. Full details are shown in the Income Questionnaire, available from the address in the introduction.

Cable/satellite television - Information on cable and satellite subscriptions is now collected from the household questionnaire rather than from the diary, leading to more respondents reporting this expenditure.

Mobile phones - Expenditure on mobile phones was previously collected through the diary. From 1996/97 this has been included in the questionnaire.

Job seekers allowance (JSA) - Introduced in October 1996 as a replacement for Unemployment Benefit and any Income Support associated with the payment of Unemployment Benefit. Receipt of JSA is collected with NI Unemployment Benefit and with Income Support. In both cases the number of weeks a respondent has been in receipt of these benefits is taken as the number of weeks receiving JSA in the last 12 months and before that period the number of weeks receiving Unemployment Benefit/Income Support.

Retrospective recall - The period over which information is requested has been extended from 3 to 12 months for vehicle purchase and sale. Information on the purchase of car and motorcycle spare parts is no longer collected by retrospective recall. Instead expenditure on these items is collected through the diary.

State benefits - The lists of benefits specifically asked about was reviewed in 1996/97. See the Income Questionnaire for more information.

Sample stratifiers - New stratifiers were introduced in 1996/97 based on standard regions, socio-economic group and car ownership.

Government Office Regions - Regional analyses are now presented using the Government Office Regions (GORs) formed in 1994. Previously all regional analyses used Standard Statistical Regions (SSRs). For more information see Appendix F.

1997-98

Bank/Building society service charges - Collection of information on service charges levied by banks has been extended to include building societies.

Payments from unemployment/redundancy insurances - Information is now collected on payments received from private unemployment and redundancy insurance policies. This information is then incorporated into the calculation of income from other sources.

Retired households - The definition of retired households has been amended to exclude households where the head of the household is economically active.

Rent-free tenure - The definition of rent-free tenure has been amended to include those households for which someone outside the household, except an employer or an organisation, is paying a rent or mortgage on behalf of the household.

National Lottery - From February 1997, expenditure on National lottery tickets was collected as three separate items: tickets for the Wednesday draw only, tickets for the Saturday draw only and tickets for both draws.

1998-99

Children's income – Three new expenditure codes were introduced: pocket money to children; money given to children for specific purposes and cash gifts to children. These replaced a single code covering all three categories.

Main job and last paid job – Harmonised questions were adopted.

1999-2000

Disabled persons tax credit replaced disability working allowance and *working families tax credit* replaced family credit from October 1999.

2000-01

Household definition – the definition was changed to the harmonised definition which has been in use in the Census and nearly all other government household surveys since 1981. The effect is to group together into a single household some people who would have been allocated to separate households on the previous definition. The effect is fairly small but not negligible.

Up to 1999-2000 the FES definition was based on the pre-1981 Census definition and required members to share eating and budgeting arrangements as well as shared living accommodation. The definition of a household was:

> One person or a group of people who have the accommodation as their only or main residence

and (for a group)

> share the living accommodation, that is a living or sitting room
> **and**   share meals together (or have common housekeeping).

The harmonised definition is less restrictive:

> One person or a group of people who have the accommodation as their only or main residence

and (for a group)

> share the living accommodation, that is a living or sitting room
> **or**   share meals together or have common housekeeping.

The effect of the change is probably to increase average household size by 0.6 per cent. A section in chapter 9 presents the information and reasoning behind this estimate.

Question reductions - A thorough review of the questionnaire showed that a number of questions were no longer needed by government users. These were cut from the 2000-01 survey to reduce the burden on respondents. The reduction was fairly small but it did make the interview flow better. All the questions needed for a complete record of expenditure and income were retained.

Redesigned diary - The diary was redesigned to be easier for respondent to keep and to look cleaner. The main change of substance was to delete the column for recording whether each item was purchased by credit, charge or shop card.

Ending of MIRAS - Tax relief on interest on loans for house purchase was abolished from April 2000. Questions related to MIRAS were therefore dropped. They included some that were needed to estimate the amount if the respondent did not know it. A number were retained for other purposes, however, such as the amount of the loan still outstanding which is still asked for households paying a reduced rate of interest because one of them works for the lender.

Appendix F

Differential grossing

Since 1998-99 results have been based on data that have been grossed differentially (re-weighted) to reduce the effect of non-response bias. This appendix shows the effect on the 2000-01 results published in this report. In previous reports this annex also showed the effect of including the spending recorded in the diaries kept by children aged 7 to 15. Inclusion of the children's data is now a permanent part of the survey methodology and no longer requires a separate analysis.

The grossing method used for the 2000-01 data is the same in principle as in previous years. As well as providing users with estimates of total spending by a single, agreed procedure, the grossing also re-weights the data. It is known from comparisons with the census (see the Appendix A section on reliability) that response rates are higher in some groups than others, leading to sampled households not being fully representative of the population as a whole. The aim of re-weighting is to compensate for this non-response bias by giving higher weights to households in the groups that are under-represented. An example of such an under-represented group is households with three or more adults and no children.

Method used to produce the weights

The weights are produced in two stages, the first of which uses results from the census-linked study of survey non-respondents (*Weighting the FES to compensate for non-response, Part 1: An investigation into census-based weighting schemes*, Foster 1994). A statistical analysis[1] was used to identify ten groups with very different response rates. A weight was then assigned to each of those groups, based on the inverse of the response rate for the group. A group with a low response rate is therefore given a high initial weight.

The second stage adjusts the weights so that there is an exact match with population estimates, for males and females in different age groups and separately for regions. An important feature of the FES grossing is that this is done by adjusting the factors for whole households, not by adjusting the factors for individuals. The population figures being matched exclude people who are not covered by the FES, that is those in bed-and-breakfast accommodation, hostels, residential care homes and other institutions. A so called calibration method[2] is used in this stage to produce the weights.

A modification to the grossing procedure adopted in 2000-01 is that it is now carried out separately for each quarter of the survey, instead of for the 12 months as a whole. The main reason is that sample sizes vary from quarter to quarter more than in the past. This is the result of re-issuing addresses where there had been a non-contact or a refusal to a new

---

[1] Chi-squared Automatic Interaction Detector

[2] Implemented by the CALMAR software package

ONS, Family Spending 2000-01, © Crown copyright 2002

interviewer after an interval of a few months, so that there are more interviews in the later quarters of the year than in the first quarter. Spending patterns are seasonal and quarterly grossing counteracts any bias from the uneven spread of interviews through the year. Quarterly grossing results in small sample numbers in some of the age group/sex categories previously used in the grossing and they have been widened slightly to avoid this.

The overall effect of differential grossing

Table F1 shows the effect of differential grossing (weighting) on the 2000-01 FES data.

Weighting increased the estimate of total average expenditure by £7.40 a week, that is by 2.0 per cent. It had the largest impact on average weekly expenditure on alcoholic drink, increasing the estimate of expenditure by 8 per cent; on fares and other travel costs, increasing the expenditure estimate by 6.3 per cent; and housing costs by 5.2 per cent. It reduced the estimate of spending on fuel and power by 2.9 per cent. Weighting also increased the estimates of average income, by £12.80 a week (3.2 per cent) for disposable household income and by £18.30 a week (3.8 per cent) for gross household income, which is the income used in most tables in the report.

Table F1
The effect of weighting on expenditure

| | Average weekly household expenditure | | | |
| | Unweighted | Weighted | Absolute | Percentage |
Commodity or service		as published	difference	difference
All expenditure groups	**378.29**	**385.72**	**7.42**	*2.0*
Housing(net)	60.76	63.92	3.15	*5.2*
Fuel and power	12.24	11.88	-0.36	*-2.9*
Food and non-alcoholic drinks	61.82	61.93	0.12	*0.2*
Alcoholic drink	13.91	15.02	1.11	*8.0*
Tobacco	6.05	6.06	0.01	*0.1*
Clothing and footwear	22.00	21.98	-0.02	*-0.1*
Household goods	32.58	32.63	0.05	*0.2*
Households services	21.73	21.96	0.23	*1.0*
Personal goods and services	14.52	14.71	0.19	*1.3*
Motoring expenditure	54.11	55.09	0.98	*1.8*
Fares and other travel costs	8.89	9.46	0.56	*6.3*
Leisure goods	19.46	19.74	0.28	*1.4*
Leisure services	49.47	50.61	1.14	*2.3*
Miscellaneous	0.73	0.72	-0.01	*-1.2*
Weekly household income:				
Disposable	396.40	409.18	12.77	*3.2*
Gross	484.27	502.52	18.25	*3.8*

The effects of weighting vary a little from year to year but in 2000-01 were similar to the effects in the previous two years. The increase in total expenditure has been about 2 per cent each year and the individual expenditure groups with the largest changes have remained the same. The effects on housing and alcoholic drink were rather larger in 2000-01 than previously but the effect on fares and travel costs was lower. The negative effect on the estimate of tobacco expenditure in earlier years has almost disappeared. The effect on the income estimates has been about the same each year. Some differences in the effect of weighting are to be expected, as the proportions of households of the types which receive different weights will differ to some extent from year to year as a result of random sampling variability. As weighting compensates at least partially for non-response bias there should be more stability in the weighted results than in results from the unweighted sample.

Re-weighting also has an effect on the variance of estimates. In an analysis on the 1999-2000 data weighting increased variance slightly for some items and reduced for others. Overall the effect was to reduce variance slightly.

Further information

Further information is available on the method used to produce the weights from the address given in the introduction.

Appendix G

Index to tables in reports on the Family Expenditure Survey in 1993 to 2000-01

2000-01 tables	Table numbers in reports for						
	1999-2000	1998-99	1997-98	1996-97	1995-96	1994-95	1993
1 Expenditure by income							
1.1 main items by gross income decile	1.1	1.1	1.1	1.1	1.1	1.1	1.1
1.2 percentage on main items by gross income decile	1.2	1.2	1.2	1.2	1.2	1.2	1.2
1.3 detailed expenditure by gross income decile	1.3	1.3	1.3	1.3	1.3	1.3	1.3
.. (housing expenditure in each tenure group)	-	-	-	1.4	1.4	1.4	1.4
1.4 main items by disposable income decile	1.4	-	-	-	-	-	-
1.5 percentage on main items by disposable income decile	1.5	-	-	-	-	-	-
2 Expenditure by age and income							
2.1 main items for all age groups	2.1	2.1	2.1	2.1	2.1	2.1	2.1
2.2 main items as a percentage for all age groups	2.2	2.2	2.2	2.2	2.2	2.2	2.2
2.3 detailed expenditure for all age groups	2.3	2.3	2.3	2.3	2.3	2.3	2.3
2.4 aged under 30 by income	2.4	2.4	2.4	2.4	2.4	2.4	2.4
2.5 aged 30 and under 50 by income	2.5	2.5	2.5	2.5	2.5	2.5	2.5
2.6 aged 50 and under 65 by income	2.6	2.6	2.6	2.6	2.6	2.6	2.6
2.7 aged 65 and under 75 by income	2.7	2.7	2.7	2.7	2.7	2.7	2.7
2.8 aged 75 or over by income	2.8	2.8	2.8	2.8	2.8	2.8	2.8
2.9 main items for all age groups of household reference person	-	-	-	-	-	-	-
3 Expenditure by socio-economic characteristics							
3.1 by economic activity status	3.1	3.1	3.1	3.1	3.1	3.1	3.1
3.2 by occupation	3.2	3.2	3.2	3.2	3.2	3.2	3.2
3.3 full-time employee by income	3.3	3.3	3.3	3.3	3.3	3.3	3.3
3.4 self-employed by income	3.4	3.4	3.4	3.4	3.4	3.4	3.4
3.5 by social class	3.5	3.5	3.5	3.5	3.5	3.5	3.5
3.6 by number of persons working	3.6	3.6	3.6	3.6	3.6	3.6	-
3.7 by age completed continuous full-time education	3.7	3.7	3.7	3.7	3.7	3.7	-
3.8 by occupation of household reference person	-	-	-	-	-	-	-
3.9 by economic activity status of household reference person	-	-	-	-	-	-	-
4 Expenditure by composition, income and tenure							
4.1 expenditure by household composition	4.1	4.1	4.1	4.1	4.1	4.1	-
4.2 one adult retired households mainly dependent on state pensions	4.2	4.2	4.2	4.2	4.2	4.2	4.1
4.3 one adult retired households not mainly dependent on state pensions	4.3	4.3	4.3	4.3	4.3	4.3	4.2
4.4 one adult non-retired	4.4	4.4	4.4	4.4	4.4	4.4	4.3
4.5 one adult with children	4.5	4.5	4.5	4.5	4.5	4.5	4.4
4.6 two adults with children	4.6	4.6	4.6	4.6	4.6	4.6	4.5
4.7 one man one woman non-retired	4.7	4.7	4.7	4.7	4.7	4.7	4.6
4.8 one man one woman retired mainly dependent on state pensions	4.8	4.8	4.8	4.8	4.8	4.8	4.7

.. Tables do not appear in the 2000-01 publication

2000-01 tables		Table numbers in reports for						
		1999-2000	1998-99	1997-98	1996-97	1995-96	1994-95	1993
4.9	one man one woman retired not mainly dependent on state pensions	4.9	4.9	4.9	4.9	4.9	4.9	4.8
4.10	household expenditure by tenure	4.10	4.10	4.10	4.10	4.10	4.10	4.9
..	household expenditure by type of dwelling	-	4.11	4.11	4.11	4.11	4.11	-
5	**Expenditure by region[1,2]**							
5.1	main items of expenditure	5.1	5.1	5.1	5.1	5.1	5.1	5.1
5.2	main items as a percentage of expenditure	5.2	5.2	5.2	5.2	5.2	5.2	5.2
5.3	detailed expenditure	5.3	5.3	5.3	5.3	5.3	5.3	5.3
..	(housing expenditure in each tenure group)	-	-	-	5.4	5.4	5.4	5.4
5.4	expenditure by type of administrative area	5.4	5.4	5.4	5.5	5.5	5.5	-
5.5	expenditure by urban/rural areas (GB only)	-	-	-	-	-	-	-
6	**Trends in household expenditure**							
6.1	main items 1974 - 2000-01	6.1	-	-	-	-	-	-
6.2	as a percentage of total expenditure	6.2	6.1	6.1	6.1	6.1	6.1	6.1
6.3	by Region[3]	6.3	6.2	-	-	-	-	-
7	**Detailed expenditure and place of purchase**							
7.1	with full method standard errors	7.1	7.1	7.1	7.1	7.1	7.1	7.1
7.2	expenditure on alcoholic drink	7.2	7.2	7.2	7.2	7.2	7.2	7.1
7.3	expenditure on food by place of purchase	7.3	7.3	7.3	7.3	7.3	7.3	-
..	expenditure on alcoholic drink by place of purchase	7.4	7.4	7.4	7.4	-	-	-
7.4	expenditure on selected items by place of purchase	-	-	-	-	-	-	-
..	expenditure on petrol, diesel and other motor oils by place of purchase	7.5	7.5	7.5	7.5	-	-	-
..	selected household goods and personal goods and services by place of purchase	7.6	7.6	7.6	7.6	-	-	-
..	selected regular purchases by place of purchase	7.7	7.7	7.7	7.7	-	-	-
7.5	expenditure on clothing and footwear by place of purchase	7.8	7.8	7.8	7.8	-	-	-
8	**Household income**							
8.1	by household composition	8.1	8.1	8.1	8.1	8.1	8.1	8.1
8.2	by age of head of household	8.2	8.2	8.2	8.2	8.2	8.2	8.2
8.3	by income group	8.3	8.3	8.3	8.3	8.3	8.3	8.3
8.4	by household tenure	8.4	8.4	8.4	8.4	8.4	8.4	8.4
8.5	by economic status of head of household	8.5	8.5	8.5	8.5	8.5	8.5	8.5
8.6	by occupational grouping of head of household	8.6	8.6	8.6	8.6	8.6	8.6	8.6
8.7	by Region	8.7	8.7	8.7	8.7	8.7	8.7	8.7
8.8	by GB urban/rural areas	-	-	-	-	-	-	-
8.9	1970 to 2000-01	8.8	8.8	8.8	8.8	8.8	8.8	8.8

.. Tables do not appear in the 2000-01 publication
1 Up to 1991 region tables covered two-year periods. From 1998-99 they cover three-year periods.
2 Up to 1995-96 region tables related to Standard Statistical regions; tables from 1996-97 relate to Government Office Regions.
3 Standard Statistical Regions

ONS, Family Spending 2000-01, © Crown copyright 2002

2000-01 tables	Table numbers in reports for						
	1999-2000	1998-99	1997-98	1996-97	1995-96	1994-95	1993
8.10 by age of household reference person	-	-	-	-	-	-	-
8.11 by economic activity status of household reference person	-	-	-	-	-	-	-
8.12 by occupation of household reference person	-	-	-	-	-	-	-
9 Households characteristics and ownership of durable goods							
9.1 households	9.1	9.1	9.1	9.1	9.1	9.1	9.1
9.2 persons	9.2	9.2	9.2	9.2	9.2	9.2	9.2
9.3 percentage with durable goods 1970 to 2000-01	9.3	9.3	9.3	9.3	9.3	9.3	9.3
9.4 percentage with durable goods	9.4	9.4	9.4	9.4	9.4	9.4	9.4-9.6
9.5 percentage with cars	9.5	9.5	9.5	9.5	9.5	9.5	9.7-9.9
9.6 percentage with durable goods by UK Countries and Government Office Regions	9.6	9.6	9.6	9.6	9.6	9.6	9.11
9.7 percentage by size, composition, age, in each income group	9.7	9.7	9.7	9.7	9.7	9.7	9.10
9.8 percentage by occupation, economic activity, tenure in each income group	9.8	9.8	9.7	9.7	9.7	9.7	9.10

Index

Italic page numbers refer to figures and tables.

ONS, Family Spending 2000-01, © Crown copyright 2002

ONS, Family Spending 2000-01, © Crown copyright 2002

Acknowledgements

Editor:	**Denis Down**

Production team: **Kay Joseland**
Nicola Sexton
Anita Premdjee
Clair Barrs
Chrisoulla Kirri
Christine Smith
Karen Reeh
Dave Wood
Maya Kara
William Hodgson
Tony King
Alison Blackwell
Reg Gatenby
Tim Burrell
Yinka Fashola

Cover artwork: **Andy Leach — onsdesign**

ONS, Family Spending 2000-01, © Crown copyright 2002